T0373200

Adventures in Translation

BABEL

Adventures in Translation

Dennis Duncan, Stephen Harrison
Katrin Kohl and **Matthew Reynolds**

Bodleian Library
UNIVERSITY OF OXFORD

First published in 2019 by the Bodleian Library
Broad Street, Oxford OX1 3BG
www.bodleianshop.co.uk

ISBN: 978 1 85124 509 3

BACK COVER: Bodleian Library, G.A. Scotl. 8° 687

Designed and typeset by Dot Little at the Bodleian Library in 10/13pt Charter
Printed and bound by Great Wall Printing Co. Ltd., Hong Kong, on 157gsm Neo matt art paper

British Library Catalogue in Publishing Data
A CIP record of this publication is available from the British Library

Contents

Prospectus Turris Babylonicæ ex Præscripto R. Adm: Patris Athanasy Kircheri Soc: Jesu.
TURRIS BABEL

Foreword

The biblical myth of Babel tells us that humankind has long dreamed of a shared 'perfect' language that would enable humans to achieve divine heights through unhindered collaboration. But the myth also highlights an even more fundamental feature of human communication: 'language' exists only in the form of specific 'languages'.

The main reason for this diversity appears to be the close relationship between language and culture. Even the era of 'global English' is by no means creating a homogeneous language landscape. 'Englishes' continue to develop and change, in the British Isles and across the world. Other languages such as Arabic, Spanish, Standard Chinese and more local shared languages continue to act as lingua francas. Moreover, communities – however small – nurture their distinctive languages because they are part of their cultural identity, and because they facilitate expression of their particular view of the world.

While the 'perfect' uniform language has remained in the realm of myth, people have got on with the job of communicating with other groups by using translation. Translation builds bridges between languages, allowing each to retain its distinctiveness and cultural base. It allows us to share stories, knowledge and ideas across different times and locations. And, unlike that mythical perfect language, translation permits and encourages adaptation to new cultural contexts and needs: it changes languages as it bridges them. Digital translation is an exciting addition to the range of translation possibilities. But it doesn't alter the fact that translation is inherently an act of interpretation and creation, as writers and artists have always understood.

The daily oral translation processes that have been happening over millennia are by their very nature ephemeral. By contrast, written texts can give us deep insights into the translation processes that have shaped our modern lives – in religion and science, politics and literature, food and health.

The Bodleian Libraries are a treasure trove of books, manuscripts, documents, maps and other materials which have grown out of transfer processes between languages.

Babel: Adventures in Translation opens up that global dimension. This innovative collection of essays, which complements an exhibition held at the Bodleian, explores religious books, scientific treatises, beast fables, road signs and of course *Harry Potter*. It examines a tablet with Linear A from ancient Crete – intriguingly still undeciphered and literally untranslatable – and takes a look at how we might communicate with people of the future, perhaps thirty millennia from now, when even the language used in this book may no longer be understood or even decipherable.

Through illustrated examples ranging from Greek papyri to illuminated manuscripts and fantasy languages, the book also tells the fascinating story of how ideas have travelled via the medium of translation into different languages and cultures, enabling collaboration, renewing narratives and stimulating creativity.

I would like to express my thanks to the curators of this exhibition – Professor Katrin Kohl, Dr Dennis Duncan, Professor Stephen Harrison and Professor Matthew Reynolds – for sifting the tens of millions of collection items in the Bodleian and finding a perfect combination for this publication and exhibition.

Richard Ovenden Bodley's Librarian

1 In this fold-out print, from Athanasius Kircher's *Turris Babel* (1679), construction of the tower is busily underway. Bodleian Library Vet. B3 b.33, between pp. 40 and 41.

Data hypothesi quantum globus terrenus
extra centru
Sem
10
Terræ
B
A
MAR DI
INDIA

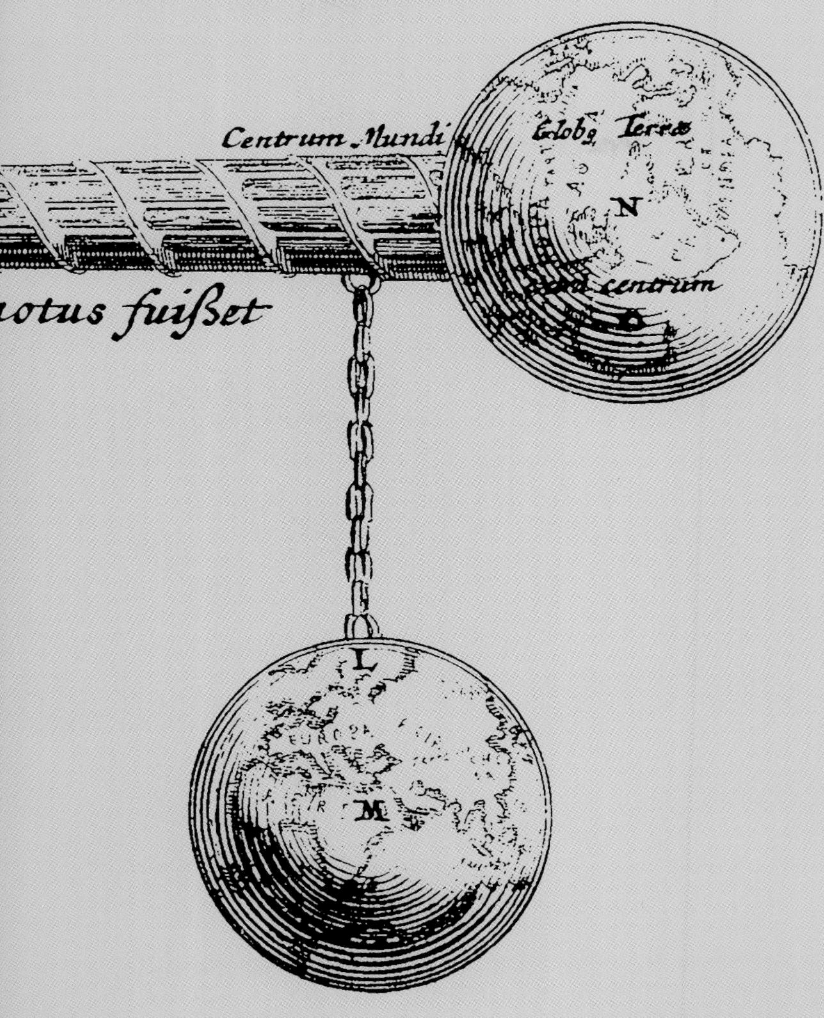

1 Babel: Curse or Blessing?

Matthew Reynolds

Babel is a paradoxical word. It is a name that was given to a city at the moment of its abandonment, and to a tower at the moment of its failure to be built. It signifies the variety of languages and yet is itself to be found unchanged in very many languages of the world. People can understand the word 'Babel'; but what it means is the disintegration of understanding. Its meaning is the confusion of meaning.

Here is the story of how this strange word came into being, as it is told in Genesis, chapter 11, in the 1611 'King James' translation of the Bible:

1. And the *whole earth was of one †language, and of one †speach.

Wis.10.5
†Hebr. lippe.
†Heb. words

2. And it came to passe as they iourneyed from the East, that they found a plaine in the land of Shinar, and they dwelt there.

3. And †they sayd one to another; Goe to, let vs make bricke, and †burne them thorowly. And they had bricke for stone, and slime had they for morter.

†Heb. a man said to his neighbour
†Heb. burne them to a burning.

4. And they said; Goe to, let vs build vs a city and a tower, whose top may reach vnto heauen, and let vs make vs a name, lest we be scattered abroad vpon the face of the whole earth.

5. And the LORD came downe to see the city and the tower, which the children of men builded.

6. And the LORD said; Behold, the people [is] one, and they [haue] all one language: and this they begin to doe: and now nothing will be restrained from them, which they haue imagined to doe.

7. Goe to, let vs go downe, and there cōfound their language, that they may not vnderstand one anothers speech.

8. So the LORD scattered them abroad from thence, vpon the face of all the earth: and they left off to build the Citie.

9. Therefore is the name of it called †Babel, because the LORD did there confound the language of all the earth: and from thence did the LORD scatter them abroad vpon the face of all the earth.

†*That is, Confusion*

The text doesn't only tell the story of Babel; it inhabits a Babelic world. Without Babel there would be no need for translation; and the Bible in English is a translation. Not only that, it draws attention to its translatedness. The little wordings given in the margin show how the translation could have been done differently, while the words in smaller script – as here in verse 6 – are shrunken to indicate that there is nothing that corresponds to them in the Hebrew source text. 'Behold, the people is one' could be 'Behold, the people one'; 'Babel' could be 'Confusion'. Here is the Babelic confounding of language at work.

As the word 'Babel' has lingered through history, and wandered into many languages, it has developed a range of meanings: a 'medley of sounds'; a 'hubbub'; a 'jumble of people or things'; a 'tall or imposing structure'; a 'visionary or unrealistic scheme'. It can be used as a hostile term in religious and political arguments: a Protestant might say that Catholic Rome is a 'Babel', while the earliest Jewish commentators on the Old Testament made a similar connection to their enemy Babylon.[1] 'Babel' is also an echo chamber for associations with other words. Its Hebrew version, *Bāḇel* (בָּבֶל), was close to the word *bālal*, which meant 'to confuse, confound', as the alternative translation in the margin of the King James Bible indicates. In English, 'Babel' is close to 'babble', and there are similar connections in many other languages: to *babbelen* in Dutch, *babbeln* in German, *babbla* in Icelandic and Swedish, *babiller* in French. The *Oxford English Dictionary* tells us that this babbling family of words has a different etymological origin from the name 'Babel': it goes back to the very beginnings of language, to 'the syllable /ba/ which is characteristic of early infantile vocalization'. But, as people have spoken and written over time, the words have overlapped and their meanings mingled.

So, just like the text of the King James translation, the history of the word 'Babel' illustrates the condition of language which the story of Babel was designed to explain. Languages continually change, split and intermingle;

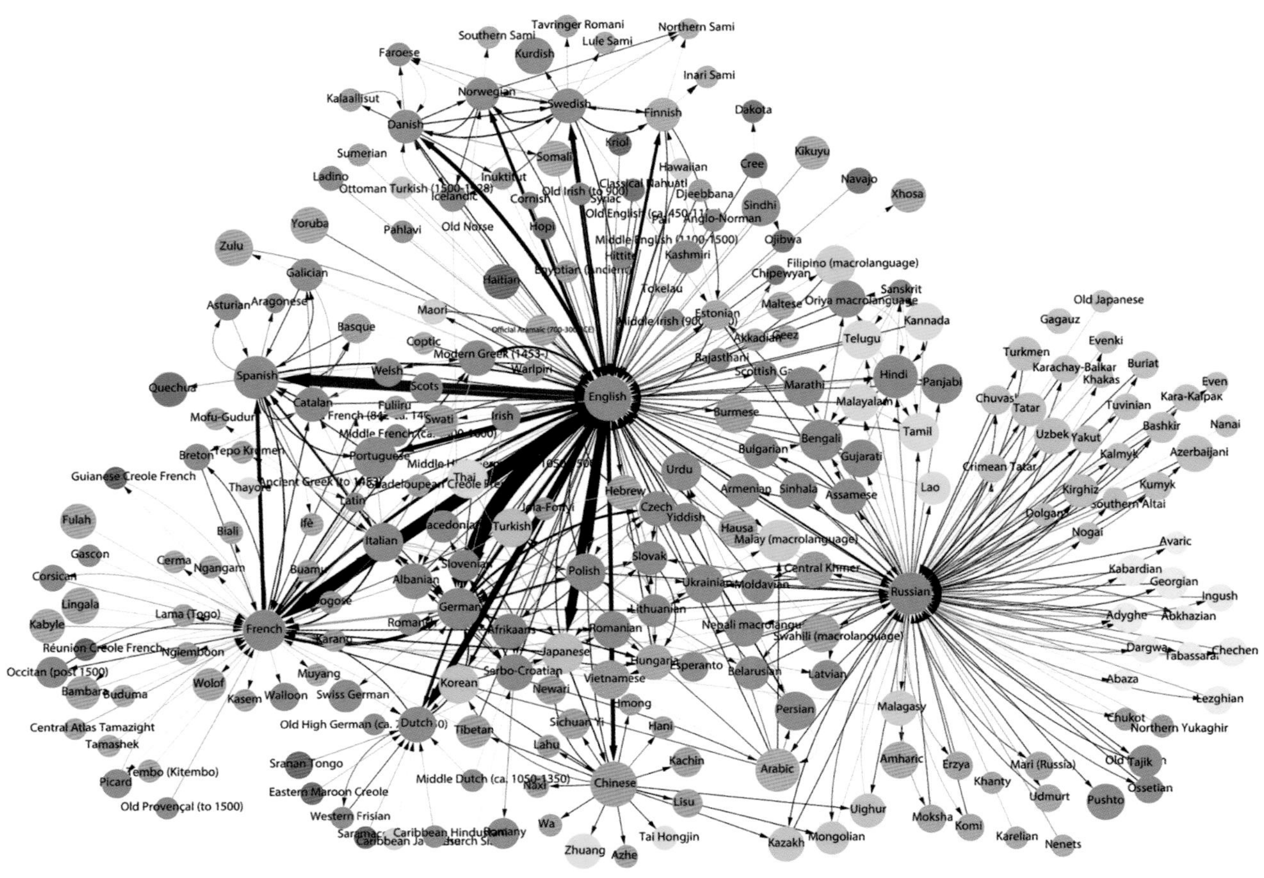

2 This diagram represents global flows of translations of books between 1979 and 2011: the size of each circle indicates the number of speakers of each language, and the thickness of the lines between them the number of translations (in both directions). From Shahar Ronen, Bruno Gonçalves, Kevin Z. Hu, Alessandro Vespignani, Steven Pinker and César A. Hidalgo, 'Links that Speak: The Global Language Network and Its Association with Global Fame', www.pnas.org/content/111/52/E5616.

and the meanings of words develop, braid and alter. There are many languages, and there are many varieties within each language. Language differences express differences between people; and because this creates misunderstanding it can seem like a curse. On the other hand, language differences come into being because people choose to speak differently, to say different things, and have new thoughts. So the variety of languages is generative: it produces understanding just as much as misunderstanding, for if there were no differences there would be nothing to understand. The process that mediates between misunderstanding and understanding, between the new and the known, the strange and the familiar, is translation. Translation is the crucial go-between in our Babelic world, mitigating the curse-like elements of Babel, and enabling its blessings to bloom (**figure 2**).[2]

Babel is at work within the history of each language as well as between languages. We can see this in the way the King James Bible seems strange to us today: in its spelling, in some of the meanings of the words, and in the way the sentences are put together. That strangeness becomes all the more visible if we compare the King James version with a recent translation of Genesis, by Mary Phil Korsak, which embodies not only a different kind of English but a different style:

1 All the earth had one lip, one speech

2 When they set out from the east
they found a dale in the land of Shinar
and settled there

3 They said, each to his companion
Come, let us brick bricks!
Let us burn them in a burning!
For them brick was stone, bitumen was clay for them

4 They said, Come, let us build ourselves a town and a tower
with its head in the skies
let us make ourselves a name
else we shall be scattered
upon the face of all the earth

5 YHWH went down to see the town and the tower
the sons of the groundling had built

6 YHWH said, Here is one people, one lip for them all!
They have begun to do this
and now nothing will check them
in all that they plan to do!

7 Come, we will go down and make their lip babble there
so that no man shall hear the lip of his companion

8 YHWH scattered them from there
upon the face of all the earth
They stopped building the town

9 So they called its name Babel
for there YHWH made the lip of all the earth babble
and from there YHWH scattered them
upon the face of all the earth[3]

Where the King James translators explained the meaning of the Hebrew *bālal* in an idiom suitable to be read out in churches and form the heart of a religious community, Korsak crafts her modern idiom into a distinctive literary style. It is, then, a combination of personal choice with the way the language has changed over time which turns 'confound the language of all the earth' into 'made the lip of all the earth babble'. Because people do not all have 'one lip, one speech', they are able to use words differently, in different times, places, languages, idioms and styles. This is a blessing of Babel.

The Bible in many tongues

People don't usually connect the word 'Bible' to 'Babel'. 'Bible' comes from a different etymological root, the Greek *βιβλία*, 'books'. Yet, just like 'babble', it has something in common with Babel, for the Bible has always moved between languages via translation: first, during the processes of its composition, between Hebrew, Aramaic and Greek; then into Latin and on into many hundreds of languages around the world.

As the Bible has travelled across languages it has generated extraordinary feats of scholarship and book-making. One of them is the 'Complutensian Polyglot' (**figure 3**), called after the Latin name, 'Complutum', for the Spanish town Alcalá, where it was created between 1502 and 1517.[4] This Bible presents the Old Testament in five different language manifestations. The upper part of the page gives St Jerome's fourth- to fifth-century Latin translation, the Vulgate, in a narrow column in the middle, flanked by the older texts from which it was derived: the Hebrew and the Greek (with Latin interlinear glosses). The lower section of the page shows the early Aramaic translation of the Pentateuch, the Targum Onkelos, together with a translation of that translation into Latin. The New Testament is treated differently because of its more straightforward linguistic make-up: the original Greek and the Latin translation are simply presented side by side. This book gives a vivid impression of the Bible as a thoroughly Babelic entity: an inherently multilingual text that is then scattered into more languages via translation.

Yet the Complutensian Polyglot also reveals the anxieties about authority which translation inevitably generates. Of all these texts, which is the correct one? Which one should I most trust? Startlingly, the prologue 'Ad lectorem', 'To the reader', argues that St Jerome's Latin translation is more authoritative than the Hebrew and Greek texts from which it emerged: it is like Jesus, and they are like the two thieves by which he was flanked at the crucifixion. The reason is that Jerome's Latin translation had become the Vulgate, the official Bible text for the Roman Catholic Church. For Cardinal Cisneros, who wrote the prologue, the authority of his Church overcame the historical precedence of the texts in Greek and Hebrew. They seemed dubious to him because they were associated with the rival beliefs of Greek Orthodoxy and Judaism.[5]

An international language

At the time of the Complutensian Polyglot, and for centuries before and after, Latin was not only the language of classical literature and the Roman Catholic Church. It was also a transnational medium used by intellectuals to communicate about all sorts of topics. In this, it was a 'global' (in fact partially global) language like English, Mandarin Chinese, Spanish, Arabic or Kiswahili today. So when, in 1679, the German Jesuit scholar Athanasius Kircher published a book in Latin about the Babel story, the language he used offered something of a remedy for the event he was investigating.[6] In *Turris Babel*, Kircher brings much systematic reasoning to bear on the Babel myth. He shows that the tower could never (as some said) have reached the moon, and illustrates the relative proportions with a diagram that looks a bit like a spear stuck into a tennis ball **(figure 4)**. He connects the confusion of tongues to later linguistic history. And he delves into the likely details of the construction process: his illustration of the tower in **figure 1**, based on a drawing by Lievin Cruyl, shows the building busily under way, with plans being examined, workers ascending the sloped, intersecting avenues, and kilns smoking as they 'brick bricks' and 'burn them in a burning' ready for use. The image presents the construction of the Babel tower as an example to learn from and perhaps emulate, rather than a prelude to catastrophe.

If it was to function as an international language, Latin needed to be thoroughly known, with its meanings fixed and calibrated against those of the vernacular languages such as English, French and German which it bridged. There needed to be dictionaries. An important element in humanism, the reform of learning which spread during the fifteenth and

Primitiua heb.	Ter. Heb.	Gen.	Ca. xi.	Trãsla. B. Hiero.	Trãsla. Gre. lxx. cũ interp. latina.

Ter. Heb. Gen. Ca. xi.

שלח ילד את עבר ולעבר ילד
שני בנים שם האחד פלג כי
בימיו נפלגה הארץ ושם אחיו
יקטן ויקטן ילד את אלמודד
ואת שלף ואת חצרמות ואת
ירח ואת הדורם ואת אוזל ואת
דקלה ואת עובל ואת אבימאל
ואת שבא ואת אופר ואת חוילה
ואת יובב כל אלה בני יקטן ויהי
מושבם ממשא באכה ספרה הר
הקדם אלה בני שם למשפחתם
ללשנתם בארצתם לגויהם
אלה משפחת בני נח לתולדתם
בגויהם ומאלה נפרדו הגוים
בארץ אחר המבול ויהי
כל הארץ שפה אחת ודברים
אחדים ויהי בנסעם מקדם
וימצאו בקעה בארץ שנער
וישבו שם ויאמרו איש אל
רעהו הבה נלבנה לבנים
ונשרפה לשרפה ותהי להם
הלבנה לאבן והחמר היה להם
לחמר ויאמרו הבה נבנה לנו
עיר ומגדל וראשו בשמים
ונעשה לנו שם פן נפוץ על פני
כל הארץ וירד יהוה לראות את
העיר ואת המגדל אשר בנו בני

Primitiua heb.: שנה · פלג · היה · ישב · שפח · ילד · פרד · Ca. xi. · היה · מצא · יהב לבן · שרף היה · בנה · גדל · עשה נפץ בנה · ראה · גדל בנה

Trãsla. B. Hiero.

de quo ortus est heber. Natique sunt heber filii duo. Nomen vni phaleg: eo quod in diebus eius diuisa sit terra: & nomen fratris eius iectan. Qui iectan genuit elmodad & saleph & asarmoth & iare & adoram & iazal & decla & hebal & abimahel: & saba & iophir: & euila & iobab. Omnes isti filii iectan. Et facta est habitatio eorũ de messa pergẽtibus vsque sephar montẽ orientalẽ. Isti sunt filii sem secundum cognationes & linguas & regiones in gentibus suis. Hec familie noe iuxta populos & nationes suas. Ab his diuise sunt gentes in terra post diluuiũ.

Erat autem (Ca. 11.) terra labii vnius & sermonum eorũdẽ. Cũque proficiscerentur de oriente inuenerunt campum in terra sennaar: & habitauerunt in eo. Dixitque alter ad proximũ suũ. Venite faciamus lateres: & coquamus eos igni. Habueruntque lateres pro saxis: & bitumen pro cemẽto. Et dixerũt. Venite faciamus nobis ciuitatẽ & turrẽ: cuius culmẽ pertingat ad celũ: & celebremus nomẽ nostrum antequã diuidamur in vniuersas terras. Descẽdit autẽ dñs vt videret ciuitatem & turrem quam edificabant filii

Trãsla. Gre. lxx. cũ interp. latina.

sale aũt genuit eber. et eber nati
σαλὰς δὲ ἐγέννησε τὸν ἔβερ. καὶ τῷ ἔβερ ἐγεν
sunt duo filij. nomen vni: phalec. quia in
ήθησαν δύο υἱοί. ὄνομα τῷ ἑνί, φαλέκ. ὅτι ἐν ταῖς
bus eius: diuisa est terra. et nomen fra
μέραις αὐτοῦ, διεμερίσθη ἡ γῆ. καὶ ὄνομα τῷ ἀδε
tri eius: iectan. iectã aũt genuit elmodad:
φῷ αὐτοῦ, ἰεκτάν. ἰεκτὰν δὲ ἐγέννησε τὸν ἰελμωδὰ
et saleph: et asarmoth: et iared: et
καὶ τὸν σαλέφ, καὶ τὸν ἀσαραμώθ, καὶ ἰεράχ, καὶ
adoram: et aizal: et decla: et ebal: et
ὀδορρὰμ, καὶ αἰζὴλ, καὶ δεκλὰ, καὶ γεβὰλ, καὶ
abimael: et saban: et vphir: et euilat:
ἀβιμεὴλ, καὶ σαβὰν, καὶ οὐφείρ, καὶ τὸν εὐειλὰ
et iobab. oẽs isti filij iectan. et facta
καὶ ἰωβάβ. πάντες οὗτοι υἱοὶ ἰεκτάν. καὶ ἐγένετ
habitatio eorũ: de messa vsque ad sephar mo
κατοίκησις αὐτῶν, ἀπὸ μασσῆ ἕως εἰς σωφηρὰ ὄρο
orientis. isti filij sem in tribubus suis
ἀνατολῶν. οὗτοι υἱοὶ σὴμ ἐν ταῖς φυλαῖς αὐτῶ
secundum linguas suas: in regiõibus suis: et
κατὰ γλώσσας αὐτῶν, ἐν ταῖς χώραις αὐτῶν, καὶ
gentibus suis. he tribus filiorũ noe fr
τοῖς ἔθνεσιν αὐτῶν. αὗται αἱ φυλαὶ υἱῶν νῶε κα
cognatiões eorũ: secundum gẽtes eorũ. ab istis
συγγενείας αὐτῶν, κατὰ ἔθνη αὐτῶν. ἀπὸ τούτ
disseminate sũt insule gẽtiũ in terra: p
διεσπάρησαν νῆσοι τῶν ἐθνῶν ἐπὶ τῆς γῆς, με
diluuiũ.
τὸν κατακλυσμόν.

Cap. [11]

Et erat oĩs terra labiũ vnũ: et vox v
καὶ ἦν πᾶσα ἡ γῆ χεῖλος ἕν, καὶ φωνὴ μ
oĩbus. et factũ est cũ mouerent ipsi ab ori
πᾶσι. καὶ ἐγένετο ἐν τῷ κινῆσαι αὐτοὺς ἀπὸ ἀνατ
te: inuenerũt campũ in terra sẽnaar: et habitauer
λῶν, εὗρον πεδίον ἐν γῇ σεννααρ, καὶ κατῴκησ
ibi et dixit homo proximo suo: ven
ἐκεῖ. καὶ εἶπεν ἄνθρωπος τῷ πλησίον αὐτοῦ, δεῦ
laterificemus laterem: et coquamus eos i
πλινθεύσωμεν πλίνθον, καὶ ὀπτήσωμεν αὐτὰς
et factus est illis later in lapidem. et bi
ρί. καὶ ἐγένετο αὐτοῖς ἡ πλίνθος εἰς λίθον. καὶ ἄσφ
men fuit illis lutũ. et dixerũt: venite edificem
τος ἦν αὐτοῖς ὁ πηλός. καὶ εἶπον, δεῦτε οἰκοδομή
nobis ciuitatẽ et turrim: cuius erit caput
μεν ἑαυτοῖς πόλιν καὶ πύργον, οὗ ἔσται ἡ κεφα
vsque ad celũ. et faciamus nobis nomen
ἕως τοῦ οὐρανοῦ. καὶ ποιήσωμεν ἑαυτοῖς ὄνομα
anteq̃ dispergamur nos a facie vn
πρὸ τοῦ διασπαρῆναι ἡμᾶς ἀπὸ προσώπου πά
uerse terre. et descẽdit dñs deus vt videret
σης τῆς γῆς. καὶ κατέβη κύριος ὁ θεὸς ἰδεῖν τὴν
uitatẽ et turrim: quã edificauerũt filij
λιν καὶ τὸν πύργον, ὃν ᾠκοδόμησαν οἱ υἱοὶ

Primitiua chal.: ילד בנה · פלג · אל יתב מטא · ילד פרש · מלל טול · שכח יהב רמה · ימד הוה בנה · קרה גדל ראש · מטא עבד בדר · גלה פרע קבה · גדל בנה

Interp. chal.

et sale genuit heber: et de heber nati sunt duo filij: nomẽ vnius phaleg: quia in diebus suis diuisa est terra: et nomẽ fratris sui iectan. Iectan aũt gẽuit elmodad et saleph et asarmoth et iare et aduram et vzal et decla et hobal et abimael et saba et ophir et euila et iobab: oẽs isti filij iectan. Et fuit habitatio eorum a messa pertingens vsque sephar montẽ orientalẽ. Isti sunt filij sem per cognationes et linguas suas in terris suis in populis suis. Iste sunt cognationes filiorum noe per generationes suas in populis suis: et ab his diuisi sunt populi in terra post diluuium. Cap. 11.

Eratque oĩs terra lingue vnius et loquele vnius. et factum est cum proficiscerentur in principio et inuenissent campũ in terra babylonis: habitauerunt ibi. Dixeruntque vnusquisque ad proximũ suũ: venite faciamus lateres: et coquamus eos igni: et erat eis later pro lapide: et bitumen erat eis pro luto. Et dixerunt: venite edificemus nobis ciuitatẽ et turrim: et culmen eius pertigat vsque ad celos: et faciamus nobis nomen: ne forte dispergamur super faciem vniuerse terre. Et apparuit dominus vt vlcisceretur sup opera ciuitatis et turris: quas edificauerunt filij

Transla. Chal.

יד ית עבר ולעבר אתיליד תרין בנין שום חד פלג ארי ביומוהי
ארעא ושום אחוהי יקטן ויקטן אוליד ית אלמודד וית שלף וית חצר
ח וית הדורם וית אוזל וית דקלה וית עובל וית אבימאל וית שבא וית
חוילה וית יובב כל אילין בני יקטן והוה מותבניהון ממשא מטי לספר
א אילין בני שם לזרעיתהון ללישניהון בארעהון לעממיהון אילין זרעית
לדתהון בעממיהון ומאילין אתפרשו עממיא בארעא בתר טופנא
והוה כל ארעא לישן חד וממלל חד והוה במיטלהון בקדמיתא
קעתא בארעא דבבל ויתיבו תמן ואמרו גבר לחבריה הבו נרמי לבנין
ורא והות להון לבינתא לאבנא וחמרא הות להון לשיע ואמרו הבו נבנה
ומגדלא ורישיה מטי עד צית שמיא ונעביד לנא שמא דלמא נתבדר
ארעא ואתגלי יי לאתפרעא על עובדי קרתא ומגדלא דבנו בני

Trāsla. Grē. lxx. cū interp. latina.

hominū. et dixit dn̄s ecce gen⁹ vnū et labiū vnū om
τῶν ἀνθρώπων. καὶ εἶπε κύριος ἰδοὺ γένος ἓν καὶ χεῖλος ἓν ἁ-
nib⁹. et hoc ceperūt facere. ꝛ nūc nō defi
πάντων. καὶ τοῦτο ἤρξαντο ποιῆσαι. καὶ νῦν οὐκ ἐκ-
cient ab eis oīa: q̄cūq̧ agressi sūt facere.
λείψει ἀπ' αὐτῶν πάντα, ὅσα ἂν ἐπιθῶνται ποιεῖν.
venite et descendētes confundam⁹ eorū linguam
δεῦτε καὶ καταβάντες συγχέωμεν αὐτῶν γλῶσσαν
vt nō audiant vnusq̄sq̧ vocē proximi. ꝛ
ἵνα μὴ ἀκούσωσιν ἕκαστος τῆς φωνῆς τοῦ πλησίον. καὶ
dispsit dn̄s ipsos inde sup faciē oīs
διέσπειρε κύριος αὐτοὺς ἐκεῖθεν ἐπὶ πρόσωπον πάσης
terre. ꝛ cessauerūt edificantes ciuitatē et
τῆς γῆς. καὶ ἐπαύσαντο οἰκοδομοῦντες τὴν πόλιν καὶ
turrim. ppt hoc vocatū ē nomē eius: confu-
τὸν πύργον. διὰ τοῦτο ἐκλήθη τὸ ὄνομα αὐτῆς, σύγχυ-
sio. q: ibi cōfudit dn̄s labia vniuerse terre: ꝛ
σις. ὅτι ἐκεῖ συνέχεε κύριος τὰ χείλη πάσης τῆς γῆς, καὶ
inde dispsit eos dn̄s sup faciem oīs
ἐκεῖθεν διέσπειρεν αὐτοὺς ὁ κύριος ἐπὶ πρόσωπον πάσης
terre. et he gñatiōes sem. sem āt erat fili⁹ cen
τῆς γῆς. καὶ αὗται αἱ γενέσεις σήμ. σὴμ δὲ ἦν υἱὸς ἑκα-
tū ānorū: qñ genuit arpharad: secūdo anno
τὸν ἐτῶν, ὅτε ἐγέννησε τὸν ἀρφαξάδ, δευτέρου ἔτους
post diluuiū. et vixit sem: postq̄ genu
μετὰ τὸν κατακλυσμόν. καὶ ἔζησε σὴμ, μετὰ τὸ γεννῆ-
it ipse arpharad: ānos quingētos. et genu-
σαι αὐτὸν τὸν ἀρφαξάδ, ἔτη πεντακόσια. καὶ ἐγέννη-
it filios ꝛ filias: et mortuus ē. ꝛ vixit
σεν υἱοὺς καὶ θυγατέρας, καὶ ἀπέθανεν. καὶ ἔζησεν
arpharad ānos cētū triginta quinq̧. et genuit
ἀρφαξὰδ ἔτη ἑκατὸν τριακονταπέντε. καὶ ἐγέννησε
cainan. et vixit arpharad: postq̄ genuit ip-
τὸν καϊνᾶν. καὶ ἔζησεν ἀρφαξὰδ, μετὰ τὸ γεννῆσαι αὐ-
se cainan: ānos quadrigētos triginta. ꝛ genu-
τὸν τὸν καϊνᾶν, ἔτη τετρακόσια τριάκοντα. καὶ ἐγέννη-
it filios ꝛ filias: et mortu⁹ ē. et vixit cai
σεν υἱοὺς καὶ θυγατέρας, καὶ ἀπέθανεν. καὶ ἔζησε καϊ-
nan ānos centū triginta. et genuit sala. et
νᾶν ἔτη ἑκατὸν τριάκοντα. καὶ ἐγέννησε τὸν σαλά. καὶ
vixit cainan: postq̄ genuit ipse sala. ānos
ἔζησε καϊνᾶν, μετὰ τὸ γεννῆσαι αὐτὸν τὸν σαλά, ἔτη
trecentos triginta. et genuit filios et fili
τριακόσια τριάκοντα. καὶ ἐγέννησεν υἱοὺς καὶ θυγατέ-
as: et mortu⁹ ē. ꝛ vixit sala ānos centū trigin-
ρας, καὶ ἀπέθανεν. καὶ ἔζησε σαλὰ ἔτη ἑκατὸν τριάκον-
ta. et genuit eber. et vixit sala: postq̄ ge
τα. καὶ ἐγέννησε τὸν ἔβερ. καὶ ἔζησε σαλά, μετὰ τὸ γεν-
nuit ipse eber: ānos trecentos triginta: et
νῆσαι αὐτὸν τὸν ἔβερ, ἔτη τριακόσια τριάκοντα, καὶ
mortu⁹ ē. et vixit eber ānos centū triginta q̄ttu-
ἀπέθανεν. καὶ ἔζησεν ἔβερ ἔτη ἑκατὸν τριακοντατέσ-
or: et genuit phalec. ꝛ vixit eber: postq̄
σαρα, καὶ ἐγέννησε τὸν φαλέκ. καὶ ἔζησεν ἔβερ, μετὰ τὸ
genuit ipse phalec: ānos trecentos septuaginta
γεννῆσαι αὐτὸν τὸν φαλέκ, ἔτη τριακόσια ἑβδομήκοντα.

Transla. B. Hiero.

adam: & dixit. Ecce vnus est populus: & vnum est labium oībus. Ceperuntq̧ hoc facere: nec desistent a cogitatiōibus suis donec eas ope cōpleāt. Venite igī descēdamus & cōfūdamus ibi liguā eorū: vt nō audiat vnusquisq̧ vocē pximi sui. Atq̧ ita diuisit eos dn̄s ex illo loco in vniuersas terras: & cessauerūt edificare ciuitatē. Et idcirco vocatū est nomē eius babel: quia ibi confusum est labiū vniuerse terre. Et inde dispersit eos dn̄s super faciē cūctarū regionū. He sunt gñatiōes sem. Sem erat centum annorum quando genuit arphaxad: biennio post diluuiū. Vixitq̧ sem postq̧ genuit arphaxad quingentis annis: & genuit filios & filias. Porro arphaxad vixit triginta quinq̧ annis: & genuit sale. Vixitq̧ arphaxad postq̧ genuit sale trecentis tribus annis: & genuit filios & filias. Sale quoq̧ vixit triginta annis: & genuit heber. Vixitq̧ sale postq̧ genuit heber quadringentis tribus annis: & genuit filios & filias. Vixit autem heber triginta quattuor annis: & genuit phaleg. Et vixit heber postq̧ genuit phaleg quadrigētis triginta annis:

Tex. Heb. Gen. Ca. xi. Pꝛitiua. heb.

האדם: ויאמר יהוה הן עם אחד
ושפה אחת לכלם וזה החלם
לעשות ועתה לא יבצר מהם
כל אשר יזמו לעשות: הבה
נרדה ונבלה שם שפתם אשר
לא ישמעו איש שפת רעהו:
ויפץ יהוה אתם משם על פני
כל הארץ ויחדלו לבנת העיר:
על כן קרא שמה בבל כי שם
בלל יהוה שפת כל הארץ ומשם
הפיצם יהוה על פני כל הארץ:
אלה תולדת שם שם בן מאת
שנה ויולד את ארפכשד
שנתים אחר המבול: ויחי שם
אחרי הולידו את ארפכשד חמש
מאות שנה ויולד בנים ובנות:
וארפכשד חי חמש ושלשים
שנה ויולד את שלח: ויחי
ארפכשד אחרי הולידו את שלח
שלש שנים וארבע מאות שנה
ויולד בנים ובנות: ושלח חי
שלשים שנה ויולד את עבר:
ויחי שלח אחרי הולידו את עבר
שלש שנים וארבע מאות שנה
ויולד בנים ובנות: ויחי עבר
ארבע ושלשים שנה ויולד את
פלג: ויחי עבר אחרי הולידו את
פלג שלשים שנה וארבע מאות

אמר
בלל חלל
עשה בצר
יהב
ירד בלל
שמע שפה
נפץ פנה
חדל בנה
ילד מאה
ילד
שנה בול חיה
ילד
חיה
רבע מאה

Transla. Chal.

אינשא: ואמר ייי הא עם חד ולישן חד לכלהון ודין דשרו למעבד וכען לא יתמנע
מנהון כל דחשיבו למעבד: הבו נתגלי ונבלבל תמן לישנהון דלא ישמעון אינש
לישן חבריה: ובדר ייי יתהון מתמן על אפי כל ארעא ואתמנעו מלמבני קרתא: על
כן קרא שמה בבל ארי תמן בלבל ייי לישן כל ארעא ומתמן בדרינון ייי על אפי כל
ארעא: אילין תולדת שם שם בר מאה שנין ואוליד ית ארפכשד תרתין שנין בתר
טופנא: וחיא שם בתר דאוליד ית ארפכשד חמש מאה שנין ואוליד בנין ובנן
וארפכשד חי תלתין וחמש שנין ואוליד ית שלח: וחיא ארפכשד בתר דאוליד ית
שלח ארבע מאה ותלת שנין ואוליד בנין ובנן: ושלח חיא תלתין שנין ואוליד ית
עבר: וחיא שלח בתר דאוליד ית עבר ארבע מאה ותלת שנין ואוליד בנין ובנן:
וחיא עבר ארבע ותלתין שנין ואוליד ית פלג: וחיא עבר בתר דאוליד ית פלג
ארבע מאה ותלתין שנין

Interp. chal.

hominū. Et dixit dn̄s. Ecce populus vnus ꝛ lingua vna est oībus illis. et hoc est qđ ceperūt facere: ꝛ nūc non prohibetur ab eis omne qđ cogitauerūt facere. Venite appareamus ꝛ cōfundam⁹ ibi linguā eorū: vt nō audiat vnusquisq̧ linguā proximi sui. Et dispersit eos dn̄s inde sup faciem vniuerse terre: ꝛ prohibiti sunt ab edificatione ciuitatis. idcirco vocatū est nomen eius babel: qm̄ ibi confudit dn̄s linguā vniuerse terre: ꝛ inde dispersit eos dn̄s sup faciē vniuerse terre. He sunt generatiōes sem: sem filius centū annoꝝ erat qñ genuit arpharad duob⁹ annis post diluuiū. Et vixit sem postq̄ genuit arpharad q̄ngētis annis: et genuit filios ꝛ filias. Et arpharad vixit triginta ꝛ quinq̧ annis: ꝛ genuit sale: ꝛ vixit arpharad postq̄ genuit sale q̄dringētis ꝛ tribus annis: ꝛ genuit filios et filias. Et sale vixit triginta annis ꝛ genuit heber: et vixit sale postquam genuit heber quadringentis ꝛ tribus annis ꝛ genuit filios ꝛ filias. Et vixit heber triginta et quattuor annis ꝛ genuit phaleg: et vixit heber postquam genuit phaleg quadringentis ꝛ triginta annis:

Pꝛitiua chal.

שרא עבד מנע
יהב גלה בלל
שמע מנע בנה
קרה בלל אל
ילד שנה תרי
חיה ילד בנה
רבע שנה חיה

sixteenth centuries, was the compilation of bilingual Latin dictionaries; the most important English example was written by Sir Thomas Elyot and published in 1538 (**figure 5**).[7] Elyot had pursued a high-profile but troubled career at court: he had served as ambassador to the Holy Roman Emperor Charles V, trying unsuccessfully to gain his support for Henry VIII's divorce from Catharine of Aragon, and had felt in danger after the execution of Sir Thomas More, who had been his friend. Still, he retained the king's favour, and the royal library was thrown open to him as a resource for his lexicographical labours. Elyot's book was the first to use the word 'dictionary' in its title, and it distinguishes itself from earlier word lists and glossaries by being fuller and more systematic, and making greater use of classical sources.[8]

Elyot's *Dictionary* presented Latin and English as separate languages: words in the one language are defined by words in the other. Yet, paradoxically, it formed part of a life's work in which English and Latin were continuously intermingling and merging. In his political career Elyot would have used both languages; and in his writing he recommends that English should increase its range and dignity by adopting words from Latin. Seven years before the *Dictionary*, he had published *The Boke Named the Governour*, a work of moral philosophy mixed with tips on education and advice for rulers: it was a massive bestseller. In it, Elyot endeavours to 'augment our Englyshe tongue' by weaving Latin vocabulary into his English in such a way that its meaning could be guessed by readers who did not know it already. Among the words he imported are many that caught on and remain in the language today, for instance 'execrate', 'superstitiously', 'articulate', 'emulation', 'beneficence', 'democracy', 'frugality' and 'society'. Others were less successful, such as 'decerpt', 'falcate', 'illecebrous' and 'humect'.[9]

3 *previous spread* The 'Complutensian Polyglot': this multilingual Bible, created in Spain in the early sixteenth century, shows the Hebrew on the left, St Jerome's Latin in the middle, Greek (with Latin gloss) on the right, and Aramaic with its Latin translation at the bottom. The book is open at Genesis 11, the story of the Tower of Babel. Bodleian Library, Byw. B 3.3.

The first English–English dictionary

Languages continually grow, change and blend: this is a major aspect of the curse and blessing of Babel. The world of language is not a jigsaw puzzle made up of separate tongues, but rather a rolling sea of usage, with the boundary lines between what count as different languages perpetually shifting. The movement of which Elyot was a leader contributed to a particularly intense moment of such intermingling, with thousands of new words being made to count as English. As a result, there was a need for

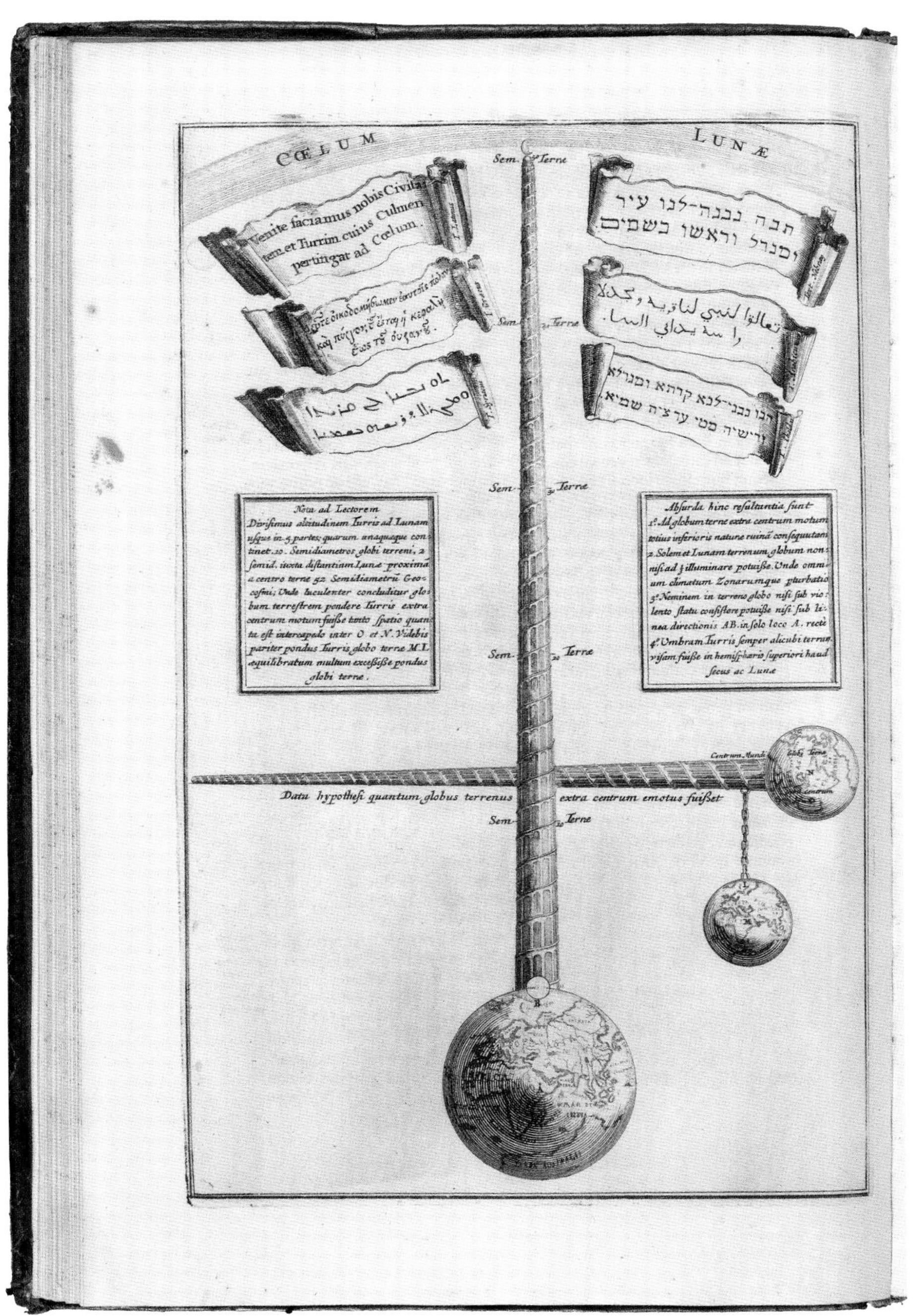

4 This image, from Kircher's *Turris Babel* (1679), pokes fun at the idea that the Tower of Babel might have been meant to reach the moon. Bodleian Library, Vet. B3 b.33, p. 38.

ble them ſelfes in frendſhyp, ſo they whiche are inferior ſhulde aduaunce and ſette them ſelfes forewarde.

Quodcunq;, what ſo euer.

Quodcunq; militum, for quotcunque milites. *Cice. atti.* Vos hortor, vt quodcũque militum contrahere poteritis, contrahatis, I aduyſe you, that as many ſouldiours as ye can gete, ye gather vnto you.

Quominus, for Vt non. *Terent. in andria.* Si poterit fieri, vt ne pater per me ſtetiſſe credat, quo minus hę fierent nuptię, volo: If it may be brought to paſſe, that my father maye beleue, that it is not in my fault, that this mariage is not concluded, I am content.

Quomodo, howe, by what reaſon, in what maner, by what meane. *Plautus in Aulul.* Quomodo tibi res ſe habet? Howe is the matter with the? *Plautus in milite.* Sed quomodo diſſimulabat? But in what maner dyd he diſſemble? *Plautus in amph.* Primulo diliculo abiſti ad legiones, By tyme in the mornynge thou wenteſt to the armye. Amph. Quomodo? In what maner or facion? alſo it ſignifieth wherfore. *Plautus in Stich.* Illa quidem nullũ ſacrificabit. G. Quomodo? quid igitur me volt? She will doo no ſacrifyce. G. wherfore? what thynge wolde ſhe than with me?

Quomodocunque, howe ſo euer it be. *Plautus in penulo.* Sed tamen quomodocunq;, quamquàm ſumus pauperculi, eſt domi quod edimus: Yet how ſo euer it be, thoughe we be poure folkes, we haue at home ſomewhat to eate.

Quomodolibet, idem.

Quondam, Sometyme, ones: ſignifyenge the tyme paſt, or tyme to come. *Verg.* Quondam tua dicere facta Tempus erit: The time ſhal be ones, whan thyne actes ſhall be declared. Alſoo it is put in the tyme preſent. *Vergili.* Quondam etiam victis redit in precordia virtus, Ye, and in them that are vaynquyſſhed, ſometyme good courage eftſones imbraceth their ſtomakes. Sometyme it ſignyfyeth allwaye. Vt quondam in ſtipulis magnus ſine viribus ignis, Lyke as in ſtubbyll or holme fyre is allwaye greate without any puyſſaunce.

Quonam, whyther. *Plautus in Trin.* Eamus intrò, ſequere. S. Quo tutè agis? C. quonam, niſi domum. Let vs go in, folowe me. S. whyther wylt thou go? whyther ſhulde I goo but home to my houſe?

Quoniam, for as moche as.

Quo officio es? what is thyne office?

Quopiam, any whyther. Iturâne Thais quopiam es? Thais, wylte thou goo any whyther?

Quoquam, any whyther.

Quoque, alſo.

Quoquo, whereſoeuer.

Q ante V.

Quoquo pacto, In any maner of wyſe. Tum ſi maxime fateatur, cum amet aliam, non eſt vtile hanc illi dari: qua propter quoquo pacto cęlato eſt opus, Than yf he vtterly cõfeſſe it, for as moch as he loueth another, it were not conuenient, that he were maryed to this woman, therfore in any maner of wyſe, this thinge muſt be kept ſecrete.

Quoquo modo, idem.

Quo quouerſum, ſeu quoquouerſum, euery waye, on euerye parte. Eius imperio claſſem quo quouerſum dimittunt, By his commaundement they dyſpeched the nauy in euery part. Rates duplices quóquouerſum pedibus triginta é regione ſolis collocabat: he ſette ſhyppes double agaynſte the ſonne, thirty feete euery waye.

Quorſum, ſeu quorſus, apud Plinium, whyther, to what place, or thinge.

Quorſum iſtuc? to what purpoſe.

Quot, how many.

Quota pars, how ſmall a porcion.

Quotannis, yere by yere, euery yere.

Quotennis? of what age? howe olde?

Quot annos natus, idem.

Quotenus, a, um, how many.

Quotidianę forma, a commune beautye or facion, euery daye ſene.

Quotidiani ſumptus, dayly expenſes.

Quotidianus, quotidiana, quotidianum, a thynge that is or happeneth dayly or daye by daye.

Quotidie, dayly, euery daye.

Quoties, howe oftentymes.

Quotieſcunq;, as often.

Quotquot, as many.

Quotuplex, how many ſortes.

Quotuplus, howe moche in meaſure or wayght.

Quotus, ta, tum, of what numbre, howe many, Hora quota eſt, what is it a clocke? Dic quotus es? Telle howe many be of you. Quotas ædes dixerit, id ego admodum incerto ſcio: How many houſes he ſpake of, I am not well aſſertayned, or I remembre not well.

Quotuſquiſque, how many.

Quouis, whyther, or to what place ye wyll.

Quouis gentium, idem.

Quouſque, how longe, how farre.

Quouſque tandem, how longe yet.

Qur, & Quor, wherfore.

Quum, ſeu qum, whan, in the whiche.

Quum primum, as ſoone.

RAbia, olde wryters vsed for Rabies.
Rabidus, da, dum, madde or woode, as a madde dogge.
Rabies, madnesse of a dogge.
Rabiosus, a, um, madde or very angry, woode angry.
Rabio, bire, to be madde or woode as a dogge. Varro.
Rabiosulus, a, um, somewhat madde.
Rabula, one which is hasty or wilfull, in any cause, ianglynge, or full of wordes.
Racemarius, a twygge of a vyne, out of the which the grapes do springe.
Racematio, the gatheringe of grapes after that the greate clusters be gathered to make wyne, the glenynge of grapes.
Racematus, ta, tum, that hath grapes.
Racemosus, full of grapes.
Racemus, a grape or a cluster of grapes.
Racha, a reprochefull worde of Hebrewe, which signifyeth, thriftlesse, braynlesse, fynally it is a rebukefull worde sygnifyenge the extreme ire of the personne that speaketh it.
Radicitus, frome the roote, or vppe by the roote, Radicitus euellere, to plucke vppe by the roote.
Radico, care, to roote or take roote.
Radicula, an herbe, the iuyce whereof is good to washe woulle: also a lytle roote.
Radio, are, to sende forth beames lyke the sunne.
Radius, a beame of the sun, or other bright sterre, sometyme of the eyes: also a rodde or yerde, that Geometricians haue to describe lynes: also a wayuers shyttell, wherwith he throweth the yern in to the webbe also the spoke of a wheele, alsoo an instrument, wherwith measures be shauen: alsoo longe olyues or oyle beryes.
Radix, dicis, a roote.
Rado, si, dere, to shaue, or make smoothe, to cut or pull vp, to hurte, to rent, to offende, to fatigate. Aures delicatas radere, to offende or fatigate delicate eares.
Radula, an instrument to shaue with.
Radulanus, a, um, that whiche is shauen of, frome any thynge.
Ragadia, & Ragades, cleftes or choppes in the fundament.
Raia, a see fysshe called Raye or skete.
Ralla, a thynne garment.
Rallum, the staffe, wherewith plowghmen in tyllynge do put the erthe frome their share.
Ramalis, le, a bowghe.
Ramale, a seryd or deed bowghe.
Ramentum, a lytle piece of any thynge.
Rameus, a, um, that whyche is of a bowgh.
Ramex, micis, a kynde of rupture, whan the bowels do fal downe into a mans coddes: also a rayle or barre, whiche goeth ouerthwart a pale or a gate.
Ramicosus, he that is broken.
Ramnus, a whyte thorne.
Ramulus, & Ramusculus, a lytell bowghe.
Ramus, a bowghe.
Rana, a frogge: also a sickenesse which doth anoy cattell.
Rana Seriphia, is a prouerbe applyed to thē that canne not speake in tyme conuenient.
Ranceo, cere, to be mouldy or putrifyed.
Rancidus, da, dum, rankled, mouldy, or putrifyed: also vnsauery, or vnpleasaunt.
Rancidulus, la, lum, a lytle mouldy or putryfyed.
Rancor, oris, rancour, fylth.
Randus, in olde tyme was taken for æs, brasse.
Randuscula porta, the brason gate.
Rantum, in the olde tyme was a quarterne of a pounde.
Ranunculus, a lytell frogge, or frosshe.
Rapa, a plant and roote called Rape.
Rapacia, rape leaues.
Rapatior, more rauenous or catchinge.
Rapacissimus, a, um, moost rauenous.
Rapacitas, raueny.
Rapaciter, rauenousely.
Rapax, acis, rauenouse.
Raphanus, a plante, and roote called Radyshe.
Rapere aliquem in ius, to arrest one, or cause hym to be arrested to appere before iuges.
Rapide, quickly.
Rapidus, a, um, very swift.
Rapina, robbery.
Rapinator, a robbar. Varro.
Rapio, pui, pere, to take by violence, hast, or fury: also to rauysshe a woman.
Rapo, Raponis, for Rapax.
Raptim, hastily.
Raptio, violent takynge of a persone.
Raptus, rauysshynge or deflourynge of a woman.
Raptito, tare, to take often violently.
Rapto, to take or drawe violently.
Raptor, toris, a rauysshour or vyolente taker.
Rapulum, a lytle rape roote.
Rapunculus, a lytle roote, whyche is eaten in salates.
Rara auis, a byrde seldome seene: wherebr is signifyed any thynge that seldome happeneth.

dictionaries to help people translate, not only between 'Latin' and 'English' but between 'English' and 'English': just because the words were being given dual nationality did not mean that they were immediately at home in their new context. The first substantial English–English dictionary was compiled by Robert Cawdrey, an uncompromising Puritan who had been expelled from the priesthood of the Church of England. It was published in 1604 as *A Table Alphabeticall: contayning and teaching the true writing, and vnderstanding of hard vsuall English wordes, borrowed from the Hebrew, Greeke, Latine, or French, &c. with the interpretation thereof by plaine English words, gathered for the benefit & helpe of ladies, gentlewomen, or any other vnskilfull persons, whereby they may the more easilie and better understand many hard English wordes, which they shall heare or read in scriptures, sermons, or elsewhere, and also be made able to vse the same aptly themselves* **(figure 6).**[10]

As its prominence in Cawdrey's title suggests, alphabetical order could still seem a novelty even though it had been adopted by earlier dictionaries such as Elyot's; and in fact it is not maintained entirely accurately throughout the *Table*'s 2,543 entries. But the book clearly met a widespread need: it was reprinted and expanded in the following years, and the gender-specific targeting was dropped.[11] A glance at Elyot's Latin–English *Dictionary* and Cawdrey's English–English *Table* makes the overlaps between Latin and the expanding English language very clear. Some words are identical in both volumes, for instance 'quondam' or 'racha'. Others have only tiny differences: 'rapina' and 'rapine', 'rapacitas' and 'rapacitie', 'quotidianus' and 'quotidian'. Like the use of Latin as an international medium, this blending of languages is both a consequence of the Babelic confusion of tongues and to some degree a cure for it.

5 *previous spread* In this important early Latin–English dictionary by Sir Thomas Elyot (1538) we can see Latin words such as *rapacitas* and *quotidianus* which were soon to appear – with only tiny changes of spelling – in monolingual dictionaries of the English language (see figure 6). Bodleian Library, 4 Δ 328, open at 'R'.

Babel and power

Knowledge is power – or *scientia potestas est*, as that phrase was first written by Sir Francis Bacon in 1597. If you know a language you have the power to join a group – for instance the Latin-speaking intelligentsia, for users of Elyot's dictionary, or the community of 'skilful users of English', for readers of Cawdrey's. If you are a leader, or other authority, this power opens onto others: not only to communicate with speakers of a language but to influence, discipline and command. So groups that want to remain opaque to the authorities concoct their own private codes or jargons: examples are cockney rhyming slang, polari (the London gay idiom that flourished until the late 1960s) and the new modes of speech invented by every generation of teenagers. Conversely, knowledge of the languages of conquered peoples has been an important tool of empire.

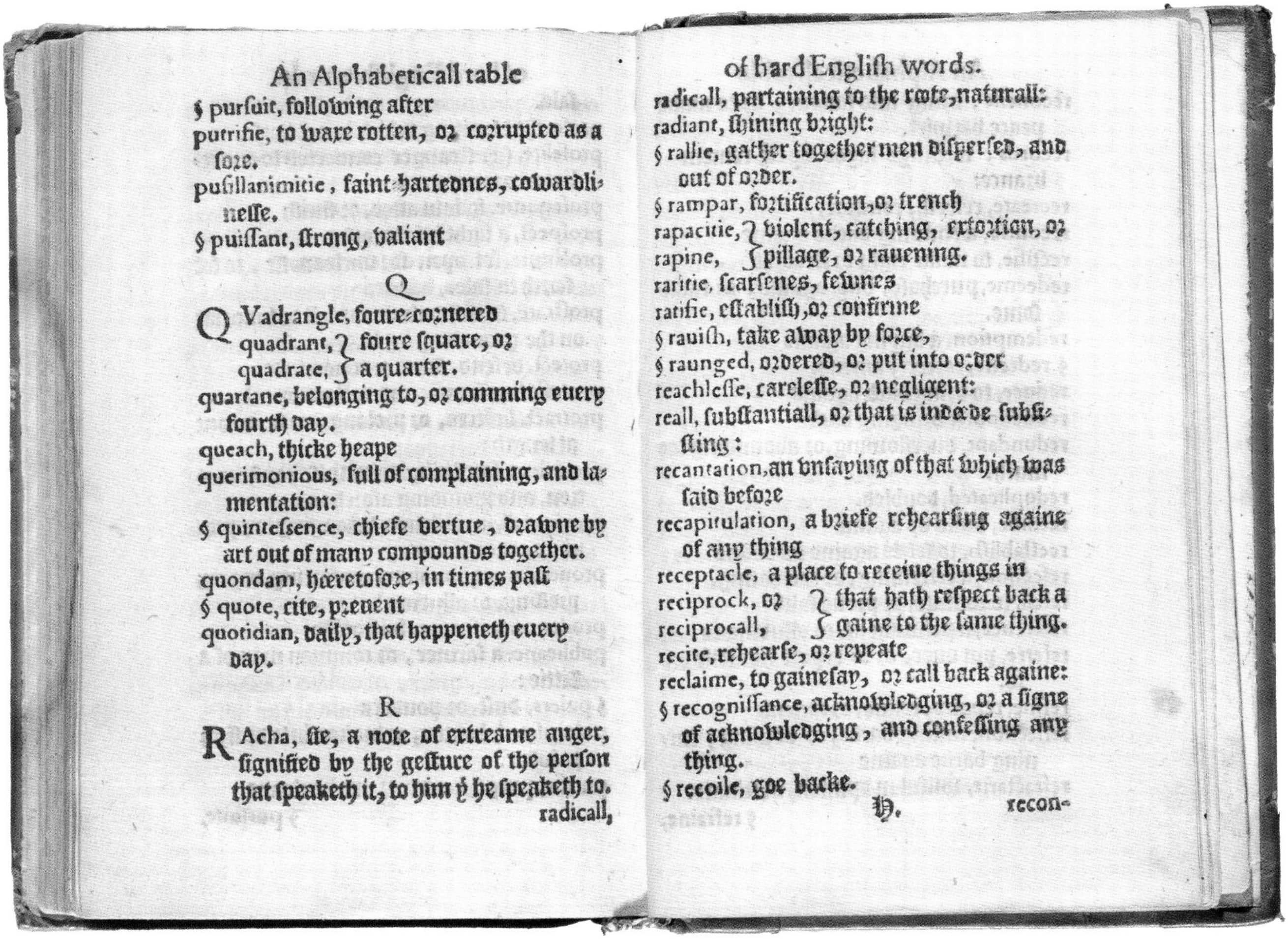

An astonishing example of this last phenomenon is the Codex Mendoza, a manuscript created for the Spanish imperial authorities in South America in 1541, twenty years after the fall of Tenochtitlan to Hernán Cortés **(figure 7)**.[12] The manuscript includes three distinct texts. Two are Mexica documents from pre-Hispanic times: a chronicle of victories and a list of tributes paid by defeated peoples. The third appears to have been created specially for

6 The first English dictionary, Robert Cawdrey's, *A Table Alphabeticall* (1604), included many words that had come into English from Latin. In figure 5 you can see *rapacitas* and *quotidianus*; here we have *rapacitie* and *quotidian*. Bodleian Library, Arch. A f.141 (2), open at 'Q'–'R'.

the Spanish: it is a sort of dictionary of Mexica life, showing details of growing up, education, priestly training, marriage, punishment and other social rituals.[13] All this is given in Mexica picture-writing. Inscribed next to the images are little glosses both in a written form of the Mexica language Nahuatl and in Spanish; on the facing page is a Spanish translation and interpretation which expands on the vignettes, filling in the contexts and clarifying the narrative structure.

This Babelic text gives a vivid impression of the sort of cultural knowledge that it was felt useful for the imperial rulers to have. It also shows the different ways that writing and speech can relate in a language community. The painted images do not allow for complex syntax, so a reader needed to draw on a pool of shared knowledge to understand what was going on in the scenes. Apparently, during the composition of the manuscript, a group of Mexica interpreters elaborated on the meaning of the images; and it was this interpretation that was then written down as the Spanish facing-page translation.

The Codex Mendoza was an attempt to overcome linguistic diversity as part of a project of imperial control. In the event, chance won out over regimentation, and the book was subjected to a Babelic scattering of its own. When it was on its way back to Spain, to the court of Charles V, it seems that pirates intercepted the convoy, and the Codex was diverted to the coffers of the French King Henri II. It became the property of the cosmographer André Thevet, and was then bought by Richard Hakluyt, an English writer and translator, author of a famous book of *Voyages* which had an influence on Shakespeare. After Hakluyt's death in 1616, the Codex passed to Samuel Purchas, another collector and author of travellers' tales, many of which he gathered into *Hakluytus Posthumus, or Purchas his Pilgrimes* in 1625. As part of this enormous publication, Purchas had the images of the Codex Mendoza remade as black-and-white woodcuts, and the Spanish translations retranslated into English. Print, of course, enabled the text to be mass-produced; and, via Purchas's English-with-woodcuts version, the Codex went on to be reworked into yet other languages: the Dutch of Johannes de Laet in 1630; the Latin of Athanasius Kircher (he of the *Turris Babel*) in 1652; the French of Melchisédech Thévenot between 1663 and 1696; and the Italian of Francisco Javier Clavijero in 1780.[14] This proliferative remaking is a blessing of Babel; for, if there were no scattering of languages, this work of imaginative understanding via translation would have no reason to be done.

7 This page from the Codex Mendoza, a manuscript in Mexica picture-writing (with translation) created for Spanish imperial authorities in South America in 1541, shows seven towns in the top right, and, across the rest of the page, the annual tribute they had to pay to their rulers in Tenochtitlan, including warrior outfits, bins of maize and beans, and a live eagle. Bodleian Library, MS. Arch. Selden. A. 1, fol. 31r.

31
xilotepec. pu
tlachco. pu
tzayanalquilpa. pu
michmaloyan. pu
tepetitlan. pu
acaxochitla. pu
tecocauhtla. pu
aguila biva / q cada bez tributo trayan / unas vezes tres / otras quatro / otras mas o menos
una pieça de armas de plumas ricas desta divisa
una pieça de armas de plumas ricas desta divisa
un a[illegible] dela de plumas ricas desta divisa
un a[illegible] dela de plumas ricas desta divisa
dos troxes de maiz y de chian
dos troxes de frisoles y de guautli

Babelic play

The crossing of languages creates all sorts of through-woven similarities and connections. Sometimes these are straightforward, as with the English 'rapacity' and 'quotidian', which were brought in from Latin, as we have seen, or a word like 'xylophone', which is made from the Greek for 'wood' and 'sound'. But there can also be startling and peculiar coincidences, as when an Italian does not live on an 'estate' but enjoys its weather (*estate* means summer), or a French person does not feel 'pain', nor sit on a 'chair', but happily eats them both (*chair* is flesh and *pain* is bread). In these cases, pronunciation reveals a difference which is invisible in writing.

This sort of cross-linguistic interference is a spur to comedy. People get used to the language or languages they habitually speak, and the way they speak them. When we are tripped up by something that seems familiar but isn't, or surprised by a well-known word among a crowd of language that is strange, we tend to smile or laugh. One lovely manifestation of this effect is *Mots d'Heures: Gousse, Rames: The d'Antin Manuscript*, published by the multilingual Hollywood actor Luis van Rooten in 1967.[15] Word for word, the title means 'Words of hours: pod (or clove), oars (or carriages, or reams)'. But the fun is in the pronunciation. Spoken in an exaggerated French accent, the words sound something like 'Mother Goose Rhymes'. From a baffling thicket of words – for the English reader – a familiar meaning emerges.

The same principle holds throughout the little book. Here is the beginning of the first 'rame':

> Un petit d'un petit[1]
> S'étonne aux Halles[2]
> Un petit d'un petit
> Ah! degrés te fallent

The footnotes provide straight-faced elucidation of the meanings of the French text, as though it were a manuscript presented by an editor. The first line, which means something like 'A little one of a little one', receives the comment: 'the inevitable result of a child marriage'. The second line, which means 'is amazed by Les Halles', prompts the reflection: 'the subject of this epigrammatic poem is obviously from the provinces, since a native Parisian would take this famous old market for granted.' Here again, it is pronunciation that gives the real key to the meaning. Read out the lines in a voice like Hercule Poirot's, and you hear not 'Un petit d'un petit' but 'Humpty-Dumpty'; and not 'S'étonne aux Halles' but 'Sat on a wall'; and so on.

Another example of fun across English and French are the columns in 'Franglais' written by the English humourist Miles Kington for *Punch* in the late 1970s and 1980s, also published as books.[16] The mixture of English and schoolchild French bubbles with unease about Britain's membership of the EEC, which it connects with economic problems and divisions in UK society. For instance, in 'Dans le Chip Shop' (**figure 8**), the customers progress through ever more unappetizing options in search of an affordable meal, from the 'Cheap Fish Range' to 'Cheap Cheap Fish Range' to 'Ultra Cheap Fish Range' to 'fish-flavoured wrapping paper' which, they are assured, is 'très populaire'. This agonizing discovery of reduced purchasing power goes along with a sort of inflation in language: a fish that 'dans les vieux jours' used to be 'un throwaway' is now being marketed as 'un New White Fish Taste Sensation'. The phrase 'dans les vieux jours' is a gruesome hybrid, made by slotting French words one by one into the framework of an English expression ('in the old days'). Kington's trick is to make marketing language like 'New White Fish Taste Sensation' sound just as out of tune.

A much more complex, subtle (and lengthy) play across languages dates back to 1499 and is called *Hypnerotomachia Poliphili*, a peculiar, Greek-based amalgam which means *The Dream-love-battle of Poliphilus*. The book is a masterpiece of early printing by the Venetian Aldus Manutius (founder of the Aldine Press);[17] and the text which it embodies is no less extraordinary. It takes the varieties of Italian that were spoken across northern Italy at the time, blends them with Latin, and sprinkles them with Greek, Arabic, Hebrew and other languages and language-games. The author is not known with complete certainty, but it seems most likely to have been Francesco Colonna, a priest who officiated in both Treviso and Venice, where he spent some time as a prior at St Mark's Cathedral. Francesco kept on being expelled from monasteries, for a range of misdemeanours, including having 'sverginata una putta' (taken a maiden's virginity); but he also kept on being rehabilitated, and is last heard of directing restoration works back at his monastery in Venice.[18]

The *Hypnerotomachia* is full of similar wandering, irreverence and interest in buildings. Its protagonist, whose name, Poliphilus, could be translated as 'lover of many things', falls asleep and, in his dream, drifts through a sensuous architectural wonderland where there is an enormous pyramid

Dans le Chip Shop

Kevin: Que manges-tu, Sheila? Je n'ai pas beaucoup d'argent ce soir, je regrette.

Sheila: Fish 'n' chips, s'il te plaît.

Kevin: Bon. Deux poisson frites, s'il vous plaît.

Fishman: Quelle espèce de poisson?

Kevin: Ah. Quelle espèce vous avez?

Fishman: Plaice, cod, haddock, skate. Tous à 90p. Avec frites, £1.15.

Kevin: C'est cher.

Fishman: C'est un give-away. Pour £1.15 vous avez aussi un Special Free Gift Offer!

Kevin: Ah, oui?

Fishman: Oui, Free Paper Wrapping Offer, maintenant avec Free Salt, Free Vinegar, Free Pepper et Free Brown Sauce!

Kevin: Hmm. Vous n'avez pas de poisson moins cher?

Fishman: Dans le Cheap Fish Range, nous avons rig, skad, plath et drit.

Kevin: ???

Fishman: Ce sont des autres noms pour rock salmon. Ou dog fish. A 70p.

Kevin: Avez-vous un Cheap Cheap Fish Range?

Fishman: Oui. Un New Line. *Onomatheicus Pseudopisces* 'n' chips. 40p.

Kevin: ????

Fishman: C'est un nouveau poisson, qu'on a trouvé dans le *Angler's Guide to Apparently Inedible Fish.* Dans les vieux jours, c'était un throwaway au quayside. Maintenant, c'est un New White Fish Taste Sensation. Nous avons fait le double-checking avec le Natural History Museum, et ce n'est pas toxique.

Kevin: Fascinant. C'est un poisson de mer?

Fishman: Oui...Eh bien, non. C'est un poisson de canal, reservoir, gravel pit et lac industriel. Il mesure 3 mètres, il a trois yeux, la bone structure est formidable et il a l'expression d'un dachshund désillusionné. Mais la viande est superbe.

Sheila: Oh, Kevin, que pensez-vous?

Kevin: Je ne sais pas ... Il y a un Ultra Cheap Fish Range?

Fishman: Mmmm ... Nous avons eeltails, à 35p, mais ce soir ils sont un peu tough. Il y a mackerel eyes à 20p. Et, à 10p, fish-flavoured wrapping paper. C'est très populaire, cela.

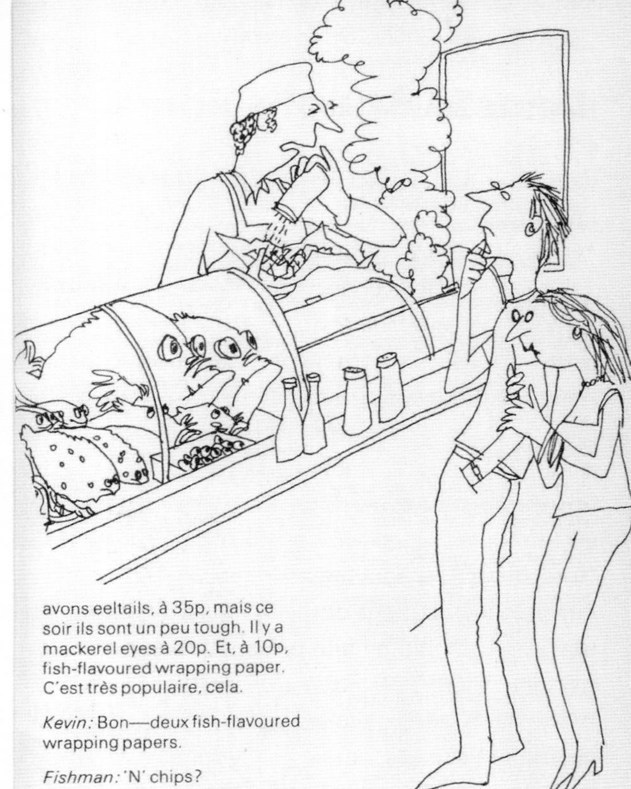

Kevin: Bon—deux fish-flavoured wrapping papers.

Fishman: 'N' chips?

Kevin: Vous avez un Cheap Chip Range?

Fishman: Oui. Chipped Turnip à 20p, Bag de Chipped Bread à 15p, et Chipped Paper Bag à 5p.

Kevin: Merci. Deux paper 'n' bags, s'il vous plaît.

Fishman: Coming up.

topped by an obelisk, statues of elephant and horse, a ceremonial gate, and fountain, and dragon, and beautiful maidens, and a queen with a sumptuous palace, and a dance. Eventually he meets Polia (whose name might be translated as 'many'), a multifaceted but indistinct nymph, with whom he falls in love. Together they experience a rite to Venus in an amazing temple; this is followed by ruins, intriguing inscriptions and a journey in a little boat. Eventually Polia gets the plague; but it is Poliphilus who dies – only she manages to resurrect him. They are rapturously reunited; but then Poliphilus awakes and Polia vanishes.

This mysterious concatenation of scenes is at once a feast for the senses and a guessing game of allegorical signification. The Babelic mixture of languages is the medium for both. For instance, **figure 9** shows pages describing a scene in which Poliphilus is inside the hollowed-out, enormous statue of an elephant. There he encounters a nude statue holding a plaque on which there is an inscription in Hebrew, Greek and Latin: these are the words next to the illustration on the left-hand page. They can be translated as: 'whoever you are, take as much as you like of this treasure, but beware: carry away the head and do not touch the body.' Here, just as with *Mots d'Heures: Gousse, Rames*, the meanings of the words are not the whole story. Poliphilus says that, despite reading and rereading the inscription, he is unable to make out its 'sophismo significato molto ambiguo' ('very ambiguous subtle meaning'). It is only a hundred pages later that he is told the explanation: the head stands for industriousness, and the body for sloth.[19]

Next, he climbs down out of the elephant and goes to study the invented hieroglyphs which you can see on the right-hand page in **figure 9**. They are carefully described in the book's habitual swirls of Latinate Italian. Then, underneath the image, Poliphilus' interpretation is given in Latin capital letters: he takes the hieroglyphs as offering advice on how to lead the soul towards God. Yet, no sooner is this wisdom gleaned than he turns away from it as a 'praecellentissima & mysteriosa & inexcogitabile factura' ('very excellent, mysterious and incomprehensible creation') and goes to gaze at the 'prodigioso Caballo' ('extraordinary horse').[20] And so Poliphilus floats on through the sea of languages, sometimes diving for meaning, sometimes enjoying the sensations of the various words and the images they evoke. This is how the *Hypnerotomachia* sees human life, oscillating between the shapes and sounds of words, and their meanings and deeper significances; tracing a zigzag course between the demands of body and soul.

8 In *Let's Parler Franglais* (1979) Miles Kington mixes English and schoolchild French to comic effect. Bodleian Library, 396941 e.37, pp. 74–5. Published by Robson Books, 1979. Copyright © Miles Kington. Reproduced by permission of the estate of the author c/o Rogers, Coleridge & White Ltd.

ſtatua ſupra ſtante di tutto, quale laltra, Se nõ che era regina, Laquale ſub-
leuato il dextro bracio cum lindice ſignaua la parte retro le ſue ſpalle, &
cum laltro teniua una tabella ritinuta cum il coperto & cum la mano ſua
indiuiſa. Nella q̃le etiam iſcripto era tale epigramma in tri idiomi.

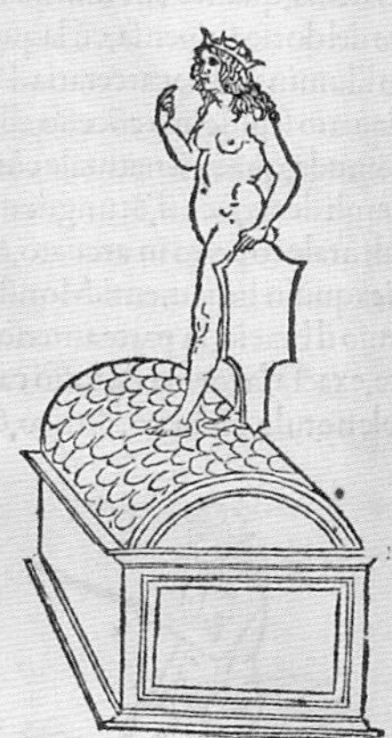

היה מי שתהיה   קח מן האוצר הזה כאות נפשך
אבל אזהיר אותך הסר הראש ואל תיגע בגופו

ΟΣΤΙΣ ΕΙ. ΛΑΒΕ ΕΚ ΤΟΥΔΕ
ΤΟΥ ΘΗΣΑΥΡΟΥ, ΟΣΟΝ ΑΝ Α
ΡΕΣΚΟΙ. ΠΑΡΑΙΝΩ ΔΕ ΩΣ ΛΑ-
ΒΗΙΣ ΤΗΝ ΚΕΦΑΛΗΝ. ΜΗ Α
ΠΤΟΥ ΣΩΜΑΤΟΣ.

QVISQVIS ES, QVANTVN
CVNQVE LIBVERIT HV-
IVS THESAVRI SVME AT
MONEO. AVFER CAPVT.
CORPVS NE TANGITO.

Di tanta nouitate digna di relato mirabondo, & degli ænigmati præle
gendoli ſæpicule, dil tutto io reſtai ignaro, & dilla iterpretatione & ſophiſ
mo ſignificato molto ambiguo. Non era auſo percio alcuna coſa perten
tare. Ma quaſi incuſſo da timore in queſto loco tetro & illumino, quan-
tunque gli fuſſe il lucernale lume. Niente di manco il ſolicito deſiderio
di contemplare la triumphante porta ſtimulante, piu legitima cauſa fue
che quiui non dimoraſſe, che altro. Dique ſencia altro fare, cum penſie-
ro & propoſito per omni modo dapo la contemplatione di eſſa porta mi
rabile, unaltra fiata quiui ritornare, Et piu tranquillamente ſpeculare tale
magnificentia de inuento dagli humani ingegni, citiſſimo allapertura
perueni. Et deſcendando uſciui fora dil exuiſcerato monſtro, Inuentio-
ne inexcogitabile, & ſencia exiſtimatione, exceſſo di faticha, & temerario
auſo humano, quale Trepano terebrare tanta durecia & contumacia di
petra, & euacuare tanta duritudine di materia, ouero altre fabrile machine poteron? Concordemente conueniendo il cauato introrſo cum la for
ma exteriore. Finalmẽte ſopra la piacia ritornato, uidi in queſto porphy-

retico baſamento in circuito inſcalpto digniſſimamẽte tali hieraglyphi.
Primo uno capitale oſſo cornato di boue, cum dui inſtrumenti agricul-
torii, alle corne innodati, & una Ara fundata ſopra dui pedi hircini, cum
una ardente fiammula, Nella facia dellaquale era uno ochio, & uno uul-
ture. Dapoſcia uno Malluuio, & uno uaſo Gutturnio, ſequẽdo uno Glo
mo di filo, iſixo i uno Pyrono, & uno Antiquario uaſo cũ lorificio obtu
rato.. Vna Solea cum uno ochio, cum due fronde intranſuerſate, luna di
oliua & laltra di palma politamẽte lorate. Vna ancora, & uno anſere. Vna
Antiquaria lucerna, cum una mano tenente. Vno Temone antico, cum
uno ramo di fructigera Olea circunfaſciato. poſcia dui Harpaguli. Vno
Delphino. & ultimo una Arca recluſa. Erano queſti hieraglyphi opti-
ma Scalptura in queſti graphiamenti.

Lequale uetuſtiſſime & ſacre ſcripture penſiculante, cuſi io le interpretai.

EX LABORE DEO NATVRAE SACRIFICA LIBER A
LITER, PAVLATIM REDVCES ANIMVM DEO SVBIE-
CTVM. FIRMAM CVSTODIAM VITAE TVAE MISERI
CORDITER GVBERNANDO TENEBIT, INCOLVMEM
QVE SERVABIT.

Babelic literature

The *Hypnerotomachia Poliphili* is at the profound extreme of possible ways of playing with language difference: it is a literary text as much as a gamesome one. In fact, all literature is a kind of serious play with language; and language difference – the curse and blessing of Babel – is at the root of it.

People often think of literature as belonging in national traditions: Japanese literature is one thing, English literature another, and French literature another again. There is some truth in this view: it matters that – to take some English examples – Christina Rossetti read Tennyson, who read Byron, who read Pope, who read Dryden, and that all these poets wrote in English. Yet they all also read and wrote in other languages too, and were influenced by authors of other tongues. They belong not only in English literary history but in a Babelic web of interconnections, whose links (to mention but a few) go from Rossetti to Dante, Tennyson to Horace, Byron to Pulci, Pope to Homer, and Dryden to Virgil. For all these writers, and for many others, the encounter with different languages was a spur to creativity. Experiencing other linguistic textures, and ways of forming meaning, prompted new ways of doing things with English; and English changed as a result. This is the last of the many blessings that have flowed from the land of Shinar: without Babel there would be no literature.

Very many examples could be given. One need think only of the multilingual modernist texts of Ezra Pound or T.S. Eliot, or the translingual writing of contemporary postcolonial and transnational authors such as Salman Rushdie or Elif Shafak, to see the point. One especially rich recent instance of literature written across languages is *Nox*, by the Canadian poet and classical scholar Anne Carson.[21] This work consists of a long strip of thick paper folded into pages which are stacked up within a box: it is half-way between an ancient papyrus roll and a modern book. When you open the box, and start handling the concertina of pages (**figure 10**), the physical experience of making your way through the text is cumbersome: you are made aware of how dealing with language involves the body as well as the mind.

The work opens with a blurry image of Catullus' poem no. 101, the famous elegy for his brother which ends 'frater, ave atque vale' ('brother, hail and farewell'). As we push on through the folds of heavy paper, we find that this poem is being very slowly translated, each word being given a dictionary-like list of equivalents in English, its meanings being unfolded like the pages of the work itself. This scholarly process is interleaved with letters, photographs

9 *Hypnerotomachia Poliphili* (1499) tells the story of a dream vision in a blend of Italian and Latin, with a scattering of other languages. In these pages the hero Poliphilus encounters an inscription in invented hieroglyphics, translates it into Latin, but can't make sense of the words. Bodleian Library, Douce C subt. 174, sig. Ci.

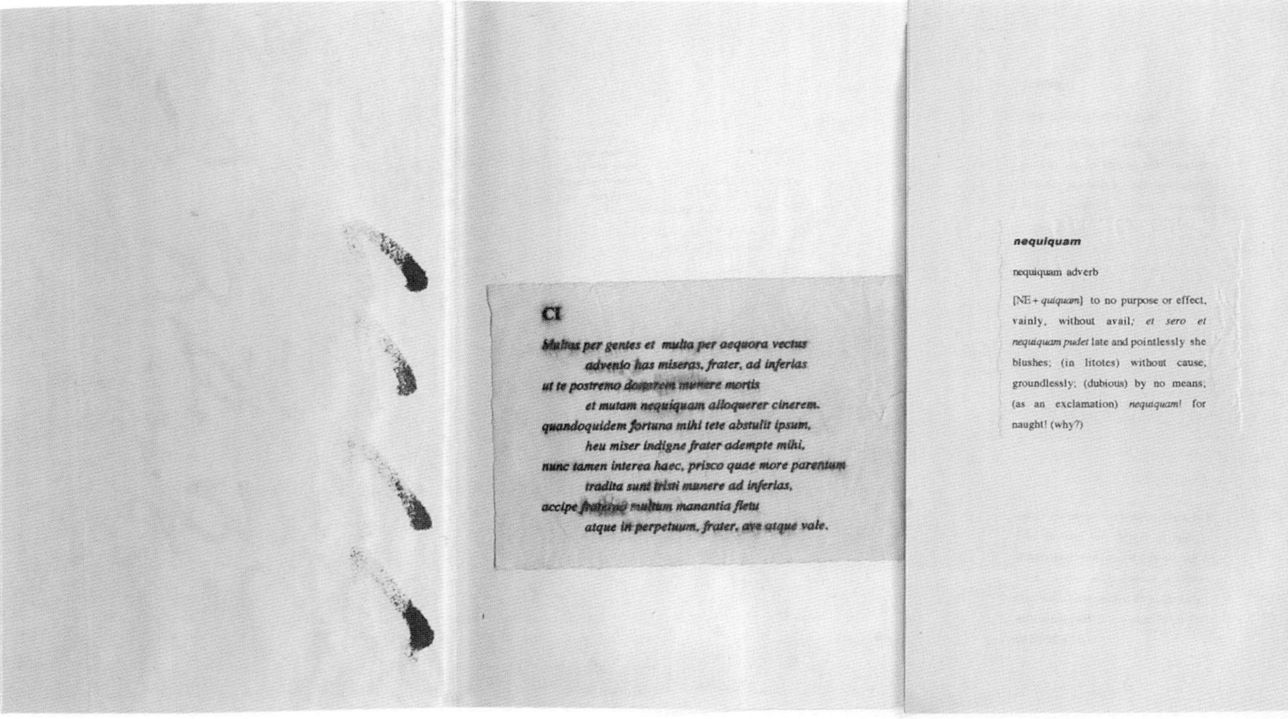

and recollections relating to Carson's own brother, who has died, and whom she is using the process of writing across languages to remember and mourn. There are moments of close connection between Catullus' words and Carson's memories, and also moments when they yawn apart. The work of translation, she says, is like 'a room, not exactly a room, where one gropes for the light switch. I guess it never ends.' Trying to know and understand her brother is the same: 'prowling the meanings of a word, prowling the history of a person, no use expecting a flood of light. Human words have no main switch.' Here, the curse of Babel – the difficulty of understanding other people's words – becomes a way of understanding the difficulty of understanding other people. Through this paradox – understanding the difficulty of understanding – Babel turns, once again, from a curse into a blessing.

Another moving and thought-provoking recent work is *translation* by John Cayley. This is a piece of digital media art which went through various iterations in 2004–05.[22] On the right-hand side of your computer screen, you see an extract from Walter Benjamin's essay 'On Language as Such, and on the Language of Man' metamorphosing letter by letter between its original

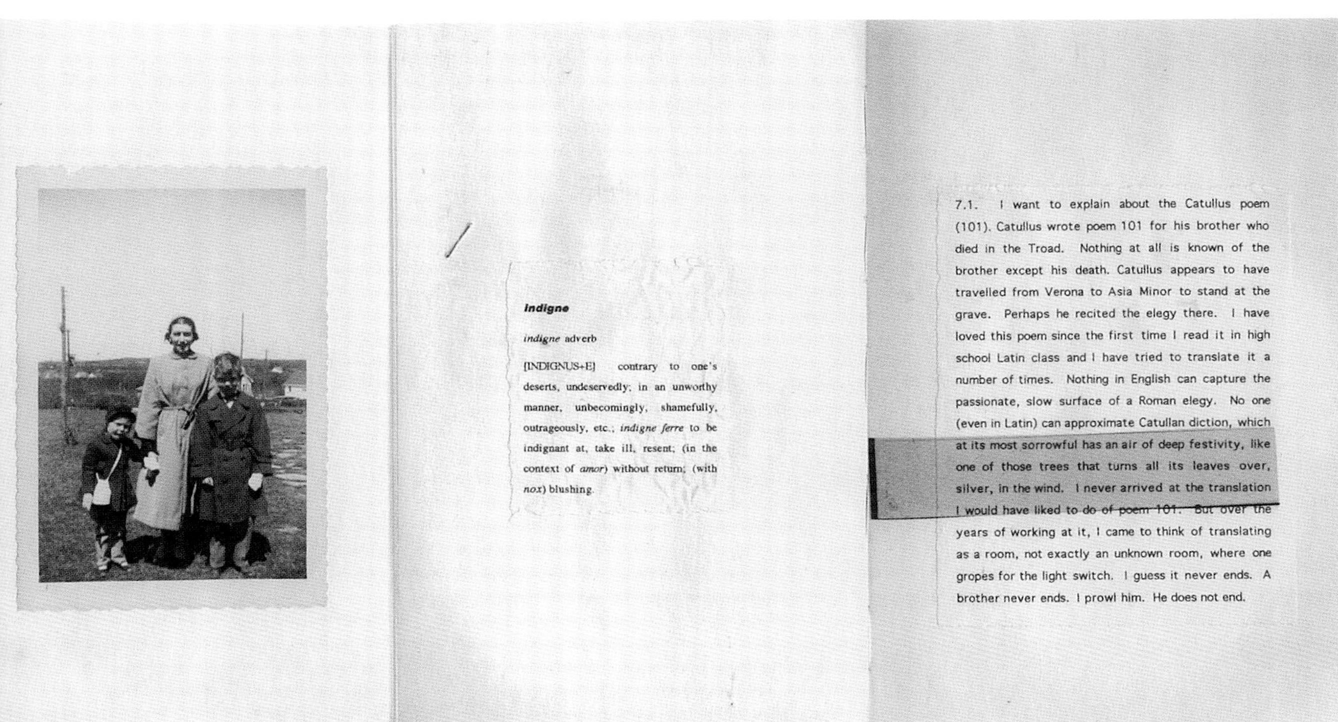

Indigne

indigne adverb

[INDIGNUS+E] contrary to one's deserts, undeservedly; in an unworthy manner, unbecomingly, shamefully, outrageously, etc.; *indigne ferre* to be indignant at, take ill, resent; (in the context of *amor*) without return; (with *nox*) blushing.

7.1. I want to explain about the Catullus poem (101). Catullus wrote poem 101 for his brother who died in the Troad. Nothing at all is known of the brother except his death. Catullus appears to have travelled from Verona to Asia Minor to stand at the grave. Perhaps he recited the elegy there. I have loved this poem since the first time I read it in high school Latin class and I have tried to translate it a number of times. Nothing in English can capture the passionate, slow surface of a Roman elegy. No one (even in Latin) can approximate Catullan diction, which at its most sorrowful has an air of deep festivity, like one of those trees that turns all its leaves over, silver, in the wind. I never arrived at the translation I would have liked to do of poem 101. But over the years of working at it, I came to think of translating as a room, not exactly an unknown room, where one gropes for the light switch. I guess it never ends. A brother never ends. I prowl him. He does not end.

German and French and English translations, occasionally taking a detour via some extracts from Proust, which again might appear in French, German or English. On the left, an array of letter-like characters, not recognizable as human language, shift one by one as well; and there is indistinctly textural background music which incorporates sung letters of the alphabet.

In this work, languages continually change and transform into others, just like the languages we use every day. Only here the process is speeded up, and it is governed by computer algorithms rather than human interactions. As you watch sentences that you know disintegrate into strange, half-legible forms like 'ba cjwjlj tube al be neccewblance', before recomposing themselves into different sentences that can be understood, you can take it as a vision of some dysfunctional future realm in which machines have corrupted the workings of language, a nightmare about Google Translate. Or else as an image of what it has always been like for humans to inhabit the Babelic world of language and languages, this shifting, varied medium, through which meaning can sometimes seem to come into bright focus, and sometimes fade to black.

10 In *Nox* (2009) the Canadian poet and classicist Anne Carson mingles fragmentary translation from Catullus with personal documents and recollections as a way of mourning the death of her brother. Bodleian Library, M10. E11771. Copyright © 2010 by Anne Carson. Reprinted by permission of New Directions Publishing Corp.

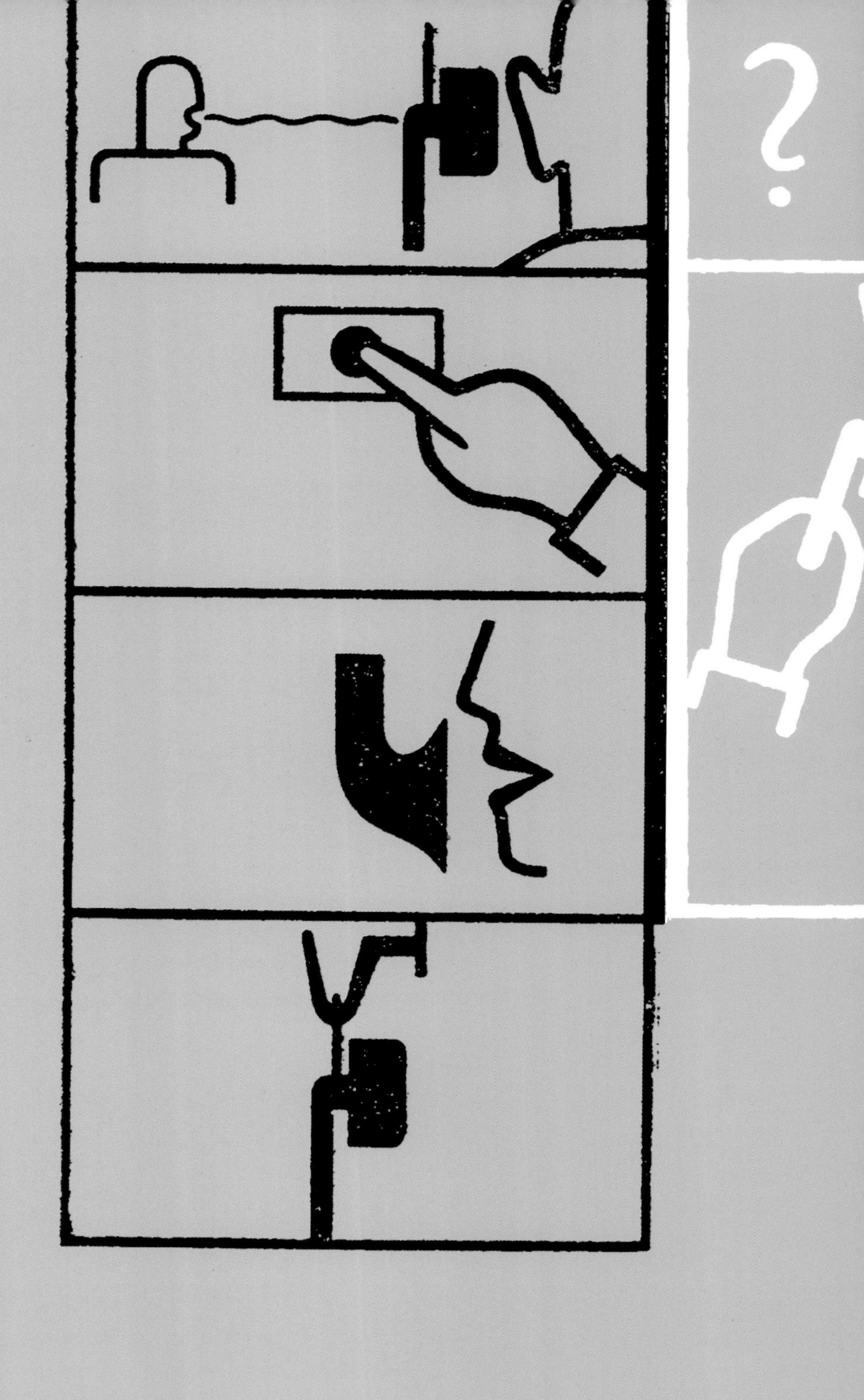

2 Debabelization: Creating a Universal Language

Dennis Duncan

In 1557 the Welsh mathematician Robert Recorde (*c*.1512–1558) published a small book on arithmetic to which he gave the title *The Whetstone of Witte*. The book is among the first in English to discuss algebra. When Recorde comes to the subject of equations – mathematical statements in which two sides, though expressed differently, are of equal value – he lets the reader into a shorthand that he has been using in his own notes for some time:

> Howbeit, for easie alteration of *equations*, I will propounde a fewe examples, bicause the extraction of their rootes, maie the more aptly bee wrought. And to avoide the tediouse repetition of these woords: is equalle to: I will sette as I doe often in woorke use, a paire of paralleles, or Gemowe [twin] lines of one lengthe, thus: =====, bicause noe .2. thynges, can be moare equalle.[23]

Henceforth, a pair of horizontal parallel lines can be taken to mean 'is equal to' (**figure 11**). But the *Whetstone of Witte* also introduces a number of other mathematical signs that are now utterly familiar to us. While they had already been used in Latin and German works for a few decades, Recorde's book is the first in English to use the symbols + and – for plus and minus. Although Recorde doesn't explain their origins as he does with the equals sign, which was after all his own invention, the + sign is thought to be a simplification of the Latin word *et*, meaning 'and'. (The same is true of the ampersand: &.) Meanwhile, following common medieval shorthand practices, the word *meno*, meaning 'minus', had been abbreviated by replacing some of its letters with a superscript bar: thus *m̄*. This was then further simplified – either by flattening the *m* or by simply extracting the bar – to the minus sign we recognize today. Thus = is an icon, that is, there is a similarity between the sign and its meaning: two lines that are equal stand for two quantities that are equal. But + and – are stylized versions of the Latin words they represent. When Recorde employs them in *The Whetstone*

11 In his mathematical textbook *The Whetstone of Witte* (1557) Robert Recorde introduced English readers to mathematical notation such as the + and – signs, as well as a symbol of his own invention: =. Bodleian Library, Savile H 12, sig. Ffi v.

as their workes doe extende) to distincte it onely into twoo partes. Whereof the firste is, *when one nomber is equalle vnto one other*. And the seconde is, *when one nomber is compared as equalle vnto. 2. other nombers*.

Alwaies willyng you to remēber, that you reduce your nombers, to their leaste denominations, and smalleste formes, before you procede any farther.

And again, if your *equation* be soche, that the greateste denomination *Coßike*, be ioined to any parte of a compounde nomber, you shall tourne it so, that the nomber of the greateste signe alone, maie stande as equalle to the reste.

And this is all that neadeth to be taughte, concernyng this woorke.

Howbeit, for easie alteratiō of *equations*. I will propounde a fewe exāples, bicause the extraction of their rootes, maie the more aptly bee wroughte. And to auoide the tediouse repetition of these woordes: is equalle to: I will sette as I doe often in woorke vse, a paire of paralleles, or Gemowe lines of one lengthe, thus: ═════, bicause noe. 2. thynges, can be moare equalle. And now marke these nombers.

1. 14.ze. —+— .15.ç ═════ 71.ç.

2. 20.ze. ——— .18.ç ═════ .102.ç.

3. 26.ʒ —+— 10ze ═════ 9.ʒ ——— 10ze —+— 213.ç.

4. 19.ze —+— 192.ç ═════ 10ʒ —+— 108ç ——— 19ze

5. 18.ze —+— 24.ç. ═════ 8.ʒ. —+— 2.ze.

6. 34ʒ ——— 12ze ═════ 40ze —+— 480ç ——— 9.ʒ

1. In the firste there appeareth. 2. nombers, that is

14.ze.

[illegible] μείζον· πάντως τέμνουσιν· καὶ οὕτως
ὁ [illegible] τῆς πυραμίδος σαφηνείᾳ ἀκόλουθος· ταῖς
[illegible] φαίνεσθαι λόγος :~
Ἐκκείσθω δὴ πυραμὶς ἐπὶ τετραγώνου τοῦ ΑΒΓΔ πυραμὶς κορυφὴν ἔχουσα τὸ Ε· καὶ περιεχομένη αὐτὴ
δίχα τῆς ἰσοσκελοῦς τριγώνοις ἴσαις πλευραῖς· ἐπεὶ δὴ
ἡ ΑΒΓΔΕ πυραμὶς ἥμισυ οὖσα ὀκταέδρου τετμήσθω
αἱ πλευραὶ ὅμως τριγώνου ἡ ΔΕ δίχα κατὰ τὸ Ζ· καὶ
ἐπεζεύχθωσαν αἱ ΒΖ ΑΖ· ἴσαι ἄρα εἰσὶν αἱ ΒΖ ΑΖ καὶ
κάθετοι ἐπὶ τὴν ΔΕ· λέγω ὅτι ἡ ὑπὸ ΒΖΔ γωνία
ἀμβλεῖά ἐστιν. ἐπεζεύχθω γὰρ ἡ ΒΔ· καὶ ἐπεὶ τετρά-
γωνόν ἐστι τὸ ΑΓ· διάμετρος δὲ ἡ ΒΔ· τὸ ἀπὸ ΒΔ δι-
πλάσιόν ἐστι τοῦ ἀπὸ τῆς ΔΑ· τὸ δὲ ἀπὸ τῆς ΔΑ
πρὸς τὸ ἀπὸ τῆς ΔΖ λόγον ἔχει [illegible] πρὸς τὸν
[illegible] ὃν δ' πρὸς [illegible]· καὶ τὸ ἀπὸ τῆς ΒΔ ἄρα
πρὸς τὸ ἀπὸ τῆς ΔΖ λόγον ἔχει ὃν ὀκτὼ πρὸς τρία·
ἴση δὲ ἡ ΔΖ τῇ ΖΒ· τὸ ἄρα ἀπὸ τῆς ΒΔ τῶν ἀπὸ
τῶν ΒΖ ΖΔ μεῖζόν ἐστιν· ἀμβλεῖα ἄρα ἐστὶν ἡ ὑπὸ
ΒΖΔ γωνία· καὶ ἐπεὶ δύο ἐπίπεδα τὰ ΑΒΕ ΔΑΕ
τέμνοντα ἀλλήλων κοινὴ τομή ἐστιν ἡ ΔΕ· καὶ πρὸς ὀρ-
θὰς αὐτῇ ἐν ἑκατέρῳ τῶν ἐπιπέδων ἠγμέναι εἰσὶν
αἱ ΒΖ ΖΔ περιέχουσαι ἀμβλεῖαν· ἡ ὑπὸ ΒΖΔ ἄρα
[illegible] ἐστὶν [illegible] δύο ὀρθῶν τῆς κλί-
[illegible] τῶν ΑΒΕ ΔΑΕ ἐπιπέδων· [illegible]
[illegible] καὶ εἴρηται ἡ κλίσις· [illegible]
[illegible] ὀκταέδρου καὶ μία [illegible]

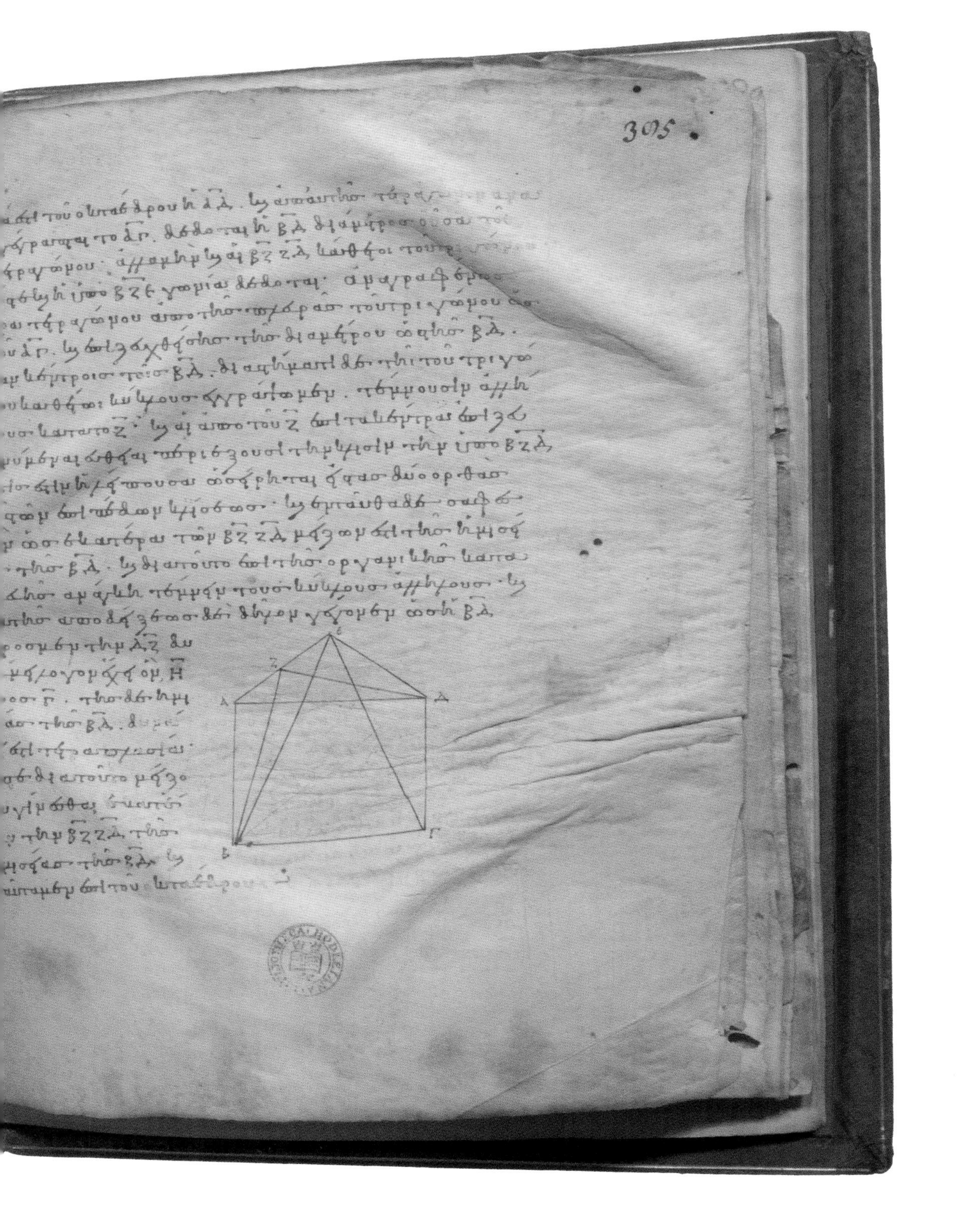
305

of Witte, however, they are scrubbed clean of this underlying Latin. This is not *translation*, but *universalizing*: the sign, unchanged, is acquiring a meaning that will become global, dependent not on language but on context. When we are dealing in mathematics, the plus, minus and equals signs are recognized around the world.

There have been a number of attempts to create universal languages, or universal sign systems, to break free of Babel's curse by finding a form of communication that all will share. Some, like mathematical notation, or the programming languages used in computing, operate within a specialized or narrowly defined field; other constructed languages, however, have been born of an altogether grander ambition, that of complementing or even replacing the natural languages we use in everyday communication, restoring the world to its pre-Babel unity of expression by 'rendring all other *Languages* and *Characters* useless'.[24]

Euclid's journey

Before we come to these, however, let us return to mathematics. The importance of Euclid's *Elements* is hard to overstate. Compiled in Alexandria at around the turn of the third century BCE, the thirteen books of the *Elements* present a comprehensive collection of definitions, theorems and proofs concerning geometry and number theory. As Richard Wallace puts it, the *Elements* formed 'the basis of all mathematical education, not only in the Roman and Byzantine periods, but right down to the mid-20th century'.[25] It is certainly the most influential and famous work of mathematics, running through a vast number of editions and languages. But the *Elements* has a surprisingly picaresque translation history. Lost to Western Europe during the Dark Ages, the *Elements* was preserved elsewhere. It was known, for example, to scholars in the Byzantine Empire, who preserved it in its original Greek, as in the manuscript MS D'Orville 301, which dates from 888 and is now held in the Bodleian Library (**figure 12**).[26] It was at around this time that the *Elements* was also discovered by the mathematicians of the Islamic world; during the ninth century Euclid's text began to circulate in Arabic translation. When the *Elements* made its eventual reappearance in Western Europe in the twelfth century, it was this Arabic version, rather than the original Greek, that formed the basis for the Latin text. Three hundred years later, in 1482, this third-generation Latin version would become the text

12 *previous spread* Though forgotten in Western Europe during the early Middle Ages, Euclid's *Elements* was preserved in the Byzantine Empire and in the Arabic world. This Byzantine copy, dating from 888, retains the Greek of the original. Bodleian Library, MS. D'Orville 301, fols 384v–385r.

of the first printed edition of the *Elements*, produced by Erhard Ratdolt in Venice (**figure 13**).[27] Given that many Western European readers had Latin but few had Greek, it would be more than half a century before an edition in the original language – the *Eukleidou Stoicheion* (Basel, 1533) – was deemed commercially viable.

In 1570 the *Elements* finally appeared in English in the translation of Henry Billingsley (**figure 14**). Billingsley worked from the original Greek rather than adding another link to the translating chain. This beautiful edition features pop-up diagrams to illustrate the three-dimensional geometry that Euclid discusses, and includes a famous 'Mathematical Preface' by the Queen's astronomer and adviser John Dee. But most importantly for our purposes, the Billingsley Euclid begins with Billingsley's own preface in which he outlines what he hoped to achieve in his translation:

> The fruite and gaine which I require for these my paines and trauaile, shall be nothing els, but onely that thou gentle reader, will greatefully accept the same: and that thou mayest receaue some prifite: and moreouer to excite and stirre vp others learned to do the like, & to take paines in that behalf. By meanes wherof, our Englishe tounge shall no lesse be enriched with good Authors, then are other straunge tounges: as the Dutch, French, Italian, and Spanishe: in which are red all good authors in a maner, found amongest the Grekes or Latines. Which is the chiefest cause, that amongst the[m] do florishe so many cunning and skilfull men, in the inuentions of straunge and wonderfull thinges, as in these our daies we see there do. Which fruite and gaine if I attaine vnto, it shall encourage me hereafter, in such like sort to translate, and set abroad some other good authors, both pertaining to religion (as partly I haue already done) and also pertaining to the Mathematicall Artes.[28]

In producing his translation, Billingsley wants to do more than simply provide a mathematical textbook for an English-speaking readership. He is hoping to set an example to other English classicists. This is a call to arms for English translators. When it comes to making the learning of the ancients accessible, English, as Billingsley sees it, lags behind all the other major European languages: Dutch, French, Italian, Spanish. And a direct acutis interiacet. Sit ergo vt trianguli. a. b. c. angulus. b. etiã sit acutus ducã: ad b. c. ppẽdicularẽ q̃ sit. a. d. que vt dictũ est cadet intra triangulũ. dico itaq3 quadratum. a. b. qd̃ subtendit angulo acuto. c. tanto minus est duobus quadratis arum linearũ. a. c. 7. c. b. quãtũ duplũ eius qd̃ fit ex. b. c. in. d. c. ¶ Vel dico q quadratum. a. c. qd̃ etiam subtenditur angulo. b. quẽ posuimus acutum quicquid rit de angulo. a. tanto minus est duobus quadratis duarum linearum. a. b. 7. quãtũ est duplum eius qd̃ fit ex. c. b. in. b. d. Erit enim per. 7. huius quadratũ cum quadrato. d. c. equale ei quod fit ex. b. c. in. d. c. bis 7 quadrato alterius sc3. b. d. quare addito vtriq3 quadrato. a. d. erit quadratũ. b. c. cũ quadratis d linearum. a. d. 7. d. c. equale quadratis duarum linearum. a. d. 7. d. b. 7 duplo quod fit ex. c. b. in. c. d. At quia per penultimam primi quadratum. a. c. est eq quadratis duarum linearu3. a. d. 7. d. c. erit quadratum. b. c. cum quadrato. a. quale quadratis duarum linearum. a. d. 7. b. d. 7 duplo eius quod fit ex. b. c. i. sed per eandem penultimam primi quadratũ. a. b. equũ est quadratis duaru nearum. a. d. 7. b. d. ergo quadratum. b. c. cum quadrato. a. c. equum est quad a. b. 7 duplo eius qd̃ fit ex. b. c. i. c. d. quare tanto min⁹ potest. a. b. duobus late b. c. 7. a. c. quantũ est duplum eius quod fit ex. b. c. in. c. d. quod est propositũ. mili modo probabis latus. a. c. qd̃ subtenditur angulo. b. acuto posse tanto n duobus lateribus. a. b. 7. b. c. quantum est duplum eius: quod fit ex. c. b. in. ¶ Notãdũ aũt per hanc 7 precedentẽ 7 penultimam primi: q cognitis later omnis trianguli cognoscit̃ area ipsius 7 auxiliantibus tabulis de corda 7 arcu gnoscitur omnis eius angulus.

Propositio .14.

Dato trigono equum quadratum describere.

¶ Sit datus trigonus. a cui nos volumus equum quadratũ desc re. Designabo superficiẽ equidistantium laterum 7 rectorum an rum equalem trigono dato s̃m quod docet. 42. primi: sitq3 super es illa. b. c. d. e. cuius si latera fuerint equalia habemus qd̃ queri ipsa eni erit q̃drata. p diffinitionẽ Si aũt latera sintineq̃lia tũc adiũgã min⁹ rum laterũ maiori s̃m rectitudinẽ. sitq3 linea. e. f. equalis minori duo⁊ laterũ c. e. adiuncta maiori quod est. b. c. s̃m rectitudinẽ. Totam. b. f. diuidam per eq lia in pũcto. g. 7 facto. g. cẽtro sup lineã. b. f. s̃m quãtitatẽ linee. g. b. describam micirculũ. b. h. f. 7 latus. e. c. pducã vsq̃quo secet circũferentiã in puncto. h. 7 q quadratũ linee. c. h. est equale trigono dato. Producã lineã. g. h. 7 q2 linea. diuisa ẽ p equalia in. g. 7 p inequalia in. c. erit p. 5. hui⁹ qd̃ fit ex ductu. b. c. i. c. q̃drato. c. g. equale q̃drato. g. f. quare 7 quadrato. g. h. quare per penultimã mi 7 duobus quadratis dua⁊ linea⁊. g. c. 7. c. h. ergo dempto vtriq3 quadrato. erit qd̃ fit ex. b. c. in. c. f. qd̃ est equale superficiei. b. e. eo q. e. f. ẽ equale. c. e. equ quadrato linee. c. h. quare quadratũ linee. c. h. ẽ equale trigono. a. qd̃ ẽ proposi ¶ Et nota q p hoc inuenit̃ lat⁹ tetragonicũ cuiuslib3 altera pte lõgioris 7 simpli ter omnis figure rectis lineis cõtente quecũq3 fuerit. qm̃ omnẽ figurã talẽ in tri gulos resoluem⁹ 7 cuiuslib3 illo⁊ triangulorum inueniem⁹ tetragonicũ latus s̃m ctrinam istius. 7 inueniemus per penultimam primi. lineam vnam que possi omnia latera tetragonica inuenta. verbi gratia volo nunc inuenire latus tetrag nicũ rectilinee figure irregularis. a. b. c. d. e. f. resoluo eam. in. 3. triangulos qui

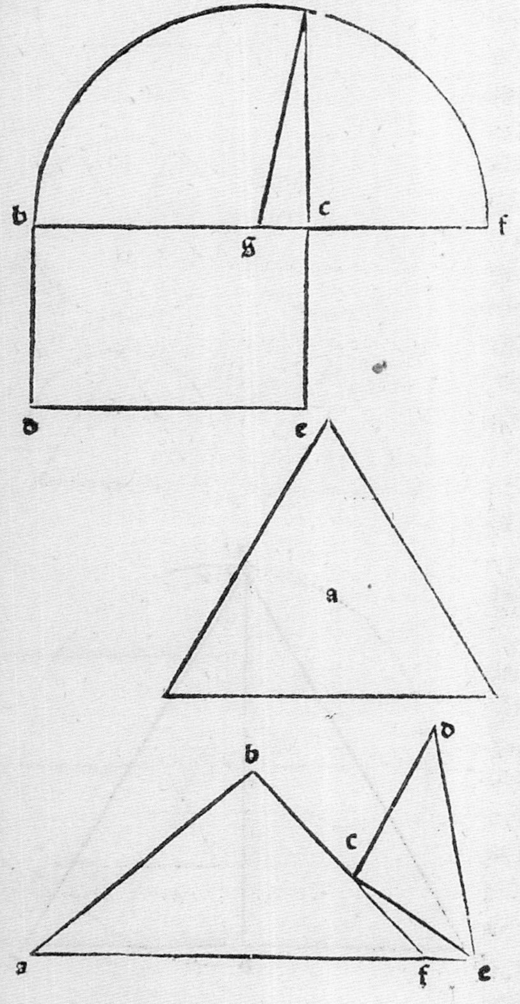

a.b.f.c.d.e.⁊.c.f.e. Jnuenio quoqꝫ ſm doctrinam iſtius tria latera tetragonica iſtoꝝ trium triangulorum.qui ſunt.g.h.h.k.⁊.k.l:⁊ erigo.h.k.perpendiculariter ſuper.g.h.⁊ produco.g.k.eritqꝫ per penultimā quadratum primi.g.k.equale quadratis duarum linearum.g.h.⁊.h.k.⁊ tertium latus.k.l.erigo perpendiculariter ſuper lineam.g.k.⁊ produco lineam.g.l.eritqꝫ per penultimam primi.g.l.latus tetragonicum totius figure rectilinee propoſite. Explicit liber ſecundus. Incipit liber tertius.

Uoꝝ diametri ſunt eq̄les.ipſos circulos eq̄les eſſe. Maiores aūt quoꝝ maiores ⁊ minores quoꝝ minores. Circulū linea ꝯtingere dicitur:que cū circulū tangat in vtraqꝫ partē eiecta.circulū non ſecat. Circuli ſeſe contingere dicunt̄ qui tangentes ſeinuicem non ſecant. Recte linee in circulo equaliter diſtare dicūt̄ a centro.cū a centro ad ipſas ducte perpendiculares fuerint equales. Plus vero diſtare a centro dicit̄.in quā ꝑpendicularis longior cadit. Recta linea portionū circuli cōtinēs corda noiat̄. Portio vero circūferentie arc⁹ nūcupat̄. Angulus aūt portionis dicit̄ q̄ a corda ⁊ arcu continet̄. Supra arcū angulus conſiſtere dicit̄.qui a quolibet pūcto arcus ad corde terminos duabus rectis lineis exeuntib⁹ cōtinet̄. Sector circuli eſt figura q̄ ſub duab⁹ a cētro ductis lineis ⁊ ſub arcu qui ab eis cōprehendit̄ cōtinet̄. Angulus aūt qui ab eis lineis ambitur ſupra centrū cōſiſtere dicit̄. Sil'es circuloꝝ portiōes dicūt̄ i quib⁹ qui ſupra arcum conſiſtunt anguli ſibi inuicē ſūt eq̄les. Arc⁹ quoqꝫ ſimiles ſunt qui equos angulos predicto modo ſuſcipiunt.

Propoſitio .1.

Jrculi ꝓpoſiti cētrū inuenire.vñ manifeſtū ē ꝙ duab⁹ rectis lineis in eodē circulo apud circūferētiā termiatis neutra illaꝝ alterā per eq̄lia orthogonal'r ſecat niſi ipſa ſuper centrum tranſierit.

Sit circulus propoſitus.a.b.c.cuius volumus centrū inuenire. duco in ipſo circulo lineā.a.c.qualitercūqꝫ contingat quā diuido per equalia i pūcto d.a quo duco perpendicularem ad lineā.a.c.quā applico circūferentie ex vtraqꝫ ꝑte.ſitqꝫ.e.d.b.quā rurſus diuido ꝑ eq̄lia in pūcto.f.quē dico eſſe centrū circuli.Si eni nō ē:erit aūt alibi aut i linea.e.b.āut extra. Jn linea.e.b.nō: ſi eni fuerit i ea vt i puncto.g.erit linea.e.f.maior linea.e.g.ps videlꝫ toto qḋ eſt ipoſſibile. Qḋ ſi fuerit extra lineā.e.b.ut in pūcto.h.ducant̄ linee.h.a.h.d.h.c.⁊ q̄r latera.h.d.⁊ d.a.trianguli.h.d.a.ſūt eq̄lia laterib⁹.h.d.⁊.d.c.trianguli.h.d.c.⁊ baſis.h.a.baſi.h.c.erit ꝑ.8.primi angul⁹.a.d.h.eq̄lis angulo.c.d.h.q̄re vterqꝫ rect⁹ ⁊ q̄r angulus.a.d.b.fuit etiā rect⁹ erit.a.d.h.eq̄lis.a.d.b.ꝑ.3.petitione ꝑmi ps videlicet toti qḋ ē ipoſſibilē.nō ē ergo cētrū dati circuli alicubi quā i pūcto.f.qḋ ē propoſitū.

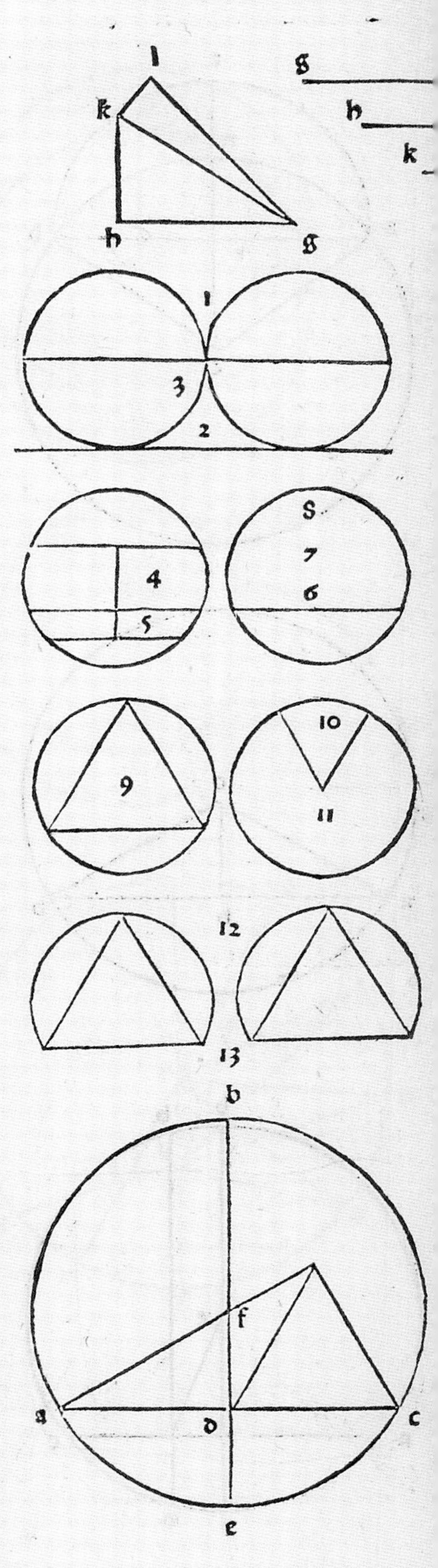

result of this lack – the fact that scientific works written in Latin and Greek are not available to the widest possible readership – is, in Billingsley's eyes, that England trails its rivals technologically: the country is not producing 'cunning and skilfull men' capable of inventing 'straunge and wonderfull thinges'. It's a strikingly modern expression of the value of translation to the national economy.

Universal characters: Lodwick and Wilkins

The economic value of translation, or rather the economic benefit of traders from different countries being able to understand each other clearly *without* translation, was surely in the mind of the merchant Francis Lodwick (1619–1694) when he self-published a work with the unwieldy but self-explanatory title *A Common Writing: Whereby two, although not understanding one the others Language, yet by the helpe thereof, may communicate their minds one to another* (1647). Lodwick points to mathematics as an example of how a universal notation can be successful: 'the Arithmeticians, whose numericall characters are still the same, although described by those of differentall Languages, as the figure of five (5) is still alike described, whether written by a Dutchman, Englishman, Frenchman, &c.'[29] Thus he wonders whether a similar principle might not be extended to language generally. As the book's title suggests, this is a *writing* system: Lodwick is keen to point out that no one will have to *speak* another language, only learn a common way of writing. In his address 'To the Reader' he makes this point as clearly as possible:

> Thou hast here presented to thy view and censure, an Essay of a Common Writing, invented, that may be common to all languages, that is, one skilled in the same, shall have no need, for what is written with this writing, to learne any other Language then his mother Tongue, which he already hath.[30]

The way this will work is by what Lodwick terms 'a kind of hieroglyphicall representation of words'. The key idea is based on the fact that many words use the same root but express different relations to it. Thus, if we think of an action – say, *drink* – then this brings with it a host of other related concepts: the agent (*drinker*), the object (*drink*), the act (*the drinking*), the profession or habitual agent (*drunkard*), the state (*drunkenness*) and the place (*drinking*

13 *previous spread* Euclid's *Elements* was immensely popular with early modern humanist scholars. This Latin version of 1482 is the first printed edition. The text is a translation of a translation: the original Greek had passed into Arabic before being translated into Latin in the twelfth century. Bodleian Library, Byw. E 1.6, sig. m4v–m5r.

14a and **14b** *also pp. 46–7* When Henry Billingsley produced the first English translation of the *Elements* he included fold-out flaps for some of the illustrations in order to demonstrate some of the three-dimensional geometry that the book discusses. Bodleian Library, MS. Savile W 5, fols 324v–325r.

THE ELEMENTS
OF GEOMETRIE
of the most aunci-
ent Philosopher
EVCLIDE
of Megara.

*Faithfully (now first) trans-
lated into the Englishe toung, by*
H. Billingsley, *Citizen of London.
Whereunto are annexed certaine
Scholies, Annotations, and Inuenti-
ons, of the best Mathematici-
ens, both of time past, and
in this our age.*

With a very fruitfull Præface made by M. I. Dee,
*specifying the chiefe Mathematicall Scieces, what
they are, and wherunto commodious: where, also, are
disclosed certaine new Secrets Mathematicall
and Mechanicall, vntill these our daies, greatly missed.*

Imprinted at London by *John Daye.*

and maketh with them right angles, wherefore (by the fourth of the first) the base F A *is e-*
quall to the base F B. *And (by the same reason) the base* F C *is equall to the base* F D. *And*
forasmuch as the line A D *is equall to the line* B C, *and the line* F A *is equal to the line* F B
as it hath bene proued. Therefore these two lines F A *and* A D *are equall to these two line*
F B *&* B C, *the one to the other, & the base* F D *is equall to the base* F C. *Wherfore also th*
angle F A D *is equall to the angle* F B C. *And againe forasmuch as it hath bene proued*
that the line A G *is equall to the line* B H, *but the line* F A *is equall to the line* F B. *Where-*
fore there are two lines F A *and* A G *equall to two lines* F B *and* B H *and it is proued tha*
the angle F A G *is equall to the angle* F B H: *wherefore (by the 4. of the first) the base* F G
is equal to the base F H. *Agayne forasmuch as it hath bene proued that the line* G E *is equa*
to the line E H, *and the line* E F *is common to them both: wherefore these two lines* G E *and*
E F *are equall to these two lines* H E *and* E F, *and the base* F H *is equall to the base* F G.
wherefore the angle G E F *is equall to the angle* H E F. *Wherefore either of the angles* G E
F, *and* H E F *is a right angle. Wherefore the line* E F *is erected, from the point* E, *perpendi*
cularly to the line G H. *In like sort may we proue, that the same line* F E *maketh right angle*
with all the right lines which are drawne vpon the ground playne superficies and touch the
point B. *But a right line is then erected perpendicularly to a plaine superficies, when it maketh*
right angles with all the lines which touch it, and are drawne vpon the ground playne super
ficies (by the 2. definition of the eleuenth). Wherefore the right line F E *is erected perpendi*
cularly to the ground playne superficies. And the ground plaine superficies is that which pas
seth by these right lines A B *and* C D. *Wherefore the right line* F E *is erected perpendicu*
larly to the playne superficies which passeth by the right lines A B *and* C D. *If therefore*
from two right lines cutting the one the other and at their common section a right line be
perpendicularly erected: it shall also be erected perpendicularly to the plaine superficies by the
sayd two lines passing: which was required to be proued.

In this figure you may most euidently conceaue the for
proposition and demonstration, if ye erect perpendicularly
ground playne superficies A C B D the triangle A F B
the triangles A F D, & C F B in such sort, that the li
angle A F B may ioyne & make one line with the
angle A F D: and likewise that the line B F of the triang
ioyne & make one right line with the line B F of the triang

¶ The 5. Theoreme. The 5. Proposition.

If vnto three right lines which touch the one the other, be erected a per-
pendicular line from the common point where those three lines touch: those
three right lines are in one and the selfe same plaine superficies.

S*Vppose that vnto these three right lines* B C, B D, *and* B E, *touching the one*
the other in the poynt B, *be erected perpendicularly from the poynt* B, *the line*
A B. *Then I say, that those thre right lines* B C, B D *and* B E, *are in one & the*
selfe same plaine superficies. For if not, then if it be possible, let the lines B D *&*
B E

B E be in the ground superficies, and let the line B C be erected vpward (now the lines A B and B C are in one and the same playne superficies (by the 2. of the eleuenth) for they touch the one the other in the point B). Extend the plaine superficies wherein the lines A B and B C are, and it shall make at the length a common section with the ground superficies, which common section shall be a right line (by the 3. of the eleuenth): let that common section be the line B F. Wherefore the three right lines A B, B C, and B F are in one and the selfe same superficies, namely, in the superficies wherein the lines A B and B C are. And forasmuch as the right line A B is erected perpendicularly to either of these lines B D and B E, therefore the line A B is also (by the 4. of the eleuenth) erected perpendicularly to the plaine superficies, wherein the lines B D and B E are. But the superficies wherein the lines B D and B E are is the ground superficies. Wherefore the line A B is erected perpendicularly to the ground plaine superficies. Wherefore (by the 2. definition of the eleuenth) the line A B maketh right angles with all the lines which are drawne vpon the ground superficies and touch it. But the line B F which is in the ground superficies doth touch it. Wherfore the angle A B F is a right angle. And it is supposed that the angle A B C is a right angle. Wherefore the angle A B F is equall to the angle A B C, and they are in one and the selfe same plaine superficies which is impossible. Wherefore the right line B C is not in an higher superficies. Wherefore the right lines B C, B D, B E are in one and the selfe same plaine superficies. If therefore vnto three right lines touching the one the one the other, be erected a perpendicular line from the common point where those three lines touch: those three right lines are in one and the selfe same plaine superficies: which was required to be demonstrated.

Demonstration leading to an impossibilitie.

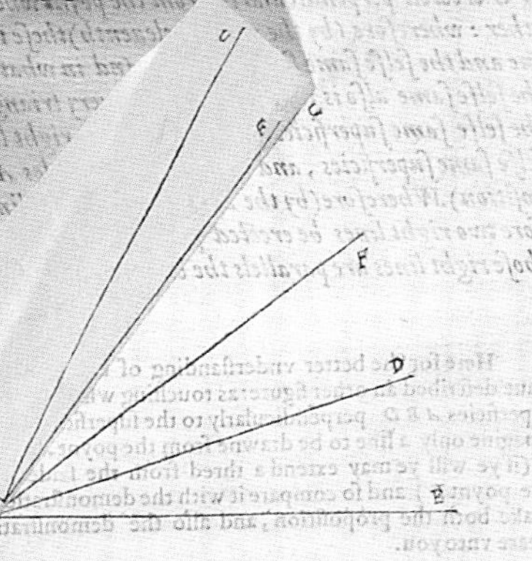

This figure here set more playnely declareth the demonstration of the former proposition, if ye erect perpendicularly vnto the ground superficies, the s[...] perficies wherein is drawne the line[...] and so compare it with the sayd d[...] stration.

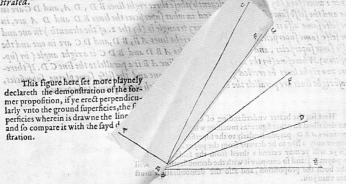

The 6. Theoreme. The 6. Proposition.

If two right lines be erected perpendicularly to one & the selfe same plaine superficies: those right lines are parallels the one to the other.

house). If we have one simple sign to indicate the root, and a series of conventional marks to indicate the relation, then each of these concepts can be expressed in relatively simple characters (**figure 15**). Not only that, but anyone reading these needs only know the roots and the general grammar of how additional marks are constructed in order to be able to decode Lodwick's script.

A Common Writing is a short work – at only thirty pages it is merely a sketch of how a universal writing system might be realized. (It does, nevertheless, end with a bravura demonstration of the opening eight verses of John's Gospel translated into just seventy-six characters.) Lodwick closes his preface apologizing for his 'harsheness of stile' and noting that he is not himself a scholar. His wish, as he states it, is that by putting the work in the public sphere he will 'allure a more abler wit and Pen, to a compleat attyring and perfecting of the subject'.[31] A few decades later, the untutored Lodwick would find himself elected to the Royal Society as a group of its members worked to hone a far vaster treatment of the common writing problem designed by one of the Society's founders, John Wilkins.

Wilkins had been considering the usefulness of a universal trade language since before the publication of Lodwick's *A Common Writing*. Nevertheless, when Wilkins's major treatment of the subject appeared in 1668 he acknowledged the influence of Lodwick on his own system. As with Lodwick, Wilkins's first goal was to produce a writing system – a character – that would straddle the languages of the world. As Wilkins puts it, the system will 'be legible by any Nation in their own Tongue'.[32] Wilkins also makes the wry aside that creating another writing system might look like a funny way of tackling the Curse of Babel: 'for any man to go about to add to their [i.e. the languages of the world] number, will be but like the inventing of a Disease, for which he can expect but little thanks from the world.'[33]

Wilkins's work, *An Essay Towards a Real Character, and a Philosophical Language*, is a rather extraordinary one. The first draft, along with most of the initial print run, was destroyed in the Great Fire of London; it is no wonder that it took Wilkins another two years to reconstruct it. His method is to organize the objects of language – the concepts, qualities and actions that we have words for – into an immense system. Here he is, describing the process:

> When after main reviews and changes I had reduced (as well as I could) into these Tables all simple things and notions, by a

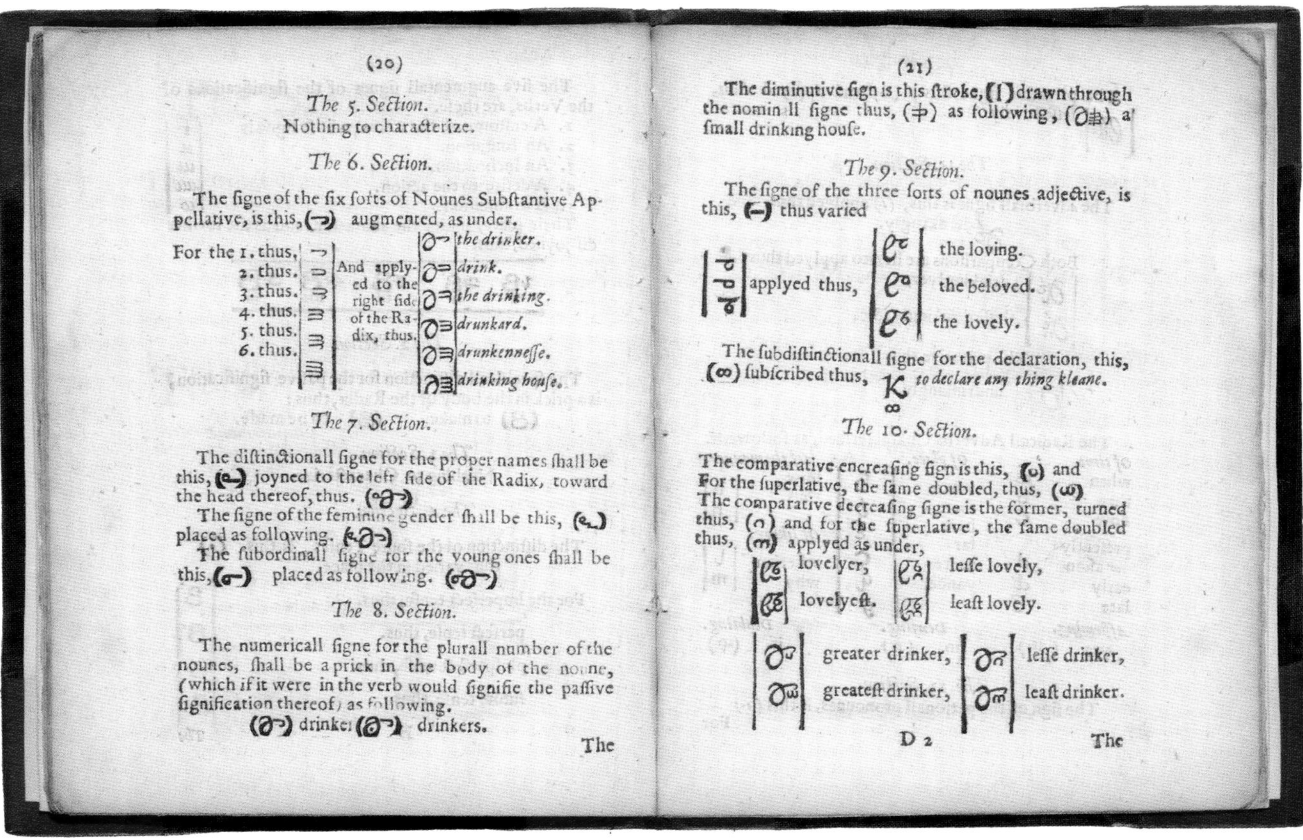
(20)

The 5. Section.

Nothing to characterize.

The 6. Section.

The ſigne of the ſix ſorts of Nounes Subſtantive Appellative, is this, augmented, as under.

For the 1. thus, 2. thus. 3. thus. 4. thus. 5. thus. 6. thus. And applyed to the right ſide of the Radix, thus. *the drinker. drink. the drinking. drunkard. drunkenneſſe. drinking houſe.*

The 7. Section.

The diſtinctionall ſigne for the proper names ſhall be this, joyned to the left ſide of the Radix, toward the head thereof, thus.

The ſigne of the feminine gender ſhall be this, placed as following.

The ſubordinall ſigne for the young ones ſhall be this, placed as following.

The 8. Section.

The numericall ſigne for the plurall number of the nounes, ſhall be a prick in the body of the noune, (which if it were in the verb would ſignifie the paſſive ſignification thereof) as following.

drinker drinkers.

The

(21)

The diminutive ſign is this ſtroke, drawn through the nominall ſigne thus, as following, a ſmall drinking houſe.

The 9. Section.

The ſigne of the three ſorts of nounes adjective, is this, thus varied

applyed thus, the loving. the beloved. the lovely.

The ſubdiſtinctionall ſigne for the declaration, this, (∞) ſubſcribed thus, *to declare any thing kleane.*

The 10. Section.

The comparative encreaſing ſign is this, and For the ſuperlative, the ſame doubled, thus, The comparative decreaſing ſigne is the former, turned thus, and for the ſuperlative, the ſame doubled thus, applyed as under,

lovelyer, leſſe lovely, lovelyeſt. leaſt lovely.

greater drinker, leſſe drinker, greateſt drinker, leaſt drinker.

D 2 The

15 Francis Lodwick's *A Common Writing* (1647) proposed a writing system that could be adopted in all countries so that 'two [people], although not understanding one the others language, yet by the helpe thereof, may communicate their minds one to another'. Bodleian Library, Vet. A3 e.350, pp. 20–21.

Consideration of them à Priori, I then judged it necessary to attempt the reduction of all other Words in the Dictionary to these Tables, either as they were *Synonymous* to them, or to be *defined* by them.[34]

It is an amazingly matter-of-fact description for such an extraordinary undertaking: to create a set of tables in which, firstly, 'all simple things and notions' have their place, and then to expand these tables to encompass every word in the dictionary! Sure enough, however, in Wilkins's *Essay*, the known universe is distilled into an immense tree diagram filling most of the fat folio book. A summary table (**figure 16**) was included as a fold-out.

Wilkins's writing system – the 'universal character' – follows the table: every word is a complex of marks derived from the path one takes through the tree diagram to get to the desired concept. So Wilkins's forty top-level 'genuses' – Metal, Beast, Motion, Judicial Relation, and so on – each have their own basic sign, and every subsequent sub-level branching adds another precisely placed notch to this. Wilkins provides a worked example – in this case the Lord's Prayer, reduced to little more than three lines. It looks not dissimilar to secretarial shorthand, but there is a crucial difference: where shorthand for the most part uses an economical system of squiggles to represent the sounds of an existing language, the squiggles of Wilkins's system are not based on pre-existing words but rather on the *characteristics* of the underlying concepts. As he puts it, his writing 'should not signifie *words*, but *things* and *notions*'.[35] In this sense it is a 'real' character (as Wilkins describes it in his title): the writing tells you directly about the thing.

16 John Wilkins's *Essay Towards a Real Character* (1668) organized 'all things and notions' into a vast tree diagram. In his 'philosophical language' words would be formed by tracing the characteristics of the desired concept through his classification system. Bodleian Library, 81.H.14, fold-out.

Wilkins's design also goes one very important step further than Lodwick's. Having reduced the knowable universe to a vast tree diagram and demonstrated how everything in it may be written, Wilkins suggests that he has already provided the basis for a spoken language: 'this Universal Character may be made effable in a distinct Language: The unfolding of which (supposing what hath been said about the Character and Grammar, to be well understood) will need but little time and pains.'[36] The spoken language can function very much as the written character did: by assigning a value to each node on the great tree diagram, only this time the values will be sounds rather than signs. First of all, then, each of the forty top-level genuses is given a syllable. Anything relating to Disease will begin with *To*; Fish will all start with *Za*; all words indicating Motion will start *Ce*, and so

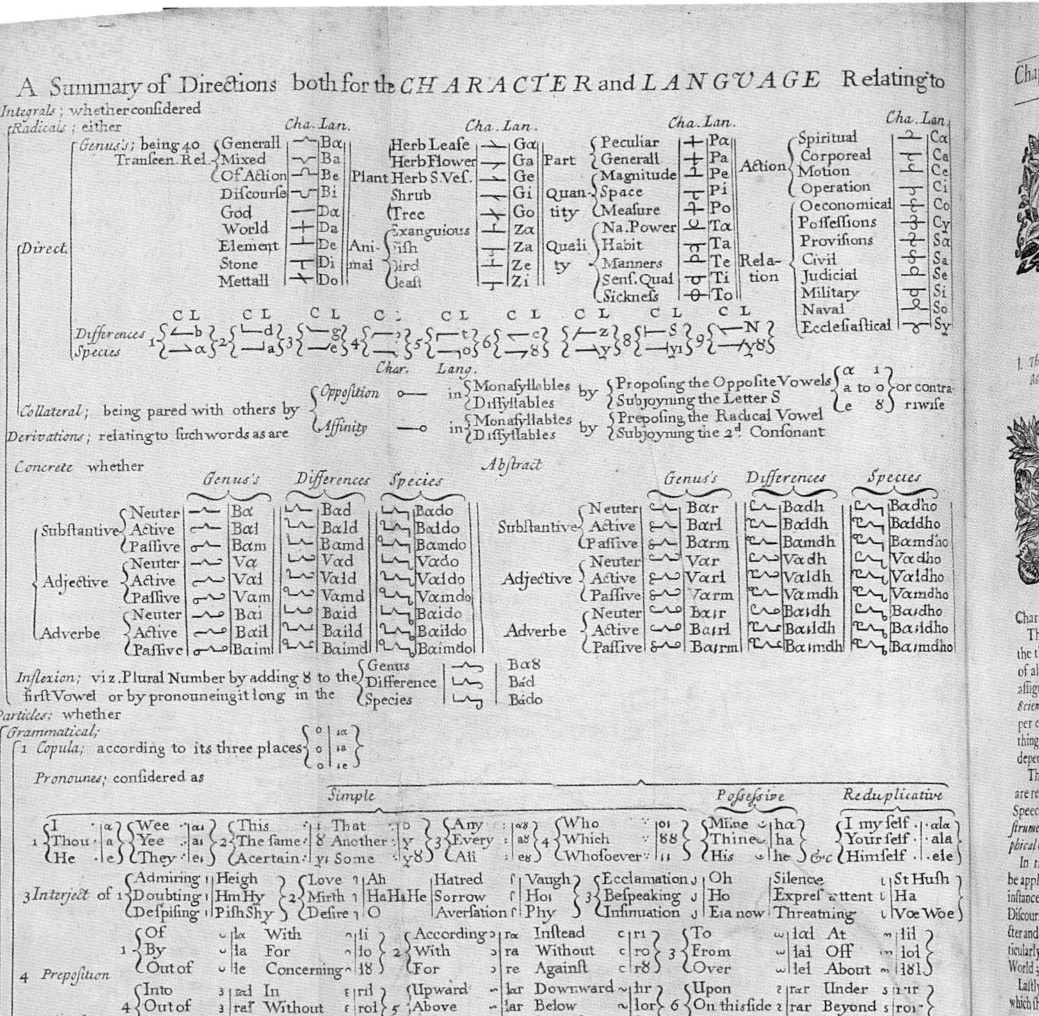

on. Within these categories, the next branch will be assigned another sound in the order B, D, G, P, T, C, Z, S, N; and further branches will accrue further sounds. So, for example,

> If (De) signifie *Element*, then (Deb) must signifie the first difference; which (according to the Tables) is *Fire*: and (Deba) will denote the first Species, which is *Flame*. (Det) will be the fifth difference under that Genus, which is *Appearing Meteor*; (Deta) the first Species, viz. *Rainbow*.[37]

Further worked examples show how a tulip will be called a *Gade*, and a salmon – belonging first of all to the genus of Fish, then the ninth branch beneath that (denoting 'freshwater'), then the second ('common to fresh and salt water') – will be *Zana*.

A Posteriori constructed languages

Wilkins's philosophical language, needless to say, did not replace the languages of the world. A doggerel poem circulated at the time mocked it as follows:

> A Doctor counted very able
> Designs that all Mankynd converse shall
> Spite o' th' confusion made att Babell
> By Character call'd Universall.
> How long this Character will be learning
> That truly passeth my discerning.[38]

The verse, though comic, hits on a real problem with Wilkins's scheme: to learn the language one would have to learn every detail of the table that underpins it. There is nothing intuitive about the fact that 'freshwater' should be the ninth distinction under Fish, as opposed to, say, the first, or the fourth. Wilkins's Universal Character is an example of what is known as an *a priori* constructed language; that is, it is designed according to a logical scheme – the language follows the system. But if such a language places a potentially intolerable burden on one's ability to memorize such an immense structure, there is an alternative: to construct a language that takes one or more existing languages as its base and simplifies them. This will be an *a posteriori* constructed language, and from the late nineteenth century a considerable number of these were developed, among them Volapük, Latino sine flexione, Basic English, and Interlingua. The best known and most successful, however, is Esperanto.

Developed by Ludovic Lazarus Zamenhof (he is said to have taken the name Ludovic himself as a teenager in tribute to Lodwick), Esperanto was first introduced to the world in 1887 in a short work now known as *Unua Libro*, which is Esperanto for *First Book*. Zamenhof's preface contains the familiar complaint about the 'time, trouble and money' that are wasted in the work of translation and could be saved if the world shared an auxiliary language.[39] Not only this, adds Zamenhof, but much of the world's political strife would disappear if we all had a common language:

> Indeed, the difference of languages is one of the most fruitful sources of the dissensions and differences among nations, for, of all things that impress a stranger in a foreign land, the language is at once the first and the greatest mark of distinction between him and them; not being able to understand or be understood, we naturally shun the contact of aliens.[40]

Other artificial languages have failed from being too hard to learn. But Esperanto has been constructed from a vocabulary of a mere nine hundred words, which 'embrace all the grammatical forms as well as all suffixes and prefixes'.[41] Its simplicity leads Zamenhof into a bold claim: 'the study of this language, rich, harmonious, comprehensible by the whole world …, does not demand, like some other tongues, the devotion of years – indeed, to learn is but the work of A FEW DAYS.'[42]

Esperanto did indeed catch on. Volapük had paved the way – the earlier auxiliary language had experienced a rapid burst of popularity in the 1880s with up to a million people learning it in Europe, before suffering an equally precipitous decline when a schism emerged over attempts to reform it. Many former Volapük clubs adopted Esperanto. In the early twentieth century, as well as the first world congress of Esperanto speakers, we find publications in Esperanto – newspapers, books, poetry pamphlets, translations of the classics – printed all over the world. A tourist brochure printed in 'Glasgo' invites readers to visit *Al Belega Skotlando*: Bonnie Bonnie Scotland (**figure 17**).[43] We can get a sense of how the language looks – its grammar and its mixture of roots – from comparing the opening to Robert Reid's poem 'Scotland' ('Skotlando') printed in a parallel translation in another Scottish Esperanto publication:

The Official Organ of The British Esperanto Association.

Vol. II.—No. 13. JANUARY, 1906. [Price One Penny (without Supplement).

La 18a internacia Kongreso Esperanto,
KONDUK- ANTO AL
BELEGA
SKOTLANDO
[BONNIE, BONNIE SCOTLAND]
Historio, Naciaj Karakterizoj, k. t. p.
Traduko Esperanta ★ Prezo, Du Pencoj.
ROTSEO, GLASGO, SKOTLANDO,
HIGGIE & KO., PRESISTOJ KAJ ELDONISTOJ.
Ĉe Librovendistoj, Jurnalvendistoj, kaj Grupoj
Esperantistaj tra la tuta Mondo.
Esperanto
Edinburgo, 1926a.
Peace, Honour,
and Good-Will!

KONDUKANTO
AL BELEGA
SKOTLANDO
[BONNIE, BONNIE SCOTLAND]
VIDAĴOJ, NACIAJ KARAKTERIZOJ, K. T. P.
Traduko Esperanta ★ Prezo, Unu Penco,
ROTHESAY, GLASGOW, SKOTLANDO,
HIGGIE & KO., PRESISTOJ KAJ ELDONISTOJ.
Ĉe Librovendistoj, Ĵurnalventistoj, kaj Grupoj
Esperantistaj tra la tuta Mondo.
OUR FIELD

1907.
SPECIALA
KONGRESO
EDITION.
KEMRBIGO,
GRANDA
BRITUJO.
KONDUKANTO AL
BELEGA
SKOTLANDO
[BONNIE, BONNIE SKOTLANDO,]
Historio, Naciaj Karakterizaj, k. t. p,
Tradukita Esperanten. ★ Prezo, Unu Penco.
ROTSE, GLASGO, SKOTLANDO,
HIGGIE & KO., PRESISTOJ KAJ ELDONISTOJ,
Aĉetebla ĉe Librovendistoj, Ĵurnalvendistoj kaj
Grupoj Esperantistoj tra la tuta Mondo.

Price, 1 Penny.
Prezo, 4 Spesdekoj.
LA UNUA GVID-LIBRO PRESITA EN ESPERANTO.
[The First Guide-Book Printed in Esperanto.]
KONDUKANTO AL
BELEGA
SKOTLANDO
(BONNIE, BONNIE SKOTLANDO),
Historio, Naciaj Karakterizaj, k. t. p.
Tradukita Esperanten. ★ Prezo, Unu Penco.
HIGGIE & CO., PRINTERS & PUBLISHERS, ROTHESAY.
To be had from Booksellers, News-agents, and Esperanto Groups throughout the world.
Aĉetebla ĉe Librovendistoj, Ĵurnalvendistoj kaj Grupoj Esperantistaj tra la tuta Mondo.
Esperanto

17a and **17b** *previous spread* Esperanto, an *a posteriori* constructed language, was created in the 1880s and still survives today. Its golden age, however, was during the first decades of the twentieth century when the British Esperanto Association published a periodical, *The British Esperantist*, and books, newspapers and pamphlets like this Scottish tourist guide *Kondukanto al Belega Skotlando* (1907) were printed all over the world. Bodleian Library, John Johnson Collection: Esperanto Box 1; Bodleian Library, G.A. Scotl. 8° 687.

Mountain and mist, lone glen and murmuring stream,
The shaggy forest and the grey hillside,
These are thy features, Scotland – these the pride
Of those that love thee, and thy minstrels' theme.

Monto kaj nebuleto, valeto silento, kaj rivereto murmuranta
La arbaro senkultura kaj la montoflanko griza,
Tiuj ĉi estas ciaj trajtoj, Skotlando, pri kiuj fieriĝas
Tiuj kiuj amas cin, kai tiuj estas la temoj de ciaj bardoj.

Perhaps those unusual accents – the circumflexes on a *c* and a *g* – jump out. Certainly they were among the features that reformers sought to remove when a simplified version of Esperanto – Ido – was adopted by a committee known as Delegation for the Adoption of an Auxiliary International Language. But between the English and the Esperanto lines we should be able to recognize plenty that would make Esperanto a far less daunting prospect than Wilkins's philosophical language.

At the same time, Esperanto and its derivatives are undeniably European in their construction (a fact which Ido's supporters turn into an unashamed selling point: 'It is not a new language to learn: *it is the quintessence of European languages*').[44] Otto Neurath's ISOTYPE (International System of Typographic Picture Education) was an auxiliary language that sought to be useful throughout the world (**figure 18**):

> In the Far East we see *one* language for writing, but a great number of languages for talking. We have made *one* international picture language (as a helping language) into which statements may be put from all the normal languages of the earth.[45]

Neurath with wry understatement sums up the long history of constructed languages with the remark that '"debabelization" is a very hard and complex work'.[46] His solution is an auxiliary language that returns to the concept of the iconic relationship (as with Recorde's equals sign: lines of equal length standing for statements of equal value). In Neurath's formulation 'WORDS MAKE DIVISION, PICTURES MAKE CONNECTION'.[47] Thus a sign telling us how to use a telephone in a series of pictures might be more useful than one which describes the process in words. The idea behind ISOTYPE is that 'pictures, whose details are clear to everybody, are free from the limits of language:

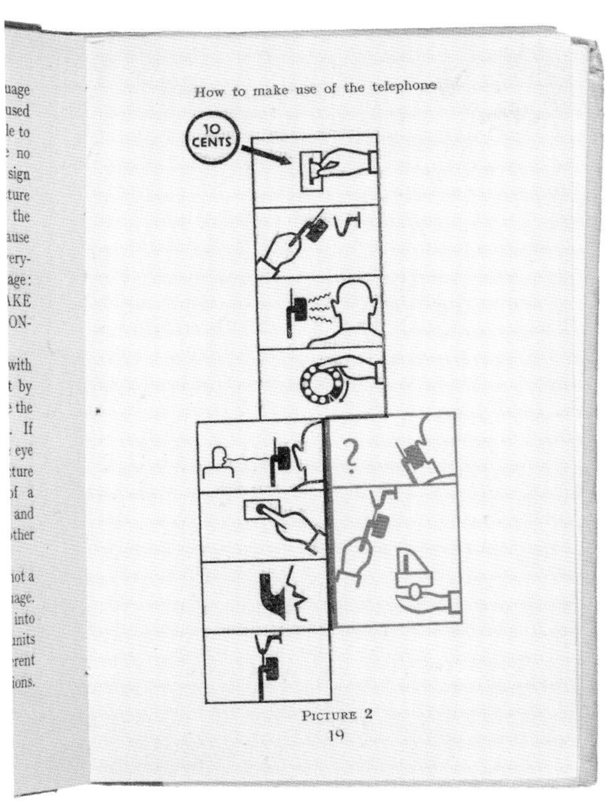

they are international.'[48] Neurath's logic here is not entirely new. The need for language-neutral pictorial road signs was felt before ISOTYPE. And if we compare our Greek, Arabic, Latin and English copies of Euclid's *Elements* we will note the similarity of the diagrams, which, barring Billingsley's innovation of using pop-ups, remain remarkably consistent across four languages and seven hundred years. A picture language like ISOTYPE, however, is more useful for some functions than for others. Neurath concedes, 'It is frequently hard to make a picture of a simple statement, … and a system of education has to see which language [i.e. word or image] is best for which purposes.'[49] We may be able to read *Moby Dick* translated into emoji, but the mapping of icons to text is a rough one to say the least.[50] As neural machine translation – via the Web or even in real time on our phones – continues to improve, it seems that translation, rather than the widespread adoption of an auxiliary language, once again holds the key to the debabelization of our global conversations.

18 'How to make use of the telephone', from Otto Neurath, *International Picture Language* (1936). Neurath fled Vienna in 1934 and developed his language ISOTYPE to promote international understanding and 'debabelization'. He explains that 'the "words" and "statements" of the picture language – signs and their order – are not the same' as in ordinary pictures because their 'organization' makes clear 'certain relations between them'. Bodleian Library, 26231 f.16, p. 19.

20 And how the high Priests and our rulers
deliuered him to bee condemned to death, and
haue crucified him.
21 But we trusted that it had bene he which
should haue redeemed Israel: and as touching
all these things, to day is euen the third day since
they were done.
22 Yea, and certaine women also of our com-
panie made vs astonied, which came early vnto
the sepulchre,
23 And when they found not his body, they
came, saying that they had seene a vision of An-
gels, which say that he was aliue.
24 And certaine of them which were with
vs, went to the sepulchre, and found it euen
so as the woman had sayde, but him they saw
not.
25 And he saide vnto them, O fooles, and
slow of heart, to beleeue all that the Prophets
haue spoken:
26 Ought not Christ to haue suffered these
things, and to enter into his glory?
27 And he began at Moses, and all the Prophets, and throughly interpreted vnto them in
all the Scriptures, those things which were
written of himselfe.
28 And they drewe nigh vnto the village,
which they went vnto, and he made as though
he would haue gone further.
29 And they constrained him, saying, Abide
with vs, for it draweth toward night, and the
day is farre passed: And he went in to tarie with
them.
30 And it came to passe, as he sate at meate
with them, he tooke bread, and [c] blessed it, and
brake, and gaue to them.
31 And their eyes were opened, & they knew
him, and he vanished out of their sight.
32 And they said one vnto another, Did not
our hearts burne within vs, while hee talked
with vs by the way, and opened to vs the Scriptures?
33 And they rose vp the same houre, and returned againe to Hierusalem, and found the eleuen gathered together, and them that were

c This word blessed, signifieth here nothing else, but to giue thankes, as appeareth by diuers places of Scripture, Luke 22.

stood in the mids of them, and saith v
Peace be vnto you.
37 But they were abashed and af
supposed that they had seene a spirit.
38 And hee sayde vnto them, W
troubled, and why doe thoughts ar
heartes?
39 Behold my hands and my feete
euen I my selfe: handle me and see,
hath not flesh and bones, as ye see me
40 And when he had thus spoken,
them his hands and his feete.
41 And while they yet beleeued n
and wondered, he said vnto them, Ha
any meate?
42 And they offered him a piece of
fish, and of an hony combe.
43 And he tooke it, and did eate be
44 And he saide vnto them, The
wordes which I spake vnto you, wh
yet with you, that all must needes b
which were written of me in the law
and in the Prophets, and in the Psal
45 Then opened he their || wits,
might vnderstand the Scriptures,
46 And said vnto them, Thus it is
and thus it behoued Christ to suffer, a
from death the third day:
47 And that repentance and remissi
should be preached in his Name amon
ons, and must begin at Hierusalem.
48 And ye are witnesses of these thi
49 *And beholde, I will send the p
my father vpon you: But tarie ye in t
Hierusalem, vntill yee be endued wi
from on high.
50 And he led them out into Beth
lift vp his hands, and blessed them.
51 *And it came to passe, as he bles
he departed from them, and was cari
heauen.
52 And when they had worshipped h
returned to Hierusalem, with great io
53 And were continually in the Tem
sing and lauding God. Amen.

Here endeth the Gospell by Saint Luke.

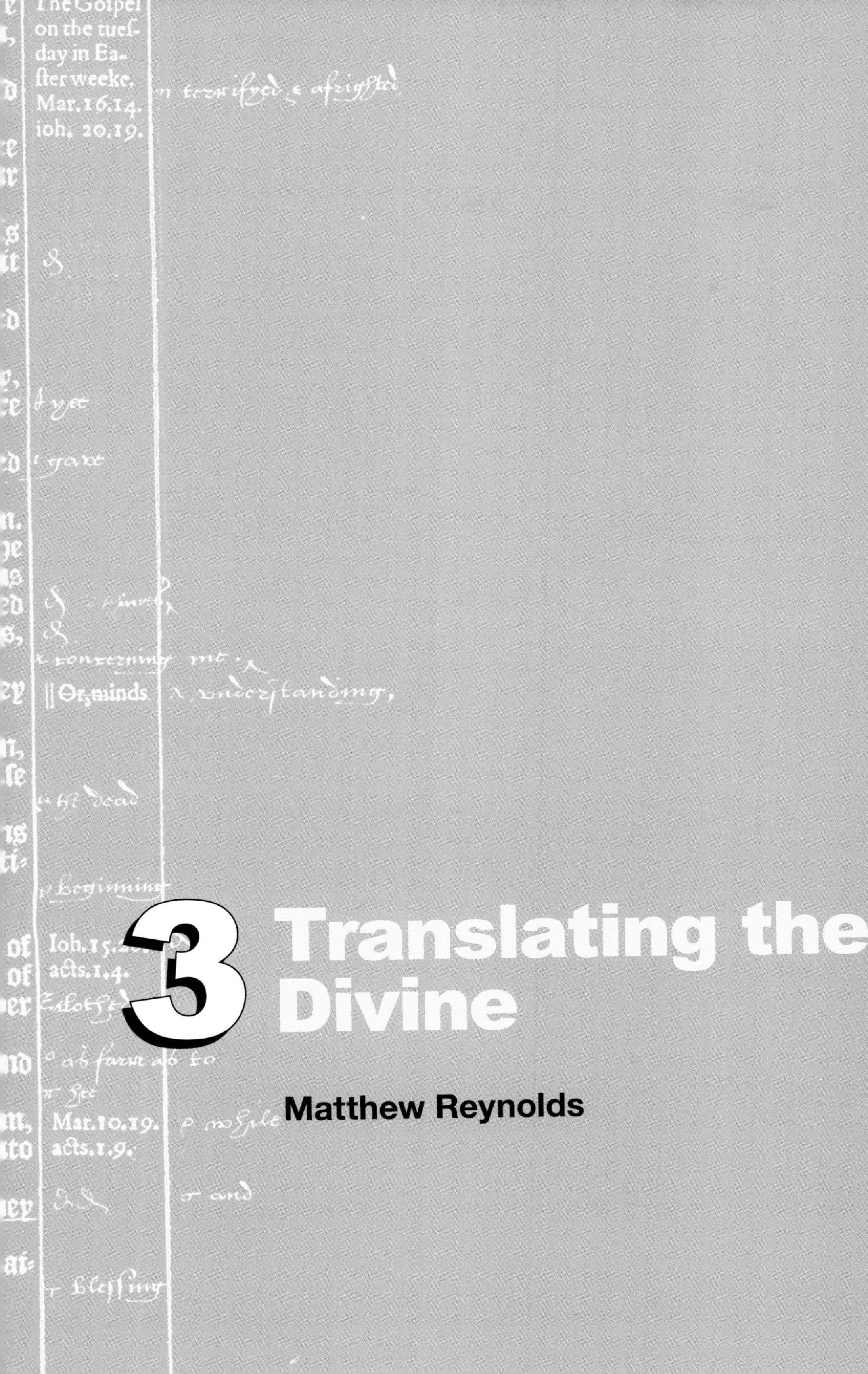

3 Translating the Divine

Matthew Reynolds

The divine becomes manifest through language and translation. In Ancient Greek tragedy, the gods typically spoke with extreme clarity and calm, displaying perfect control of human language as of the universe and of themselves.[51] More recently, in the Church of Jesus Christ of the Latter-day Saints, the *Book of Mormon* is believed to have come into being via a process of perfect translation. Following directions from the angel Moroni, in 1827, a farmhand called Joseph Smith uncovered gold plates, inscribed in an unknown tongue that is said to have looked a bit like Hebrew and a bit like Egyptian hieroglyphics. Fortunately, he also discovered a miraculous translation machine alongside them: a pair of diamond-like stone discs in a spectacle-like frame. Using this early version of Google Translate he was able to read the mysterious source text and put it swiftly into English. Soon afterwards, the gold plates disappeared; but it did not matter because 'the voice of God spoke out of heaven saying that the book was true and the translation correct.'[52]

These examples of easy translation between human and divine contrast with other instances where communication is complicated, indirect or impossible. The Greek gods also spoke through prophets and oracles whose interpretation was frequently opaque and whose fulfilment was generally disastrous (as when Agamemnon had to sacrifice his daughter in order to pursue the Trojan War, or when Oedipus murdered his father and married his mother). In the New Testament of the Bible, divine teaching is often conveyed indirectly, through the veiled medium of parable. And, in later Christian belief, there is a long tradition of conceiving of God as being wholly beyond words, describable only by what He is not: this is often called 'negative theology'.

Perhaps the most elaborate and beautiful example of negative theological writing is Dante's 'Paradiso', the last *cantica* of his *Commedia*. Dante tells of how he floated up through the heavens, accompanied by Beatrice his guide, as blessed souls mediated God's truths to him via a dazzling variety

19 This nineteenth-century illustration, by Gustave Doré, provides a visual translation of Canto 31 of Dante's 'Paradiso', which is itself presented as a verbal translation of a divine vision. Dante Alighieri, *The Vision of Hell (Purgatory and Paradise)*, trans. H.F. Cary, illus. G. Doré, London, 1893. Wikimedia Commons.

of signifying strategies. They converse; they sing; they dance; they spell out words in the sky. By a kind of synchronized flying, they gather together into the form of an eagle, which then itself seems to speak. Later, they rearrange themselves in a sparkling river, and then into the image of a luminous rose which seems to be giving sustenance to innumerable irridescent bees. This scene inspired a startling illustration by Gustave Doré (**figure 19**).[53]

Yet, when Dante reaches the summit of paradise, and comes face to face with the divine, both words and images fail. He can explain that he saw a face like a human face, and an arrangement of three circles; but what he mainly says is how thoroughly he cannot translate his experience into words. He is a geometer failing to come up with the formula for measuring a circle; he is an infant at the breast; one moment of that experience was as vast as the twenty-five centuries which (he says) separate him from the moment when Neptune looked up from the depths of the ocean and saw the first ever ship, the *Argo*, casting its shadow on the surface of the water above him. Words are incapable of rendering the memory in his mind; and that memory is virtually nothing compared to the reality of what he saw.

This moment of untranslatability between divine and human has been translated from human to human, not only through the many hundreds of translations of the *Commedia* that have been done into a multitude of languages, but also through the more fragmentary and diffuse processes of translation which constitute poetic influence. For instance, in Tennyson's *In Memoriam*, a work of mourning for a deceased friend, the poet has a vision of 'empyreal heights of thought' and the 'deep pulsations of the world', which he endeavours to describe; only, like Dante, he is stricken by the inadequacy both of his language and of his memory:

> Vague words! But ah, how hard to frame
>   In matter-moulded forms of speech,
>   Or ev'n for intellect to reach
> Thro' memory that which I became …[54]

Yet, differently from Dante, Tennyson then finds an analogue to his supernatural experience in the natural world. At dawn, a breeze comes and shakes the elms and roses and lilies in a rhythm that echoes the deep pulsations of the world; it seems to speak 'the dawn, the dawn'; and then East and West brighten together, and 'broaden into boundless' day in an image of eternity. Language may not be able to render the divine directly, but it can describe the book of nature, through which the divine is partially translated.

The inimitable Qur'an

The Qur'an stands in contrast to these Christian linguistic veils and layerings. Muslims believe that the Qur'an was revealed word by word to Muhammad through the intermediary of the angel Jibril (Gabriel): in consequence, it is 'inimitable'. This does not mean that the Qur'an is not allowed to be translated; but it does change how the translations are used and understood. Muslims must get to know the Qur'an in Arabic, and (unless they are unable to do so) use the Arabic text for religious purposes such as prayer. A translation could not take the place of the sacred book, as translations of the Christian Bible have done in hundreds of languages around the world. But translations can be used to interpret and spread knowledge of the Qur'an, and indeed they have a vital part to play in those processes. As Travis Zadeh has noted, 'the practice of orally explaining the Qur'an in languages other than Arabic stretches back to the earliest periods of Islamic history', when, in eastern Iran and central Asia, there was an 'extensive network of Muslims who negotiated scripture across linguistic frontiers'. Written, interlinear translations into Persian also date from that time.[55]

For many Muslims, the inimitability of the Qur'an is rooted not only in its origin, but in the unique beauty and intricacy of its language. In the tenth century CE Hamd b. Muhammad Al-Khattābī gave a full account of this view. He wrote that humans would never be able to produce an equivalent to the Qur'an for a range of reasons:

> Among these reasons is the fact that their knowledge does not encompass all the nouns and words of the Arabic language which are the receptacles and conveyors of meaning; their understandings do not grasp all the meanings of the things conveyed by these words; and their knowledge is not complete enough to exhaust all the modes of arrangement by which these words are composed and linked together so that they might try and choose the best and the most beautiful of them and produce a speech like it. Indeed, speech is composed of these three things: a word which conveys, a meaning which subsists in it, and a linking which arranges the two. If you contemplate the Qur'ān you will find these things to be the

لبعض ظهيرا لو انزلنا
هذا القرآن على جبل لرأيته خاشعا
متصدعا من خشية الله وتلك
الأمثال نضربها للناس لعلهم
يتفكرون

قال الله سبحانه وتعالى
قل لئن اجتمعت الانس والجن على
ان ياتوا بمثل هذا القران لا
ياتون بمثله ولو كان
بعضهم

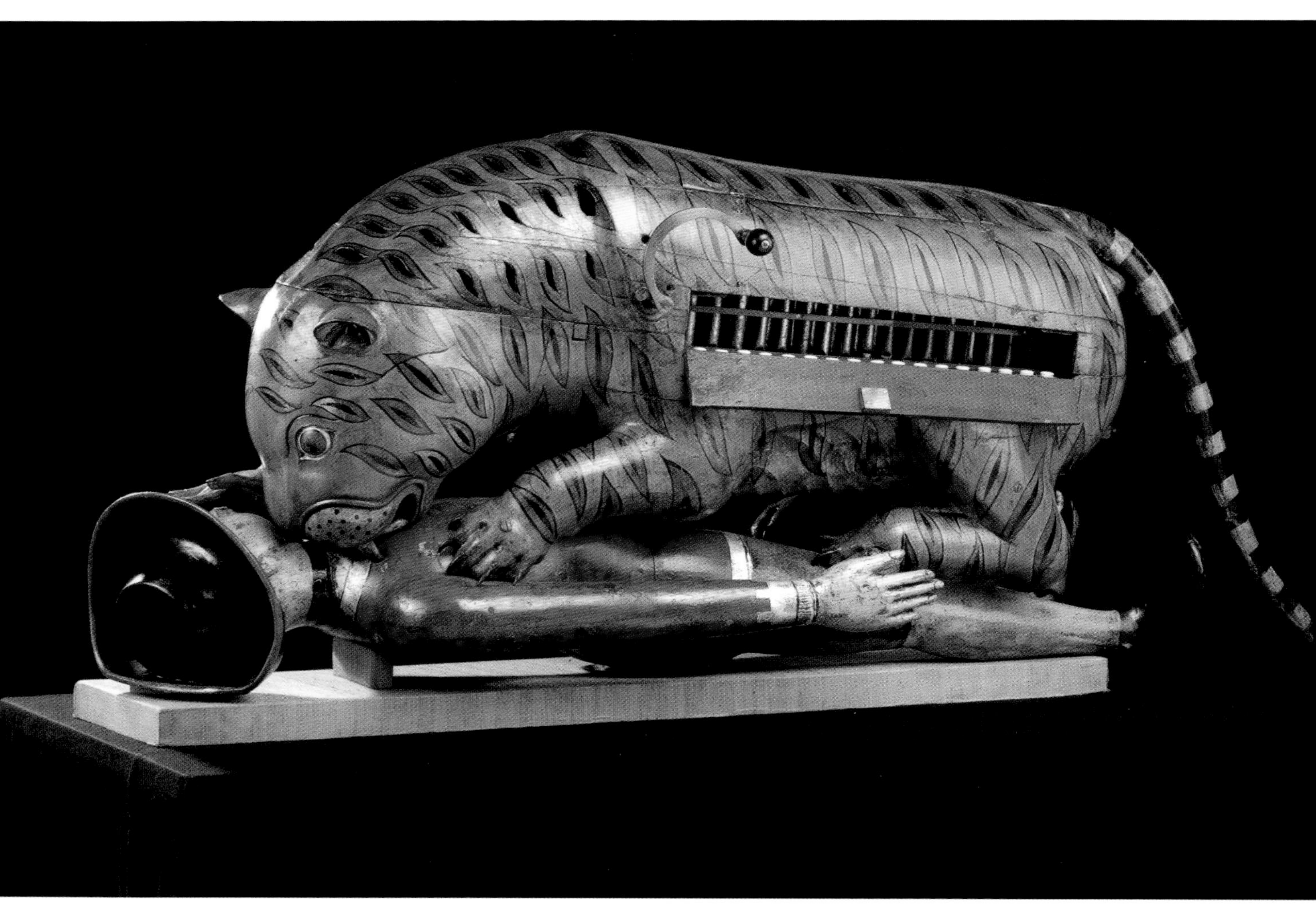

20a *previous spread* In this sixteenth-century manuscript of the Qur'ān the beautifully intricate combination of words and pattern asserts the inimitability of the sacred Arabic text. Bodleian Library, MS. Bodl. Or. 793, fols 8b–9a.

20b *above* 'Tipu's Tiger', a playful representation of Tipu Sultan's resistance to the incursions of the East India Company. When a handle is turned the soldier's arm moves up and down and the organ inside the tiger produces sounds that imitate his dying groans. © Victoria and Albert Museum, London.

> height of nobility and virtue so that you will not see any words more eloquent or lucid or sweeter than its words, and you will not see any arrangement more beautifully composed and more harmonious and congruent than its arrangement. As for the meanings, it is obvious to one possessed of a mind that the intellects testify that they are foremost in their field, and ascend to the highest degrees of merit in their properties and attributes ... Therefore you should now understand and know that the Qur'ān is an inimitable miracle because it came with the most eloquent of expressions, in the most beautiful forms of composition, containing the most authentic meanings.[56]

There are similarities between this account of untranslatability and the descriptions by Dante and Tennyson of the failure of, first, their memory and then their language to reproduce their experience of the divine. Only, for Al-Khattābī, the barrier falls within language: between the inimitable text of the Qur'an and any other human words.

This idea is beautifully exemplified in **figure 20a**, a sixteenth-century Qur'an which once belonged to Tipu Sultan, who was born in 1750 and ruled Mysore, in southern India, from 1783 until his death at the hands of the British in 1799.[57] Woven into the complicated pattern is the verse of the Qur'an which asserts its inimitability. No less than Doré's illustration to Dante, this dazzlingly intricate illumination offers a vivid image of the untranslatable divine.

Yet, though the text is presented as inimitable, the book in which it appeared was of course not immune from being possessed and transported to a different land. Like the Codex Mendoza (discussed in Chapter 1) this Qur'an arrived in the Bodleian as the result of the upheavals of empire. Tipu Sultan led resistance to the incursions of the East India Company, and was known as 'The Tiger of Mysore'. He had a mechanical, musical statue created in honour of this appellation: it represents a tiger savaging the supine body of a British man **(figure 20b).** But Tipu was eventually defeated and killed at the fall of the fortress of Seringapatam (now Srirangapatna). His mechanical tiger was claimed as booty and ended up on display in the Victoria and Albert Museum (where it can still be seen); and his library of over two thousand books was appropriated and dispersed among various institutions and individuals. The splendid Qur'an was donated to the Bodleian by the directors of the East India Company in 1806. So divine books can be translated by violence between different continents and powers.

Travelling religions

Divine texts are also transported as believers travel and non-believers are converted. Religions spread, and translation plays a crucial role in that process. **Figures 21, 22** and **23** all give haunting witness to the intertwined activities of linguistic and geographical translation.

Figure 21 shows a manuscript of a Buddhist tantric work, the *Mañjuśrīnāmasaṅgīti*, or 'Recitation of the Names of Mañjuśrī'.[58] It consists of 162 verses associated with Mañjuśrī, who was the bodhisattva of wisdom. The work was popular in central Asian Buddhism and this book, which probably dates back to the seventeenth or eighteenth century, provides evidence of its travels across the region. The manuscript was written in Mongolia, but shows the influence of southern Asian culture in the landscape format of the paper, which imitates manuscripts made from dried palm leaves. The black writing that runs horizontally is Tibetan, and reads from left to right. The translation into Mongolian dangles underneath, since Mongolian traditional script was written vertically. Originally, this writing in black ink was all that the manuscript contained. The red writing was probably added at a later date: it is Sanskrit, but written in a Nepalese script rather than the more common Devanāgarī script that was used for Sanskrit manuscripts and printed books in India. This is a trace of the route taken by Nepalese Buddhist traditions as they moved north via Tibet.[59]

In **figure 22** we see the product of a religious translation enterprise about which more is known. The book dates from 1852, and is an early example of an Anglican Bible translated from English into Maori.[60] It is open at the beginning of the Gospel according to St Mark (*Ko te Rongo pai a Maka*): at the start of verse 3 you can read the Maori for 'the voice of one crying in the wilderness' (*he reo no tetahi i te koraha e karanga ana*).

Missionaries had been present in New Zealand since Christmas Day 1814, when the Rev. Samuel Marsden, invited by Maori chief Ruatara, had preached at the Bay of Islands in the far north of the country. Over the following few years, missionaries had concentrated on sharing practical skills with Maori people, on the principle that relationships of exchange and trade would make Maori well disposed towards Christianity. However,

21 This seventeenth- or eighteenth-century manuscript of the Buddhist tantric work the *Mañjuśrīnāmasaṅgīti*, or 'Recitation of the Names of Mañjuśrī', includes Tibetan, Mongolian and Sanskrit written in a Nepalese script: this linguistic complexity is a trace of the journey taken by Buddhist traditions as they moved north to Mongolia. Bodleian Library, MS. Asiat. Misc. d. 8.

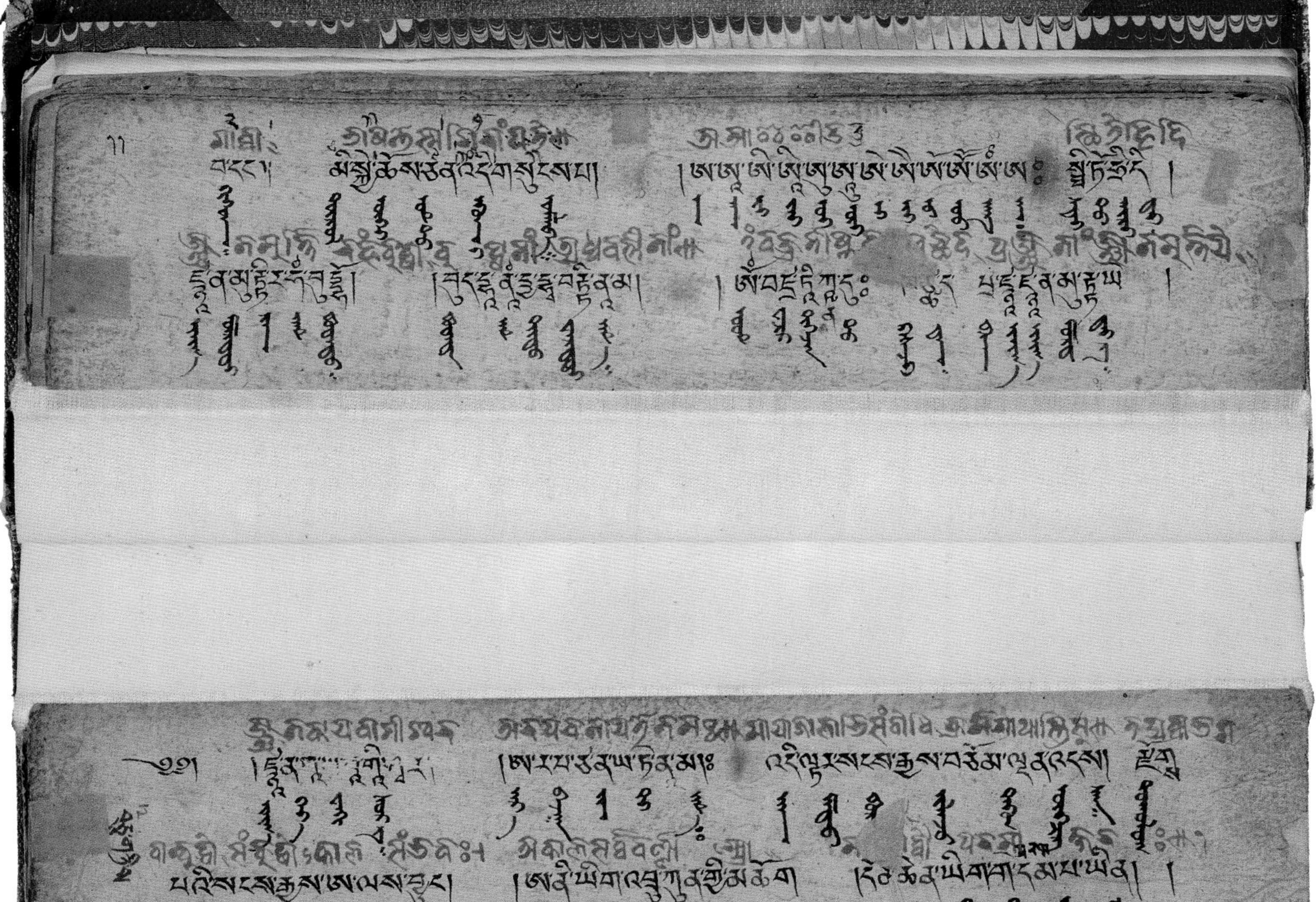

51 Na, te arai o te temepara kua pakaru, e rua nga wahi, o runga a puta noa ki raro; runa a te whenua, pakaru ana nga kamaka;

52 Tuwhera noa hoki nga urupa; a he maha nga tinana i ara mai o te hunga tapu kua moe,

53 A puta ake ana i nga urupa i muri iho o tona aranga mai, haere ana ki roto ki te pa tapu, he tokomaha hoki te hunga i kitea ai ratou.

54 Na, te kitenga o te keneturio, me ona hoa tiaki i a Ihu, i te ru, me nga mea i meatia, nui atu to ratou wehi, ka mea, He pono ko te Tama a te Atua tenei.

55 A he tokomaha nga wahine i reira e matakitaki mai ana i tawhiti, nga mea hoki i aru mai i a Ihu i Kariri, a i mahi mea mana:

56 I roto i a ratou a Meri Makarini, a Meri whaea o Hemi raua ko Hohi, me te whaea hoki o nga tamariki a Heperi.

57 ¶ A ka ahiahi, ka haere mai tetahi tangata taonga nui o Arimatia, ko Hohepa te ingoa, ko ia ano hoki he akonga na Ihu:

58 I haere ia ki a Pirato, a tonoa ana e ia te tinana o Ihu. Na, ka mea a Pirato kia hoatu te tinana.

59 Na, ka tango a Hohepa i te tinana, a takaia ana e ia ki te rinena ma,

60 A whakatakotoria ana ki tana urupa hou, i haua e ia ki roto ki te kamaka: na, whakataka atu ana e ia tetahi kohatu nui ki te kuwaha o te urupa, a haere ana.

61 A i reira ano a Meri Makarini, me tera Meri, e noho ana i te ritenga atu o te tanumanga.

62 ¶ Na, i te aonga ake i muri i te takanga *hakari*, ka haere mai nga tohunga nui me nga Parihi ki a Pirato,

63 Ka mea, E mara, e mahara ana matou ki ta tera tangata tinihanga i mea ai, i a ia ano i te ora, Kia taka nga ra e toru ka ara ahau.

64 Na, whakahaua atu kia tiakina te tanumanga, a tae noa ki te toru o nga ra, kei haere atu ana akonga i te po, tahae ai i a ia, a ka mea ki te iwi, Kua ara i te mate: penei kino atu i to mua to muri he.

65 Ka mea atu a Pirato ki a ratou, He kai tiaki ano a koutou: haere, kia puta a koutou whakaaro kei taea atu *ia*.

66 Na, haere ana ratou, hiritia ana te kohatu, me *te whakanoho ano i* nga kai tiaki, kei taea atu te tanumanga.

UPOKO 28.

I TE mutunga o te hapati i te mea meake puao te *ra* tuatahi o te wiki, ka haere a Meri Makarini me tera Meri atu kia kite i te tanumanga.

2 Na, he nui te ru i puta mai: i heke iho hoki tetahi anahera a te Ariki i te rangi, a haere mai ana, whakataka atu ana e ia te kohatu i te kuwaha, a noho ana i runga.

3 Rite tonu tona ahua ki te uira, i ma tonu hoki tona kakahu, ano he hukarere:

4 A wiri noa iho nga kai tiaki i te wehi ki a ia, whakatupu tupapaku ana.

5 Na, ka oho mai te anahera, ka mea ki nga wahine, Kei wehi korua: e mahara ana hoki ahau, e rapu ana korua i a Ihu i ripekatia.

6 Kahore ia i konei: kua ara hoki, kua pera me tana i mea ai. Haere mai kia kite i te wahi i takoto ai te Ariki.

7 A, hohoro te haere, korerotia atu ki ana akonga, kua ara mai ia i te mate; tena ia te haere atu na i mua i a koutou ki Kariri; ko reira koutou kite ai i a ia: na, kua korero atu nei ahau ki a korua.

8 A hohoro tonu to raua haere mai i te urupa, wehi ana, hari ana, a oma ana ki te korero ki ana akonga.

9 ¶ A i a raua e haere ana ki te korero ki ana akonga, na, ka tutaki a Ihu ki a raua, ka mea, E ia ma. Na, ka haere mai raua, ka pupuri i ona waewae, a koropiko ana ki a ia.

10 Katahi a Ihu ka mea ki a raua, Aua e wehi: haere, korerotia atu ki aku teina kia haere ki Kariri, ko reira hoki ratou kite ai i a au.

11 ¶ A i a raua e haere ana, na, kua tae atu etahi o nga kai tiaki ki te pa, a korerotia atu ana ki nga tohunga nui nga mea katoa i meatia.

12 Na, ka mine mai ratou me nga kaumatua, ka runanga, a he nui te moni i homai e ratou ki nga hoia,

13 I mea hoki ratou, Me ki atu e koutou, I haere mai ana akonga i te po, a tahaetia ana ia, i a matou e moe ana.

14 A ki te rangona tenei e te kawana, ma matou ia e whakapati, a ka ora koutou.

15 Na, ka tango ratou i nga moni, a meinga ana nga mea i akona ai ratou: heoi e korerotia ana ano tenei e nga Hurai a taea noatia tenei ra.

16 ¶ Na, ka haere atu nga akonga tekau ma tahi ki Kariri, ki te maunga i whakaritea e Ihu ki a ratou.

17 A, to ratou kitenga i a ia, ka koropiko ki a ia: ko etahi ia i rapurapu.

18 ¶ Na, ka haere mai a Ihu, ka korero ki a ratou, ka mea, Kua tukua katoatia mai ki a au te mana o te rangi o te whenua.

19 Na, haere koutou, meinga hei akonga nga iwi katoa, iriiria i runga i te ingoa o te Matua, o te Tamaiti, o te Wairua Tapu:

20 Akona ratou kia mau ki nga mea katoa, i whakahaua atu e ahau ki a koutou: na, ko au tena hei hoa mo koutou i nga ra katoa, a te mutunga ra ano o te ao. Amine.

KO TE

RONGO PAI A MAKA.

UPOKO 1.

KO te timatanga o te rongo pai o Ihu Karaiti, o te tamaiti a te Atua;

2 Ko te mea hoki ia i tuhituhia i roto i nga poropiti, Na, ka tonoa e ahau taku karere i mua i tou aroaro, mana e whakapai tou ara ki mua i a koe.

3 He reo no tetahi i te koraha e karanga ana, Whakapaia e koutou te huarahi o te Ariki, whakatikaia ona ara.

4 I te koraha a Hoani e iriiri ana, e kauwhau ana i te iriiringa o te ripeneta hei murunga hara.

5 Na, ka haere atu ki a ia te whenua katoa o Huria, me nga tangata o Hiruharama, a iriiria katoatia ana e ia ki te awa o Horano, me te whaki ano i o ratou hara.

6 Na, te kakahu o Hoani, he huruhuru kamera, he hiako hoki te whitiki o tona hope; a tana kai, he mawhitiwhiti, he honi koraha;

7 A i kauwhau ano ia, i mea, Tenei te haere mai nei i muri i a au tetahi e kaha rawa ana i a au, e kore ahau e tau ki te piko iho wewete ai i te here o ona hu.

8 Ko au nei, he iriiri taku i a koutou ki te wai: mana ia koutou e iriiri ki te Wairua Tapu.

9 A i aua ra, ka haere mai a Ihu i Nahareta o Kariri, a ka iriiria e Hoani ki Horano.

10 Na, tika tonu ake ia i te wai,

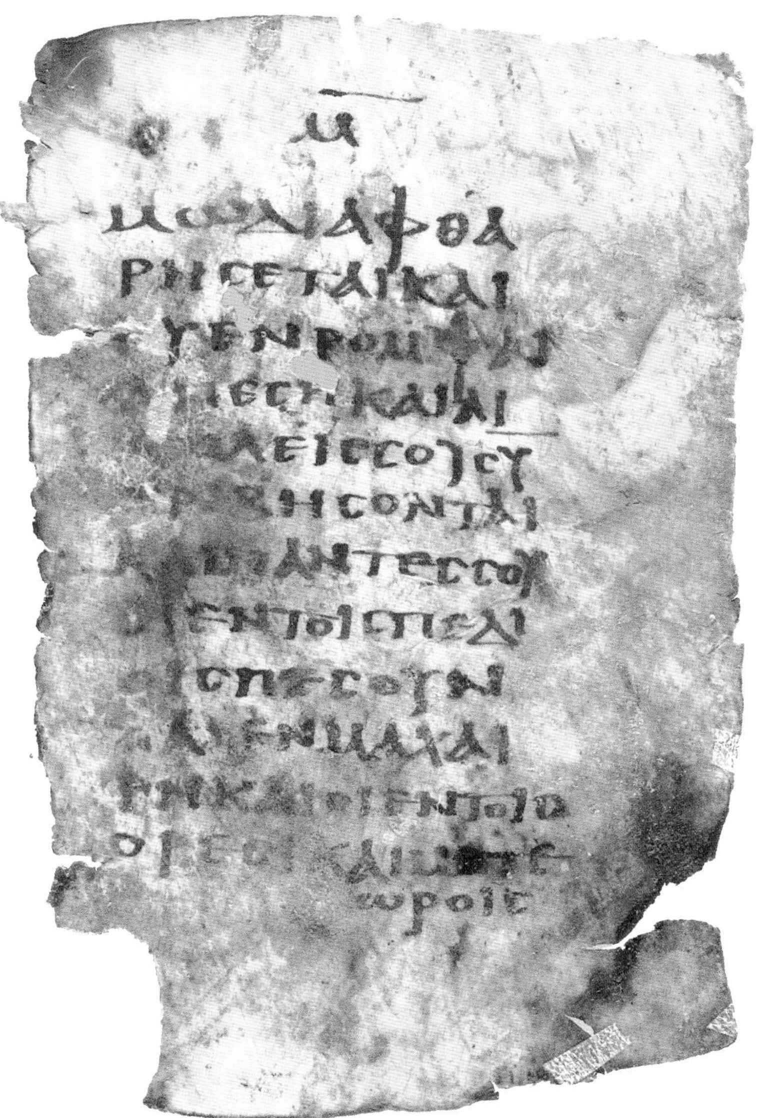

22 *far left* The New Testament translated into Maori (1852), open at the Gospel according to St Mark (*Ko te Rongo pai a Maka*). Bodleian Library (RHO) 850.871 r. 5, pp. 46–7.

23 A parchment fragment of a Greek translation of the biblical Book of Ezra, fourth century CE, dug out of a rubbish dump in the ancient Egyptian city of Oxyrhynchus (modern-day el-Bahnasa). The Hebrew original is lost. Bodleian Library, MS. Gr. bib. g. 3(P) recto.

the strategy was not working, and in the first decade of the mission not a single Maori had been converted (personal disputes among the missionaries had also played their part). The missionaries' efforts were redirected towards language-learning and translation by Henry Williams, who took over as leader in 1823. Four years later, a small selection of Bible texts in Maori was printed in Sydney; then, in 1834, William Colenso took the first printing press across to New Zealand. In 1835 a sixteen-page edition of Ephesians and Philippians was published there; and in the following year the production of complete Maori New Testaments – like the one in **figure 22** – began.[61]

In this brief history we can see how Christians' wish to spread news of their God can have profound effects on a language. Before the missionaries' arrival, Maori was a spoken tongue, existing in a continuum of speech practices which varied from group to group. In order to produce a Maori Bible, missionaries had first to find a way of noting down the words of the Maori from whom they were learning: this is how the Maori language gained a written form. Once books were made using that form, what had been a variable mode of speech took on the fixity of print. Then, when the books were distributed across the country, what had been a local variety of language spread far and wide. Missionaries needed to teach Maori to read so they could understand it. Standardization of the Maori language had begun; and the need for literacy went along with it.

In many other countries at about the same time, Christian missionaries were trying to spread the good news via translation; and they are still doing it today. An American evangelical website claims that the Bible has been completely translated into 500 languages and partially into another 1,300; translation projects are apparently getting started in a further 2,300. Even allowing for the possibility of exaggeration, it is an amazingly ambitious enterprise. Many of these languages were (or are) oral: in them, the Bible was (or will be) not only the first book ever translated, but the first book ever written down and printed. The endeavour to translate the divine has played – and is playing – a major part in the history of the world's languages.[62]

Figure 23, in contrast, shows the fragility of some of the earliest biblical texts, and the happenstance by which they were preserved. It is a fragment of parchment, discovered among the sands covering a rubbish dump outside the ancient Egyptian city of Oxyrhynchus (now el-Bahnasa). The dump at Oxyrhynchus was discovered in 1896, and since then has yielded as many as

5,000 fragments – mainly papyri – which form the most astonishing verbal treasury of the ancient world, including everything from court records, bills and horoscopes to texts by Sappho, Plato and Menander. The parchment leaf shown in **figure 23** contains a bit of a Greek translation of the biblical Book of Ezra.[63] The Hebrew original has been lost; and this little scrap is the oldest surviving witness of the Greek translation.

Communal translation and the King James Bible

More than a millennium before the creation, in Mongolia, of the trilingual Buddhist manuscript of the *Mañjuśrīnāmasaṅgīti*, Buddhist teaching was being translated in China. Typically, it was done by large assemblies of scholars – as many as a thousand in some cases. A monk, who might have travelled from India, and who might well not know Chinese, would recite a sutra by heart, perhaps in Sanksrit, perhaps in one of several possible intermediary languages. All the monks present would ponder and discuss until an agreed translation was reached; at which point it would be written down.[64] This practice gives a vivid picture of how, when a religious text is felt to belong to a community, translation can become a group activity. This is different from the usual mode of translation of literary texts, where individual vision and style are typically prized, and single translators generally take on the work of re-creating them in another language.

The 'Authorized' or 'King James' translation of the Bible, which was published in 1611, was created by a communal process that has something in common with the Chinese Buddhist model. Following a conference called by the king in 1604, around fifty translators were gathered to undertake the work. They were divided into six 'companies', two based in Cambridge, two in Oxford and two in Westminster. Each company was given a different stretch of the Bible to translate; but, within each company, individuals worked at the same passages and then gathered to compare notes. A provisionally agreed version was then considered by all the companies together.[65]

The process of arriving at the final, communally sanctioned version did not only involve the individual translators who belonged to the companies. It also took in many of the texts that had been produced during the long history of Bible translation into English and other languages. In the British Isles, translations of parts of the Bible can be found in

Anglo-Saxon times: they were typically interlinear, functioning as aids to interpretation in rather the same way as the early Persian translations of the Qur'an. Church authorities were often worried about the unorthodox ideas that might develop if 'unlearned' people read Bible texts in English for themselves, without the guidance of a priest. But there was little opposition to translation per se. In the late fourteenth century the sustained shared enterprise that produced the group of manuscripts known as the Wycliffite Bible did attract ecclesiastical condemnation; but this was due less to the translation than to the radical beliefs of the endeavour's leader John Wycliffe. In any case, the condemnation was not very effective. The Wycliffite Bible seems to have been widely read, and survives in about 250 examples, substantially more than any other medieval work.[66]

There were similar complexities during the sixteenth century, when English Bibles were created in the context of the Reformation, and of a Europe-wide surge in translation. Between 1466 and 1522 there were twenty-two editions of the Bible in High and Low German; and the Bible was put into Italian in 1471, Dutch in 1477, Spanish in 1478, Czech around the same time, and Catalan in 1492.[67] Luther's famous version, published in 1522, was revolutionary not because it was a translation but because it was in brilliantly compelling colloquial German, and (like the Wycliffite Bible before it) was associated with fierce criticism of the Church. The same was true of Tyndale's English version, done in exile during the 1520s and 1530s. It was condemned by royal proclamation in 1530, and Tyndale was captured and executed as a heretic in Brussels in 1535. But, in that same year, his translation was completed by the fugitive Augustinian friar Miles Coverdale, and printed in a form that became known as the Coverdale Bible. This translation was welcomed and promoted by the Archbishop of Canterbury Thomas Cranmer on behalf of Henry VIII, who perhaps never noticed its roots in the work of the hated Tyndale.[68]

Over the ensuing decades, the Tyndale–Coverdale Bible was revised and reprinted in different forms: as the 'Great Bible' in 1541 and the 'Bishops' Bible' in 1568. Other translations also appeared: the more Protestant 'Geneva Bible' in 1560, and the Roman Catholic Douai–Rheims New Testament in 1582. Of all these texts, it was the Bishops' Bible that most underpinned the King James version. Sections of it were distributed to the companies, and the translators were instructed to follow its wording unless another translation was felt to 'agree better with the text'.[69] **Figure 24** is a record of this process. It shows a 1602 edition of the Bishops' Bible, together with marginal notes made by some of the King James translators.[70]

Despite all the alterations and different publications through which it passed, large stretches of Tyndale's translation survive in the King James Bible, and his stylistic signature is stamped upon it. Here, for instance, is the beginning of the Gospel according to St John in Tyndale:

> In the beginninge was that worde and that worde was with god / and god was that worde / The same was in the beginninge with god. All thyngis were made by yt and without it was made no thinge / that made was. In yt was lyfe / And lyfe was the light of men. And the lyght shynneth in darcknes / and darcknes comprehended yt not.[71]

And here is the same passage in the King James version:

> In the beginning was the Word, & the Word was with God, and the Word was God.
> The same was in the beginning with God.
> All things were made by him, and without him was not any thing made that was made.
> In him was life, and the life was the light of men.
> And the light shineth in darknesse, and the darknesse comprehended it not.[72]

Tyndale decided not to diminish the repetition in the source, nor to alter its parataxis (the repeated use of 'and'); and he managed to combine these brave translation choices with a compelling rhythm and haunting turn of phrase. When the King James translators chose to follow him so closely, they produced a text which struck many contemporaries as unidiomatic and strange. Yet, over the decades and centuries that followed, as this communally adjusted version of Tyndale's distinctive language was declaimed in churches across the country, and pondered quietly by believers at home, it became the texture of a religious community. It moulded the imaginations of Anglicans just as it had guided the King James translators in their shared labour. This work of divine translation was also a literary masterpiece.

24 *following spread* A 1602 edition of the 'Bishops' Bible', first published in 1568. The pencil notes in the margin were made by translators working on the King James Bible (1611), who took this earlier translation as their main source. Bodleian Library, Bib. Eng. 1602 b.1, fols 429v–430r.

28 But Jeſus turning backe vnto them,
ſayd, Yee daughters of Hieruſalem, weepe not
for me, but weepe for your ſelues, and for your
children.
29 For behold, the dayes are comming, in the
which they ſhall ſay, Happie are the barren, and
the wombes that neuer bare, & the paps which
neuer gaue ſucke.
30 Then ſhall they beginne to ſay to the
Eſa.2.19. mountaines, *Fall on vs, and to the hilles, Co-
oſee.10.8. uer vs.
apo.16.16. 31 For if they doe theſe things in a moiſt tree,
what ſhall be done in the drie?
Mat.22.38. 32 *And there were other two euill doers, led
with him, to be put to death.
Mat.27.38. 33 *And after that they were come to the
mar.15.27. place which is called Caluarie, there they cruci-
iohn 19.18. fied him, and the euill doers, one on the right
hand, and the other on the left.
34 Then ſayd Jeſus, Father, forgiue them,
for they wote not what they doe: And they parted his raiment, and caſt lots.
35 And the people ſtoode beholding, and the
rulers mocked him with them, ſaying, He ſaued
other men, let him ſaue himſelfe, if hee be verie
Chriſt, the choſen of God.
36 The ſouldiers alſo mocked him, comming
to him, and offering him vineger,
37 And ſaying, If thou bee the king of the
Jewes, ſaue thy ſelfe.
38 And a ſuperſcription was written ouer
him with letters of Greeke, and Latin, and Hebrewe, THIS IS THE KING OF THE
IEWES.
39 And one of the euill doers, which were
hanged, railed on him, ſaying, If thou be Chriſt,
ſaue thy ſelfe and vs.
40 But the other anſwering, rebuked him,
ſaying, Feareſt thou not God, ſeeing thou art in
the ſame damnation?
41 And we truely are righteouſly puniſhed, for
we receiue according to our deeds, but this man
hath done nothing amiſſe.
42 And he ſayd vnto Jeſus, Lord, remember
me when thou commeſt into thy kingdome.
43 And Jeſus ſaid vnto him, Uerely I ſay vnto thee, to day ſhalt thou be with me in paradiſe.
44 And it was about the ſixt houre, and there
was a darkeneſſe ouer all the earth, vntill the
ninth houre.
45 And the Sunne was darkened, and the
vaile of the temple was rent, euen thorow the
middes.
46 And when Jeſus had cried with a loude
Pſal.30.6. voice, hee ſayd, *Father, into thy hands I will
commend my ſpirit: And when he thus had ſaid,
he gaue vp the ghoſt.
47 When the Centurion ſaw what was done,
he glorified God, ſaying, Uerely this was a righ-
teous man.
48 And all the people that came together to
that ſight, when they ſawe the things which
were done, ſmote their breaſts, and returned.
49 And all his acquaintance, and the women
that followed him from Galilee, ſtood afarre off,
beholding theſe things.
Mat.27.25. 50 *And beholde, there was a man named
mar.15.43. Joſeph, a counſeller, and hee was a good man,
iohn 19.38. and a iuſt,
51 (The ſame had not conſented to the coun-
ſell and deed of them) which was of Arimathea,
a citie of the Jewes, which ſame alſo waited for
the kingdome of God.
52 He went vnto Pilate, and begged the body of Jeſus.
53 And when he had taken it downe, he wrap-
ped it in a linnen cloth, and layd it in a ſepulchre
that was hewen in ſtone, wherein neuer man
before was layd.
54 And that day was the preparing of the
Sabboth, and the Sabboth drew on.
55 The women that followed after, which
had come with him from Galilee, beheld the ſepulchre, and how his body was layd.
56 And they returned, and prepared ſweete
odours and ointments, but reſted the Sabboth
day, according to the commandement.

The xxiiij. Chapter.

13 Chriſt appeareth to the two diſciples that went to
Emaus.

BUT [a] vpon the * firſt day of the a That is, the firſt day of the weeke.
Sabboths, very early in the
morning, they came vnto the ſe- Mar.16.1.
pulchre, bringing the ſweete o- iohn 20.21.
dours, which they had prepared,
and other women with them.
2 And they found the ſtone rolled away from
the ſepulchre.
3 And they went in, but found not the bodie
of the Lord Jeſu.
4 And it came to paſſe, as they were amazed
thereat, beholde, two men ſtood by them in ſhi-
ning garments.
5 And as they were afraid, and bowed down
their faces to the earth, they ſayde vnto them,
Why ſeeke ye the liuing among the dead?
6 He is not here, but is riſen: *Remember Mat.17.23.
how he ſpake vnto you when he was yet in Ga- mar.9.31.
lilee, luke.9.22.
7 Saying, The Sonne of man muſt bee deliuered into the hands of ſinful men, and be crucified, and the third day riſe.
8 And they remembred his words,
9 And returned from the ſepulchre, and told
all theſe things vnto thoſe eleuen, and to all the
remnant.
10 It was Marie Magdalene, and Joanna,
& Marie Jacobi, & other that were with them,
which told theſe things vnto the Apoſtles.
11 And their wordes ſeemed to them fayned
things, neither beleeued they them.
12 *Then aroſe Peter, and ranne vnto the Iohn 10.6.
ſepulchre, and when he had looked in, hee ſawe
the linnen clothes layd by themſelues, and departed, wondring in himſelfe at that which was
come to paſſe.
13 *And behold, two of them went that ſame The Goſpel
day to a village called Emaus, which was from on the
Hieruſalem about threeſcore [b] furlongs. Munday in
14 And they talked together of all theſe things Eaſter
that had come to paſſe, weeke.
15 And it came to paſſe, that while they com- Mar.16.12.
muned together, and reaſoned, Jeſus himſelfe b That is, 7. miles and an halfe.
drew neere, and went with them.
16 But their eyes were holden, that they
ſhould not know him.
17 And he ſayd vnto them, What manner of
communications are theſe that yee haue one to
another as ye walke, and are ſad?
18 And the one of them, whoſe name was
Cleophas, anſwering, ſayd vnto him, Art thou

onely a stranger in Hierusalem, and hast not
knowen the thinges which are come to passe
there in these dayes?
19 He saide vnto them, What things? And
they said vnto him, Of Jesus of Nazareth,
which was a Prophet, mightie in deede & word
before God and all the people,
20 And how the high Priests and our rulers
deliuered him to bee condemned to death, and
haue crucified him.
21 But we trusted that it had bene he which
should haue redeemed Israel: and as touching
all these things, to day is euen the third day since
they were done.
22 Yea, and certaine women also of our com-
panie made vs astonied, which came early vnto
the sepulchre,
23 And when they found not his body, they
came, saying that they had seene a vision of An-
gels, which say that he was aliue.
24 And certaine of them which were with
vs, went to the sepulchre, and found it euen
so as the woman had sayde, but him they saw
not.
25 And he saide vnto them, O fooles, and
slow of heart, to beleeue all that the Prophets
haue spoken:
26 Ought not Christ to haue suffered these
things, and to enter into his glory?
27 And he began at Moses, and all the Prophets, and throughly interpreted vnto them in
all the Scriptures, those things which were
written of himselfe.
28 And they drewe nigh vnto the village,
which they went vnto, and he made as though
he would haue gone further.
29 And they constrained him, saying, Abide
with vs, for it draweth toward night, and the
day is farre passed: And he went in to tarie with
them.
30 And it came to passe, as he sate at meate
with them, he tooke bread, and [c] blessed it, and
brake, and gaue to them.
31 And their eyes were opened, & they knew
him, and he vanished out of their sight.
32 And they said one vnto another, Did not
our hearts burne within vs, while hee talked
with vs by the way, and opened to vs the Scriptures?
33 And they rose vp the same houre, and returned againe to Hierusalem, and found the eleuen gathered together, and them that were
with them,
34 Saying, The Lord is risen indeede, and
hath appeared to Simon.
35 And they tolde what things were done in
the way, and how he was knowen of them in
the breaking of the bread.
36 *And as they thus spake, Jesus himselfe
stood in the mids of them, and saith vnto them,
Peace be vnto you.
37 But they were abashed and afraide, and
supposed that they had seene a spirit.
38 And hee sayde vnto them, Why are yee
troubled, and why doe thoughts arise in your
heartes?
39 Beholde my handes and my feete, that it is
euen I my selfe: handle me and see, for a spirit
hath not flesh and bones, as ye see me haue.
40 And when he had thus spoken, he shewed
them his hands and his feete.
41 And while they yet beleeued not for ioy,
and wondered, he said vnto them, Haue ye here
any meate?
42 And they offered him a piece of a broyled
fish, and of an hony combe.
43 And he tooke it, and did eate before them.
44 And he saide vnto them, These are the
wordes which I spake vnto you, while I was
yet with you, that all must needes be fulfilled
which were written of me in the law of Moses,
and in the Prophets, and in the Psalmes.
45 Then opened he their || wits, that they
might vnderstand the Scriptures,
46 And said vnto them, Thus it is written,
and thus it behoued Christ to suffer, and to rise
from death the third day:
47 And that repentance and remission of sins
should be preached in his Name among all nations, and must begin at Hierusalem.
48 And ye are witnesses of these things.
49 *And beholde, I will send the promise of
my father vpon you: But tarie ye in the citie of
Hierusalem, vntill yee be endued with power
from on high.
50 And he led them out into Bethanie, and
lift vp his hands, and blessed them.
51 *And it came to passe, as he blessed them,
he departed from them, and was caried vp into
heauen.
52 And when they had worshipped him, they
returned to Hierusalem, with great ioy:
53 And were continually in the Temple, prai-
sing and lauding God. Amen.

The Gospel on the tues-day in Easter weeke. Mar.16.14. ioh. 20.19.

|| Or, minds.

Ioh.15.26. acts.1.4.

Mar.10.19. acts.1.9.

Here endeth the Gospell by Saint Luke.

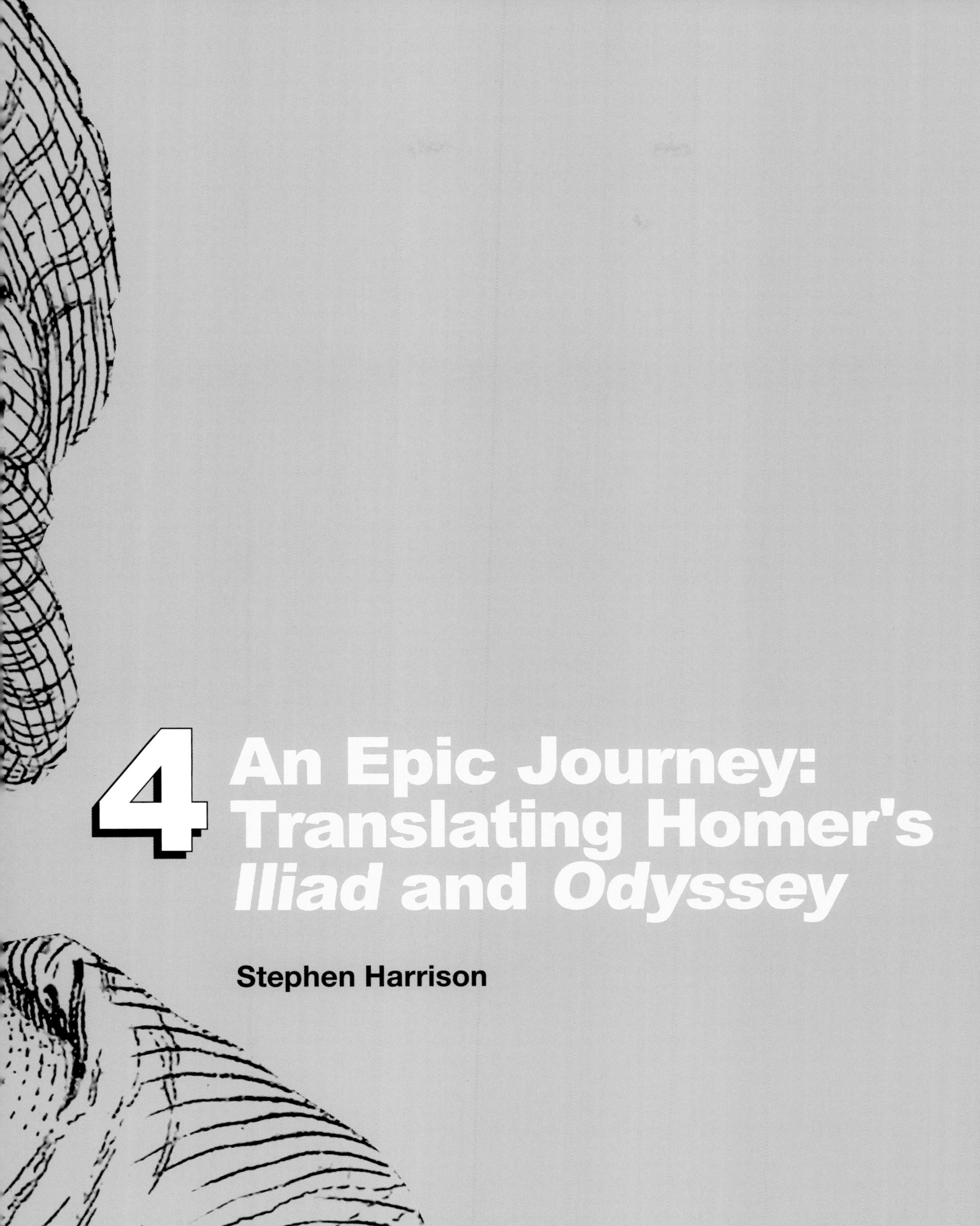

4 An Epic Journey: Translating Homer's *Iliad* and *Odyssey*

Stephen Harrison

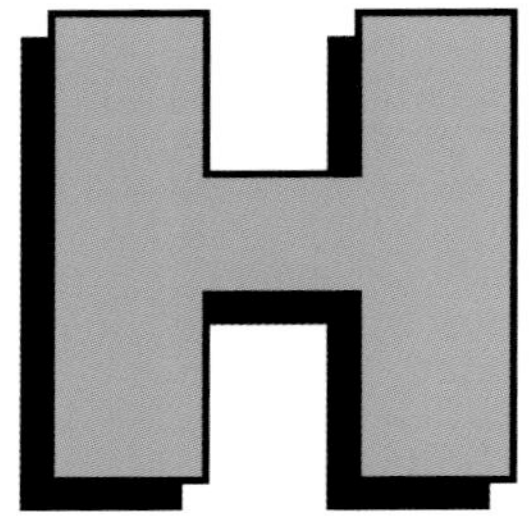

omer (eighth century BCE), probably the earliest and certainly the most celebrated of the preserved Ancient Greek poets, is the author of two of the greatest long poems in world literature, stirring epic stories of heroic, tragic and futile war (the *Iliad*) and return, survival and revenge (the *Odyssey*). Translation and adaptation of the classic texts of Greek and Latin literature helped to establish the literary traditions in the modern European languages, and has been a constant inspiration for writers across the ages.[73]

A preserved text is of course a precondition for translation. Though our main source for his text lies in later medieval parchment manuscripts from Greece, we have more papyri of Homer recovered from the saving sands of Egypt than of any other Ancient Greek author (more than 1,500 fragments of the *Iliad* alone); this is a strong indication of the poet's popularity in the Greek-speaking part of the Roman Empire before the Arab conquests of the seventh century CE. One of the most important of these is the Hawara papyrus, preserving part of the first book of the *Iliad*, a beautiful calligraphic copy surely written for an important client in the second century CE (**figure 25**).[74]

Homer in antiquity and early printings

No full translation of Homer into Latin survives from the Roman Empire, perhaps because the education of the Roman elite classes usually involved learning Greek to a high level; but one Latin abbreviation was done in a single book, the *Ilias Latina* of Baebius Italicus in the second century CE. This text later became vital for the transmission of the outline plot of the *Iliad* in the long centuries where very few could read Greek in Western Europe, from the fall of the Western Roman Empire in the fifth century CE to the rise of humanism in the fifteenth century CE. Equally important were the Late Latin versions of the originally Greek prose works on the fall of Troy presented under the names of Dictys of Crete (fourth century CE) and Dares of Phrygia (fifth to sixth century CE). They were supposed eyewitnesses to the Trojan War on either side, and they were themselves translated and adapted (with romance-style treatment) into many vernaculars in the medieval period. An example is the enormous twelfth-century *Le Roman de Troie* by Benoît de Sainte-Maure, a poem nearly three times as long as the *Iliad* and a source (via Boccaccio's *Il Filostrato*) for Chaucer's *Troilus and Criseyde* (1380s). Even the Greek-speaking Byzantine Empire, which lasted until the fall of Constantinople in 1453, found Homer's ancient poetic Greek difficult of access; the scholar Michael Psellos in the eleventh century CE wrote a prose paraphrase of the *Iliad* in contemporary Byzantine Greek, which shows both Homer's continuing classic status and the need for a modern reading aid.

For the translation of Homer, as for much else, the invention of printing in the mid-fifteenth century was a major watershed. The first printed edition (*editio princeps*) of Homer's *Iliad* and *Odyssey* appeared in Florence in 1488/89, edited by the Greek scholar Demetrius Chalcondyles; this massive work was then used in the first octavo (pocket-sized) edition of Homer (1504), issued by the great and enterprising Venetian printer Aldus Manutius (1449–1515). He brought many Greek classics to print for the first time, popularized portable editions and introduced the italic font.[75] Within a generation, Andrea Divo di Capodistria produced a close Latin translation of both poems (Venice, 1537) which followed the pagination of the Aldine edition, in effect creating the first parallel translation once placed next to its Greek original. This was an important step forward in the early modern understanding of Homer, and of Ancient Greek.

Vernacular translations

Translations into a range of European vernaculars followed. The first complete translation of the *Odyssey* into a vernacular language was the German version by Simon Schaidenreisser published in 1537, while Gonzalo Pérez's complete Spanish version was published in Antwerp in 1556. The first complete version of the *Iliad* in French verse, by Hugues Salel (who had published part of it earlier in 1545) and Amadis Jamyn was published in 1580, while Lodovico Dolce's looser Italian version of the *Iliad* was published posthumously in 1570 (along with his version of Virgil's *Aeneid*).

In English, it was George Chapman (1559–1633), contemporary and poetic rival of Shakespeare, who produced the first complete translation

465 ΝΤΟΣΚΑ

470

490

490

 495

 500

 505

Far-left column:
...ΕΙ
...Ρ
...ΩϹΙ
...ΟΜΙ...
...ΑΡΕΙϹ
...ΗΥΤΕΒ...
ΤΑΥΡΟϹΙ...
...ΙΟΝΑΙ
...ΙΠΡΕΤ...
...ΠΕΤΕΠ...
...ΑΕΙϹΤΑ...
...ΜΕΙΕΔ...

Middle-left column:
...ΑΙΟΙ
...ΤΕϹ
...ΡΙΑΝΔΡ...
...ΕΩϹΙΝ
...ΚΑΙΕΝΘΑ
...ΛΛΕΙΠΩ
...ΙΚΕΡΑΥΝ...
...Ι
...ΟΠΑΝΤΩΝ
...ΑΡΟΜΕΝΗΙϹΙ...
...ΑΓΙΚΕΙΝΩΙ
...ΗΛΦΕϹϹΙΝ
...ΛΛ...ΜΑΤΕΧΟΥϹΑΙ
...ΓΕΤΕΠΑΝΤΑ
...ΥΛΕΤΗΔΛΜΕΝ

Right column:
ΕΝΠ...
ΤΕΤΙΠΟ...
ΝΕΜΟΝ...
ΕϹΚΩΛΟ...
ΤΡΑΙΑΝΤΕ...
ΜΕΝΕΜΟΝΤ...
ΝΕΙΧΟΝΗΔΥ...
ΝΜΕΔΕΩΝ
ΕΥΤΡΗϹΙΝΤΕ...ΟΝ
ΚΟΡΩΝΕΙΑΝΚΑ...
ΠΛΑΤΑΙΑΝΕΧΟΝΗ...
ΠΟΘΗΒΑϹΕΙΧΟΝΕ...Ο
ΗϹΤΟΝΘΙΕΡΟΝΠΟ...ΟΝ
ΠΟΛΥϹΤΑΦΥΛΟΝ
ΑΝΤΕΖΑΘΕΗΝΑΝΘ...ΙΑΝ

ΤΟΠΟΡΘ

ΑΙΝΕΕϹ
ΚΑΙΕΠΙϹ
ΑΥΒΟΛΙΔΑ
ΘΩΝΑΤΕΙ
ΛΙΔΑΚΑΙΠΑ
ΩΠΟΛΙΝΑΜΦ
ΗΦΙϹΟΝΔΙΟΝΕΝ
ΓΗΝϹΕΠΙΚΗΦΙϹ
ΑΜΕΛΑΙΝΑΙΝ
ΙΧΑϹΙϹΤΑϹΑΝΑ
ΝΕΠΑΡΙϹΤΕΡΑΘ
ΕΥΕΝΟΙΑΜΟϹΤΑΧΥϹ
ΟϹΟϹΤΕΛΑΑΙΩΝΙΟ
ΛΙΓΟϹΜΕΝΕΗΝΑ
ΠΑΝΕΛΛΗΝΑϹΚ

ΙΝΘΟΙ
ΕΚΑΡΥϹΤ
ΟΝΑΥΘΗΓΕ
ΛΚΩΔΟΝ
ΩΙΔΑΜΑΒΑ
ΑΙΧΜΗΤΑΙΜΕ
ΘΩΡΗΚΑϹΡΗΞΕ
ΤΩΙΔΑΜΑΤΕϹϹΑ
ΟΙΔΑΡΑΘΗΝΑϹ
ΔΗΜΟΝΕΡΕΧΘ
ΘΡΕΨΕΔΙΟ
ΕΝΘΑΔΕΜΙΝ
ΚΟΥΡΟΙΑΘΗΝ
ΤΩΝΑΥΘΗΓΕ
ΤΩΙΧΘΥΠΩ

ΛΑ
ΗΟϹ
ϹΑ
ΕΝΚ
ΜΕΛ
ΕϹϹΙ
ΝΗϹΕΠΙ
ΙΠΟΛΙ
ΟΝΤΟΤΑ
ΩΡΟϹΑΡΟΥ
ΙΛΛΟΝΤ
ΕΝΩΝΕΝ
ΟΜΕΝΕϹ
ΝΙΟϹΓΕΝ

of all of Homer (1616) (**figure 26**). This was made famous two centuries later by the Greekless John Keats's celebratory sonnet 'On First Looking into Chapman's Homer' (1816). Chapman taught himself Greek, referring as he worked to Spondanus's parallel Latin translation (1583) and to Scapula's Greek–Latin lexicon (1580), but he did not provide mere literal English versions of his originals; Odysseus, for example, became a humanist hero who seeks salvation, regeneration and enlightenment. Here as often translation is a mode of reception and interpretation, moulding Homer's text to contemporary sensibilities as well as rendering it linguistically. This is the opening of his *Odyssey*:

> The man, O Muse, inform, that many a way
> Wound with his wisdom to his wished stay;
> That wandered wondrous far, when he the town
> Of sacred Troy had sack'd and shivered down;
> The cities of a world of nations,
> With all their manners, minds, and fashions,
> He saw and knew; at sea felt many woes,
> Much care sustained, to save from overthrows
> Himself and friends in their retreat for home;
> But so their fates he could not overcome,
> Though much he thirsted it.[76]

A century later, Alexander Pope (1688–1744) put both Homer and himself on the map with translations of the *Iliad* (1715–20) and *Odyssey* (1726, in collaboration with others) into heroic rhyming couplets (like Chapman). These translations made him a rich man: his earnings from his versions of Homer have been estimated at £200,000 in 1976 values (some £1.5 million today).[77] Pope's translation was of seminal importance for poetry in English: Samuel Johnson wrote that it 'may be said to have tuned the English tongue, for since its appearance no writer, however deficient in other powers, has wanted melody'.[78] The edition shown from 1771 presents Homer and Pope facing each other as a double frontispiece, giving equal billing to the translator and poet and showing how important Pope's translation had become after half a century (**figure 27**).[79] Pope worked from the Greek, and also from a range of other translations. They included a translation into French prose by Mme Anne Dacier (*Iliad*, 1699; *Odyssey*, 1708), perhaps the most significant Homeric version by a woman until the twenty-first century (see further below).[80] I cite the opening of Pope's *Iliad*:

25 *previous spread* Hawara Homer (second century CE, found in 1888 in the Fayum area of Egypt): columns from this beautiful Ancient Greek papyrus book with lines from Homer, *Iliad* 1. Bodleian Library, MS. Gr. class. a. 1 (P), plate 9r.

Achilles' wrath, to Greece the direful spring
Of woes unnumber'd, heavenly goddess, sing!
That wrath which hurl'd to Pluto's gloomy reign
The souls of mighty chiefs untimely slain;
Whose limbs unburied on the naked shore,
Devouring dogs and hungry vultures tore.
Since great Achilles and Atrides strove,
Such was the sovereign doom, and such the will of Jove![81]

Translations after Pope

The lasting authority of Pope's version deterred potential successors as poetic translators of Homer. The 1791 *Iliad* and *Odyssey* of William Cowper, best remembered as the poet of Anglican hymns such as 'Oh! for a Closer Walk with God' and 'God Moves in a Mysterious Way', imitate John Milton in Latinate style, unusual word order and laborious blank verse, showing that Cowper deemed *Paradise Lost* the central model for English epic – see, for example, the opening of his *Iliad*:

Achilles sing, O Goddess! Peleus' son;
His wrath pernicious, who ten thousand woes
Caused to Achaia's host, sent many a soul
Illustrious into Ades premature,
And Heroes gave (so stood the will of Jove)
To dogs and to all ravening fowls a prey,
When fierce dispute had separated once
The noble Chief Achilles from the son
Of Atreus, Agamemnon, King of men.[82]

In the nineteenth century the greatest English poets discussed rather than practised Homeric translation. Significant here was the debate about the best metre for Homer in English conducted by Matthew Arnold in his Oxford poetry lectures of 1860, published as *On Translating Homer* (1861–62). Arnold suggested some form of English hexameter as an appropriate medium to render Homer's key characteristics of rapidity, plainness, and nobility; Johann Heinrich Voss had had some success with German accentual hexameter versions of Homer in the eighteenth century (*Odyssey*, 1781; *Iliad*, 1793). This metrical recommendation was soon rejected by Arnold's poetic rival Alfred Tennyson, who incredulously expostulated, 'These lame hexameters the strong-winged music of Homer!' (1863,

GEORGIVS CHAPMANVS HOMERI METAPHRASTES. ÆTA: LVII. M.DC.XVI.
CONSCIVM EVASI DIEM
Optimus hic sese, qui nouit cuncta Magistro,
Prospiciens rerum fines Meliora sequutus
De Homero Rediuiuo. Hes:
Seuen Kingdoms stroue, which Theirs should Homer call,
And now one Chapman, ownes him, from them all. Scotiæ Nobilis
Eruditorum Poetarum huius Æui, facile Principi Dno Georgio Chapman;
Homero (velit nolit Inuidia) Rediuiuo. I. M. Tessellam hanc
Χαριστήριον. D. D.
Ille simul Musas, et Homerum scripserit ipsum,
Qui scribit Nomen, Magne Poeta, tuum.

ICH DIEN
ILIAS
MUSAR: HERCUL: COLUM:
ODYSSÆA
NE VSQUE.
To the Imortall Memorie, of the Incomparable
Heroe, HENRYE Prince of Wales.
And so tis kept: Not thy thrice sacred will
Sign'd with thy Deathe; moues any to fullfill
Thy Just bequests to me: Thow, dead, then;
Liue deade, for giuing thee Eternitie:.
Ad Famam
To all Tymes future: This Tymes Marck extend:
Homer, No Patrone founde: Nor Chapman, freind:
Ignotus nimis omnibus;
Sat notus, moritur sibi:.

26 George Chapman, *The Whole Works of Homer* (1616) – the first complete English translation, by a contemporary and literary rival of Shakespeare. Bodleian Library, Mal. 9, frontispiece and title page.

27 Alexander Pope's translation of the *Iliad*, with Pope facing Homer (London, 1771). First published in 1715–20, this was a bestseller then and is still in print. By permission of the President and Fellows of Corpus Christi College, Oxford, *The Iliad of Homer* LD.13.d.1.5, pp. iii–iv.

‘On Translations of Homer. Hexameters and Pentameters’). He himself produced some effective brief samples in blank verse around this time,[83] but did no more; his much earlier blank-verse poem ‘Ulysses’ (1833), combining Homer’s returned Odysseus with the restless Ulisse of Dante (*Inferno*, Canto 26), is perhaps his most Homeric in style. Arnold himself had likewise already produced his most Homeric work in his blank-verse ‘Sohrab and Rustum’ (1853), a tragic war poem adapting material from the Persian medieval *Shanameh* with many Iliadic touches.[84] The most successful translations after this debate about verse form were (perhaps understandably) in prose, especially the so-called ‘biblical’ versions of the *Odyssey* by Butcher and Lang (1879) and the *Iliad* by Lang, Leaf and Myers (1883). They appropriated the style and cultural authority of the 1611 King James Bible, both picking up the archaic tinge of Homer which would have been perceived by Greeks of later periods and suggesting that Homer was in some sense the sacred book of the Greeks.

The modern era: adaptations and intermedial translation

The modern era saw a more flexible approach to Homeric versions: the most famous of these from the twentieth century is James Joyce’s 1922 novel *Ulysses*, where the journey of the anti-hero Leopold Bloom across Dublin on 16 June 1904 is carefully mapped onto particular episodes of the *Odyssey* in one of the masterpieces of modernist fiction. The artist Henri Matisse had no problem in seeing Joyce’s work as the *Odyssey*: the illustrations he executed for a 1935 New York limited edition of Joyce’s novel (it would not appear in the UK until 1936 owing to its supposedly obscene character) plainly show that he thought he was illustrating Homer’s original (see his depiction of Odysseus’ erotic dalliance with the nymph Calypso, **figure 28**).[85]

Translation can thus take place between media as well as between languages. This had been happening since the Greek world, where Homeric scenes often appear in art, especially on ceramics;[86] one example is the Athenian black-figure lekythos (olive oil jar) of the second half of the sixth century BCE on which Odysseus is depicted escaping the blinded Polyphemus by tying himself under the belly of a giant ram (**figure 29**).[87] This tendency to translation between media has continued in the modern world, especially in cinema. In many ways this is the contemporary form of epic: the film of *Troy* (2004), directed by Wolfgang Petersen and starring Brad Pitt as Achilles and Eric Bana as Hector, is a costume version of the *Iliad* with the addition of the sack of Troy (anticipated but not narrated in Homer's poem) and with some interesting changes such as the deaths at Troy of both Agamemnon and Menelaus.[88] The Coen brothers' *O Brother, Where Art Thou?* (2000) stars George Clooney as the escaped convict Ulysses Everett McGill and transposes a plot loosely based on the *Odyssey* to the American South of the 1930s; the Cyclops episode, for example, becomes a blackly comic picnic lunch with the villainous one-eyed Bible salesman Big Dan Teague, played by John Goodman.[89]

New technologies and translation: paperback, film, radio

Just as the coming of printing in the mid-fifteenth century had been a key moment in the editing and translation of the classics (see above), so too was the emergence of the durable paperback in the mid-twentieth century and the possibilities it opened up for mass-circulation cheaper classical translations.[90] The latter-day Aldo Manuzio for the UK was Allen Lane,[91] who in 1935 founded Penguin Books, the first high-quality and moderate-price paperback publisher, and in 1945 launched the Penguin Classics under the editorship of the classicist E.V. Rieu. The first volume to be published was Rieu's own version of the *Odyssey* (1946), which sold more than 2 million copies in its first twenty years; until Penguin's publication of D.H. Lawrence's *Lady Chatterley's Lover* in 1960 it was the best-selling paperback of any kind in the UK.[92] Rieu aimed 'to make Homer easy reading for those who are unfamiliar with the Greek world'.[93] Homer's epic poem is rendered as a lively narrative in modern prose, with the books headed not 'Book I' but 'I' with a summarizing heading, looking like the chapters of a novel, the most popular form of paperback literature of the time. The easy reading is clear from the opening of the *Odyssey*:

> The hero of the tale which I beg the Muse to help me tell is that resourceful man who roamed the whole world after he had sacked the holy citadel of Troy. He saw the cities of many people and he learnt their ways. He suffered great anguish on the high seas in his struggles to preserve his life and bring his comrades home. But he failed to save those comrades, in spite of all his efforts.[94]

28 Henri Matisse's illustration of Odysseus with Calypso, from a 1935 New York edition of James Joyce's *Ulysses*; the artist chose to illustrate an episode from the Homeric original rather than Joyce's transformation of the plot. Bodleian Library, Limited Editions Club 71, p. 140. © Succession H. Matisse/ DACS 2019.

(Calypso) Henri Matisse
Calypso – Lithog. étude III
Henri Matisse

uarantor. Rein-
, that we go on
h, that we lived
n. That we all
ds of years ago
have forgotten
past lives.
urdling spirals
er of the word:
d be better. An
the bed. Given
of *Photo Bits:*
urs. Tea before
with her hair
I gave for the
e over the bed.
instance all the
what the ancient
eve you could be
e, for instance.
nple.
the sugar. She
ng through her
said. Did you
y.
his inner pocket
ne broken com-
smell, stepping
ied stork's legs.
jet from a side
f the fork under
ned it turtle on
tossed it off the
ty brown gravy
ut and buttered
the burnt flesh
t a forkful into
nent the tooth-
A mouthful of
l, sopped one in
What was that
a picnic? He
eading it slowly
of bread in the

Another rising post-war technology which gave opportunity for the production and diffusion of classical translations was radio. The Anglo-Irish poet Louis MacNeice produced many classical radio plays for the BBC in the 1940s and 1950s, which involved a considerable amount of adaptation and some translation of classical texts.[95] In 1952 he was commissioned to produce a verse translation of the whole of the *Iliad* for BBC radio, but in the end only a few sample drafts were forthcoming.

Recent versions: Logue, Walcott, Oswald

In 1959 the poet Christopher Logue was similarly commissioned by the then BBC producer and later classics professor Donald Carne-Ross to produce a verse version of Book 21 of the *Iliad* for BBC radio.[96] This was the beginning of what became *War Music*, Logue's loose translation of the *Iliad* written over half a century. In its final version[97] it covered Books 1–2 (*Kings*), 3–4 (*The Husbands*), 5–6 (*All Day Permanent Red*), 7–9 (*Cold Calls*) and 16–19 (*War Music*); there are some fragmentary versions of parts of Books 10–24 (*Big Men Falling a Long Way*, including the original Book 21 translation). Logue, who like Keats could not read Greek, worked from published translations, including those of Pope and Rieu (above) as well as (initially) a literal version by Carne-Ross. Logue's versions vary between fairly close poetic paraphrase to widely allusive poems with an increasingly loose relationship to the original narrative, with a free, forceful, vividly colloquial and quasi-cinematic approach and typography related to Pop Art; his Homer lays bare the ignoble human urges and motives behind the war and its fundamental brutality, clear to him as a pacifist and anti-nuclear campaigner. His extraordinary handwritten drafts for the project are set out on continuous rolls of computing paper; the final posthumous edition of the collected *War Music* (2015) depicts an Apache attack helicopter, a key tool of modern military airpower, which makes clear the relevance of Homer's war poem to today's world (**figure 30**).

In 1992 Derek Walcott was awarded the Nobel Prize in Literature, primarily for his long poem *Omeros* (1990) (**figure 31**).[98] Like Joyce's *Ulysses*, and as its title suggests, *Omeros* contains characters and episodes loosely adapted from Homer set in the writer's own place and time, the 1980s on the island of St Lucia, transposing the heroic narrative of colonizing Europe to the contemporary colonized Caribbean (though with some anachronies

29 Odysseus escapes from the blinded cyclops Polyphemus, tied under a huge ram from the monster's flock; this typically cunning exploit is often illustrated in Greek art. Athenian black-figure lekythos (oil jar), 550–500 BCE. © Ashmolean Museum, University of Oxford, AN1943.249.

MASS: (SCAM, D) … horses drinking… men drinking beside them…

(i) (POSSIBLE CUTAWAYS IN THE SEQ? – NOT REALLY) (SEE FROM T. ROV AT…?) E: RETREAT CRUMBLES AT RIVER.

SCAMANDER'S FORD:

SOME GS (LED BY, PURSUED BY? – FAM|PLACE DETAILS? AEN? – ARE MAJOR ACTS?) TRY TO HOLD THE SCAM'S LOW (TROY) SIDE (WILLOWS. BULRUSHES, SEE A. FIGHTS RIV. SELECTED p. 134)

SEAWARD

THEY ARE DRIVEN BACK ACROSS THE GOLDEN SAND INTO THE SCAM. THEN UP THE STEEP W. BANK, WHERE THEY HAD HOPED ('A. WILL HELP US NOW' MOTIF?) FOR

(i) MASS … about 300 men went… T'S COMING UPON THEM: (SCAM?) … (ENEMY) proved to be much nearer than expected

'… ran down the (T-side slope of the Scam)
… slithered up the.. (sea-side slope)

(CRANE) SCAM TURNS WINE COLOURED STREAKED AT FIRST THEN ONLY STREAKED WITH CLEAR THEN

(ii + iii) H. to loose first close friend at middle - end of 8. CAG. TO KILL. MIX There after he will loose more and more friends. This increases his madness

LUTIE? WITH p. 62.

(i) ~~[struck]~~ LAYKON – IN 21/3 BK 3/333. TO BE INTRODUCED IN THIS SECTION: ~~His~~ BROTHER – YOUR L'S MOTHER (21/84) (FORD OF SCAM. SCENE OF HIS CONCEPT BINDING MORE OF, ✓

AT WHICH POINT DOES SCAM DEEPEN HIMSELF? p. 57

① H. PRESSING ATTACK. (+ AENEAS)

TROY

THROUGH THE DARKNESS – HOW DEEP IS IT? HOW LONG: E. Ap. TO REMOVE.

CHY. PRESSING (AFTER LONG CHARIOT CHARGE OF 'C' AND 'D')

① SOME GKS (LED BY (AND?) OD.) TRY TO HOLD THE LOW SE. BANK | WHILE REST CROSS.

SCAM.

MAIN GR. FORCE ① CROSSING HERE + BOMB. + ? OD. COVERING THEIR BACKS.

FORDS

DIO AND CHARIOTS. ①

TAKE UPPER FORD TO ATTACK H'S LEFT – CHY'S CHARIOTS.

HIGH BANKS

FLAT → DITCH → PALISADE → SHIPS

HOPE FOR HELP FROM CAMP HIGH BANKED ON CAMP SIDE

5-15 'D' USE 'OWEN' OFFICER IN A-CHRON O INCIDENT 'BIOS'

FLOWER MEADOWS BY SCAM. WILLOWS | RUSHES | SAND BANKS | DUCKS |

MASS: The sand was deep. The water was warm. SCAM.

path ascents

(i E) COMPARE WITH iii A BEFORE WRITING

NO OMENS (LIST IN MONDRIAN, p. 19) UNTIL FIGHTING AT (D–E). BOTH SIDES INTERPRET FAVOURABLY. WHICH LEAD – WHEN GKS CONTINUE TO LOOSE – PROVOKES AB'S LAST ANTI-GOD OUTBURST.

(i) END.
H. (IN 'E'?) (BEFORE TEERING AT D(o)) LOOSES HIS DRIVER. ESTABLISH DRV
ESTAB. EARLY: 'PROGRESSIVE' IS IN OPENING SEQ: 'LUTIE'

97

5-15 (i) X-REF. AT (13|iii-) THE GATE IS ATTACKED BY AXE MEN. FEATURE THE AXE MEN (WHOSE? FROM WHERE? THEIR APPEARANCE, CRIE?) IN (i) - AT THE SCAM?

DETAILED GK|T. SEQ'S REQUIRED HERE. X-REFS 80%.

(WHO?) TAKES THE FOOTFIGHTERS ACROSS (WHO AT REAR?)
(WHO?) " " CHARIOTS|CAVALRY " SLIGHTLY UPSTREAM TO A SMALLER FORD.
SCAM. THEN DEEPENS
HIMSELF SO THE GKS
CANNOT GET ACROSS. DID CHARGES (CHY? IT HAS TO BE CHY - ON LEFT OF T. ADVANCE.) ONCE, TWICE, THRICE - ALWAYS BEATEN BACK. (ONE OF H'S SUDDEN APPEARENCES?) WHEEL LEFT TO JOIN BACK TO THE FOOTFIGHTERS...

(YES: SHOULD HAVE BEEN ESTABLISHED)

SCAM. HEARS THE CALL. INCREASES HIS FLOW (SIM?) AND SWEEPS (DID - IF IT IS HE - ONTO THE FOOTMEN) THEM TOWARDS FOOTFIGHTERS.

30 *previous spread* Christopher Logue, handwritten drafts from *War Music* ('Row in Heaven', adapting parts of *Iliad* Book 21). Working papers for this remarkable modern version of Homer's war poem. © The Estate of Christopher Logue.

31 Front cover of Derek Walcott's *Omeros* (Farrar, Straus & Giroux, New York, 1990) with an illustration by the author. A magnificent novel-length poem which draws extensively on the *Odyssey*; it brought its author the Nobel Prize in Literature for 1992. Jacket design by Cynthia Krupat, copyright © 1990. Reprinted by permission of Farrar, Straus & Giroux. Cover illustration by Derek Walcott, Courtesy of The Estate of Derek Walcott.

and shifts of time). The poor fishermen Achille and Hector compete for the love of the housemaid Helen in a version of the *Iliad*'s plot, and there are clearly further Homeric elements, such as the local athletics competition (as in *Iliad* Book 23 and *Odyssey* Book 8) or the cyclone seen as the Odyssean Cyclops. But it is a rich amalgam of many strands, in which the poet both conjures up the sensuous beauty and post-colonial difficulties and squalor of his homeland and uses Homer and classical literature to reflect on his own poetic activity and status as a poet torn between the worlds of European and Caribbean culture. The work is divided into seven books containing a total of sixty-four chapters, a compromise perhaps between the books of an epic poem and the chapters of a novel (which it matches in length), while its three-line stanzas look to the terza rima metre of another great epic poem, Dante's *Divina Commedia*.

In 2011 the English poet and Oxford Classics graduate Alice Oswald published *Memorial*, an extraordinary part-translation of the *Iliad* which follows more or less the sequence of the poem but cuts out all the narrative apart from the obituaries of its victims and its similes (**figure 32**).[99] The similes themselves are all translated twice in a row, which makes for a strikingly incantatory effect, especially in the author's remarkable live performance;[100] the obituaries are more loosely paraphrased. The main part is prefaced by a bare list in capital letters of the names of all those killed in the narrative of the poem (211 names), one per line over seven pages, which clearly relates to the title: *Memorial* begins with the visual form of a war memorial. This Homeric version thus picks out the very elements in the poem which are often deemed to be diversions from the main narrative, the obituaries and similes; some of the latter are arrestingly updated, with Hector at one point compared to 'a man rushing in leaving his motorbike running'. The effect is very striking: the poem becomes much more reflection about nature and loss, and much less a battle narrative or a representation of warrior prowess: Achilles, Homer's chief hero, is barely mentioned, as he is not among those killed in the poem, and the victims especially important for the shape of the Homeric plot (Sarpedon, Patroclus) are treated with little more emphasis than the others.

This recent poetic version is likely to be a lasting work, combining a lyric sensitivity for nature in the similes with a tragic view of conflict in the obituaries in a way which resonates with the wars of our times. And even now, more conventional Homeric translation continues to break new boundaries: in 2017 the British, US-based classical scholar and translator Emily Wilson became the first woman to publish a verse version of the *Odyssey,* a full rendering in traditional iambic pentameters but a contemporary and accessible style.[101] I cite her opening:

> Tell me about a complicated man.
> Muse, tell me how he wandered and was lost
> when he had wrecked the holy town of Troy,
> and where he went, and who he met, the pain
> he suffered in the storms at sea, and how
> he worked to save his life and bring his men
> back home.[102]

Wilson's version is palpably modern too in its ideological approach, bringing out the poem's issues of power, class and gender by, for example, emphasizing the slave status of the domestic staff in Penelope's palace and showing some sympathy for the disabled Cyclops.[103]

We have seen how European writers from the Renaissance through to today have simultaneously translated from the Homeric epics and emulated them in adaptations and original works. The epics of Homer, perhaps because they have been consistently seen as the earliest foundations of Western literature, have been the beneficiary of a particularly rich set of receptions in the European vernacular languages, in a tradition which shows no sign of exhaustion in the twenty-first century.

32 A scene from the world premiere of Chris Drummond and Yaron Lifschitz's stage version of Alice Oswald's 2011 *Memorial: An Excavation of the Iliad*, Brink Productions, Adelaide, March 2018. Oswald's poem presents an extraordinary version of the *Iliad* which strips the Homeric epic down to the obituaries of war's victims and its similes from the peacetime world. Brink Productions, photo © Shane Reid.

5 Translating Tales: Beast Fables around the World

Stephen Harrison

ne type of literature which has been very widely diffused via translation and adaptation is that of the beast fable, a form found in most Indo-European cultures. Such tales usually consist of animals speaking and/or behaving like humans, and they are commonly used for moralizing or didactic purposes. Recent examples have been prominent in children's literature: for example, the tales of Beatrix Potter from the early twentieth century (see below) or even *The Very Hungry Caterpillar* by Eric Carle (1969). Two especially influential and frequently translated beast-fable traditions, which to some degree merge in early modern Europe, are the tradition of the Sanskrit *Panchatantra* and the tradition of the Greek stories attached to the name of Aesop.[104]

Panchatantra: the Sanskrit tradition

Some 200 versions of some kind of this work exist in fifty languages, making it one of the most frequently translated or adapted texts in history. The oldest (lost) version was written in Sanskrit in the Indian subcontinent *c.*300 CE;[105] its title *Panchatantra* means 'five discourses'. In the standard reconstruction[106] the five books of the original are set in a frame narrative in which a king enlists the help of a wise Brahmin to educate his three dull sons in the arts of government; the Brahmin undertakes to do this in six months and composes the five books for the purpose. The five books are entitled 'On Causing Dissension Among Allies', 'On Securing Allies', 'The Story of the Crows and the Owls', 'On Losing What You Have Gained' and 'On Hasty Actions'; in each of them practical lessons are delivered to the recalcitrant princes through animal stories. For example, the first two tales in Book 1, told by jackal ministers to a lion king (one of a number of embedded structural frameworks in the collection), are entitled 'The Monkey That Pulled the Wedge', in which a monkey comes to grief through playing with something that does not belong to him, and 'The Jackal That

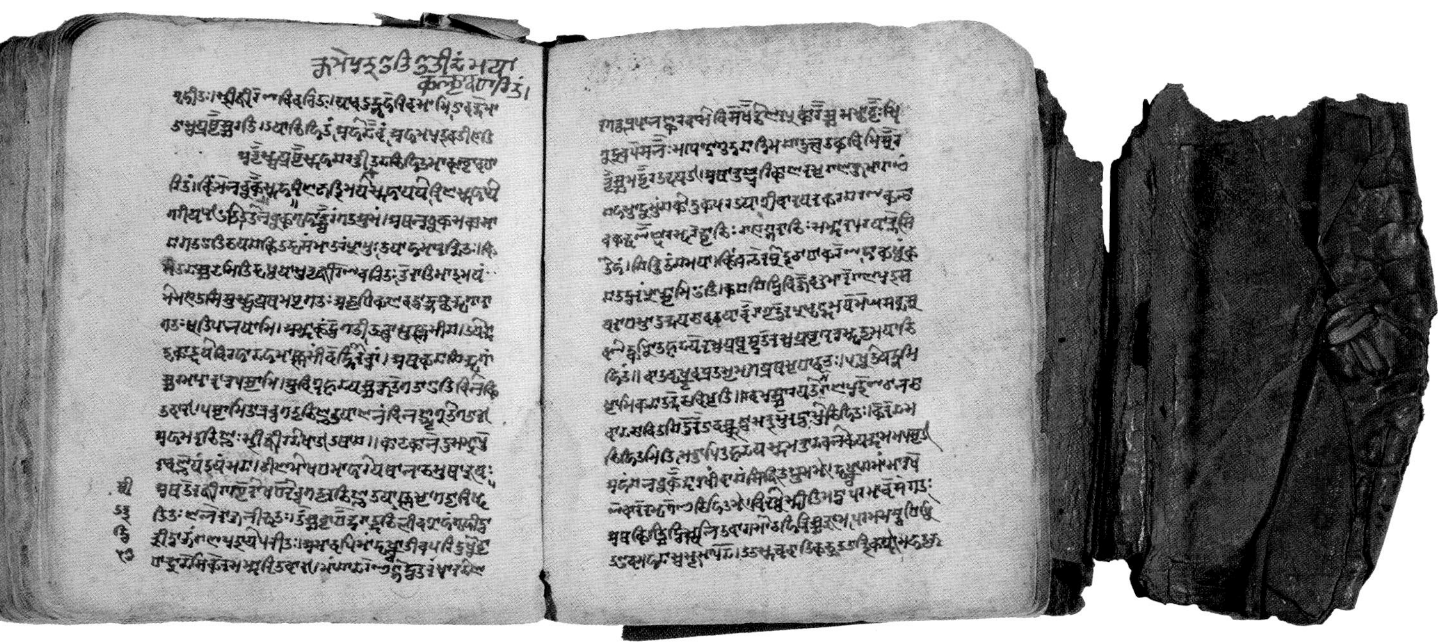

Tried to Eat a Drum', in which a jackal conquers his fear of a drum's noise. They are generally narrated in prose, but are embedded in extensive dialogues between the jackal ministers, who draw out the moral lessons of the stories and cite further proverbs and pieces of wisdom, usually in verse.

The stories themselves are relatively brief and often not without humour. Here is a typical extract from 'The Monkey That Pulled the Wedge':

> In a certain country there was a city near which a merchant had started to build a temple. One day the architect and the other workers employed in this project went into the town around midday for lunch. It so happened that a carpenter had split a log of Arjuna wood half-way and driven a wedge of acacia wood into it with a machine. When they left for lunch, he left that half-split log there held apart by the wedge. In the meantime a large herd of wild monkeys, who were frolicking at will here and there on tree tops, temple towers and wood piles, happened to come to that spot. One of those monkeys, whose end was near and who was frivolous by nature, sat on that log with his testicles hanging down in the slit. 'Who in the world drove that wedge in here? It is in the wrong place,' the monkey thought. So he took hold of the wedge with both his hands and began to yank it out. I don't have to tell you what happened when the wedge popped out![107]

33 Tantrākhyāyikā: seventeenth-century manuscript of the Sanskrit text in its original binding, the medieval Kashmiri recension of the much older Sanskrit animal tales of the *Panchatantra*. This was the seventeenth-century Kashmiri Sanskrit scholar Rajanaka Ratnakantha's personal copy. Bodleian Library, MS. Stein Or., f. 2.

Animal fables of various kinds used for similar didactic purposes are to be found in earlier Sanskrit literature such as the *Rig Veda*, the hymn collection partly going back to the second millennium BCE, and the philosophical *Upanishads* and the great epic *Mahābhārata* from the first millennium BCE (the last includes in Book 8 the fable of the crow who rashly seeks to match swans in flight).[108] As well as these Hindu sources, there are also traces of stories from the *Jātaka* tales of the previous incarnations of the Buddha in animal forms, which may go back to the fourth century BCE. One of these *Jātaka* tales is similar to one in Aesop (Perry *Aesopica* 188), the story of the ass who is disguised by his master in a lion's skin but gives himself away when he brays; in the *Panchatantra* (Book 3, Story 1) we find a leopard rather than a lion, but essentially the same story. It has been plausibly suggested that these similarities between fables may ultimately be owed to a common Mesopotamian origin.[109]

For the last century, most scholars have held that the medieval Kashmiri recension of the *Panchatantra* known as the *Tantrākhyāyika* is the extant text closest to the original version.[110] The copy of this work once owned by the seventeenth-century Kashmiri Sanskrit scholar Rajanaka Ratnakantha, on multicoloured paper, was used by Johannes Hertel for his first printed edition of the book (**figure 33**).[111]

Panchatantra: translations and adaptations from Persia to La Fontaine[112]

The Sanskrit *Panchatantra* went through a remarkable chain of translations in the millennium between its emergence and the invention of printing in the fifteenth century, covering multiple languages and multiple religious cultures, from Hinduism via Persian Zoroastrianism to Islam and Judaism. A Pahlavi (Middle Iranian) version is now lost; it was produced by the doctor Burzoë for the Parthian Sassanian Emperor Chosroes I (Khosrow I), who reigned 531–579 CE and was an opponent of the Roman emperor Justinian. It was itself soon rendered into Old Syriac by the priest Bud *c.*570 CE, but the key translation was that from the Pahlavi version into Arabic. This was done in the mid-eighth century CE by Ibn al-Muqaffa', an Islamic convert born in Persia. He worked in the Iranian civil service under both Umayyad and Abbasid rulers but was forced to suicide under the Caliph al-Mansur in 756 or 759. This extant version had the title *Kalila wa-Dimna*, using the Arabic

versions of the names of the two jackal counsellors of the frame narrative of Book 1 (see above). It is widely considered the first masterpiece of Arabic prose and still read in schools and universities as a literary classic.[113] The Bodleian holds a beautifully illustrated copy from 1354 (**figure 34**).[114]

The *Kalila wa-Dimna*, having become an Arabic classic, was widely translated in its turn as a 'mirror for princes' and collection of moral examples. It was popular with Jewish writers in the West: the doctor Simeon Seth of Antioch in modern Turkey did a rendering into Byzantine Greek for the Emperor Alexius I Comnenus at the end of the eleventh century CE, and

34 *Kalila wa-Dimna* – the influential Arabic version of the *Panchatantra*, a 1354 illustrated manuscript, depicting a version of 'How the Battling Rams Killed the Greedy Jackal' (*Panchatantra*, Book 1, Story 3). Bodleian Library, MS. Pococke 400, fols 45v–46r.

one Rabbi Joel produced a Hebrew version in the early thirteenth century CE. The cultured reign of Alfonso X the Wise of Castile saw several versions towards the end of the thirteenth century. In 1283 the distinguished Toledo intellectual Jacob ben Eleazar wrote a Hebrew version in rhymed verse, which is partly preserved, and around the same time Isaac ben Solomon Ibn Sahula wrote *Meshal ha-qadmoni* ('The Fable of the Ancient'), an original Hebrew work using the framework and structure of the *Kalila wa-Dimna*, aimed at replacing it. A closer version of the Arabic work in early Castilian Spanish, *El libro Di Calila e Dimna*, was also produced at this time. In the East, a Persian version *Anvar-e Sohayli*, notorious for its obscure and exaggerated style, was written in Herat in western Afghanistan in the fifteenth century at the court of its Timurid rulers.[115] In the late sixteenth century it was rewritten in soberer form in the same language as *'Iyar-e Danesh* for the great Mughal emperor Akbar.[116]

The lost Hebrew version of Rabbi Joel, mentioned above, was influential as the source for the first Latin translation by the Jewish convert Giovanni di Capua (*c.*1270). This had the portentous title *Liber Kalilae et Dimniae: Directorium Vitae Humanae Alias Parabola Antiquorum Sapientium* (The Book of Kalila and Dimnia: The Steering of Human Life, Otherwise the Parables of the Wise Ancients) and was eventually printed in Strasbourg in 1489. It was translated into German and Spanish in the early days of print, as *Das Buch der Beispiele der alten Weisen* ('The Book of Examples from the Wise Men of Old') by Antonius von Pforr in Germany in 1480–82, and as *Exemplario contra los enganos y peligros del mundo* (Example Against the Deceits and Perils of the World) in Zaragoza in 1493. This last was the source for Anton Francesco Doni's Italian *Filosofia Morale* (1552), itself the source for Sir Thomas North's *The morall philosophie of Doni, popularly known as the Fables of Bidpai* (1568) (**figure 35**).[117] This became the key English translation, executed by the author of the version of Plutarch's *Lives* (1579) famously used by Shakespeare.[118]

In the French *Fables* of Jean de La Fontaine (1668–1694) we reach the point at which our first case study for the translation of beast fables, that of the Sanskrit *Panchatantra*, meets our second, that of Aesop's Greek tales. In the preface to the third volume of 1678 La Fontaine claims that many of the fables in the later books are drawn from 'Pilpay sage indien' (i.e. Bidpai, as in North's title, one of the many names given to the original wise Brahmin of the *Panchatantra*);[119] in fact, some twenty can be identified as derived from

of Morall Philosophie 82

deedes to goe about the destruction of any. For hee that diggeth a pit for others, many times falleth into it himselfe.

THe Sea Crabbe disposed to play with a foole, was contented to be ridden of him, but he like a Cockes combe (not knowing she went backwarde,) put a Bridle in hir mouth, and

it went to hir tayle, and spurring hir forwardes, the Crabbe went backwardes. I am a foole (quoth the foole) to thincke to doe well with thee, since I know not thy nature nor condicion.

Now listen what chaunced to an vngracious traueyler, and then consider well of the matter.

P.ij. Two

35 Illustration of the fable of a fool riding a 'sea crabbe' from Thomas North's version of *The morall philosophie of Doni*, H. Denham, London, 1570: an English collection of moral stories deriving through a complex linguistic chain from the Sanskrit *Panchatantra*. Bodleian Library, Douce S 195, p. 82.

the Sanskrit tradition. One source for La Fontaine's 'Pilpay' was the French version of the Persian *Anvar-e Sohayli* (see above) published in Paris in 1644 by Gilbert Gaulmin under the title *Le Livre des lumières ou la Conduite des Roys* ['The Book of Enlightenment or the Conduct of Kings'], *composée par le sage Pilpay Indien, traduite en français par David Sahid, d'Ispahan, ville capitale de Perse*. Another was the Latin version of the same Persian text by Father Pierre Poussines, *Specimen sapientiae Indorum veterum* ('A Sample of the Wisdom of the Ancient Indians'), published in Rome in 1666.[120] But the majority of the fables in the first six books of the *Fables* (published together in 1668) are derived from the Greek animal tales of Aesop, to whom we now turn.

Aesop: Greek beast fable and its early reception

Aesop may have been a real person who lived in the sixth century BCE and was associated with the Greek island of Samos.[121] He is referred to by Herodotus in the fifth century BCE as a 'maker of stories' (*logopoios*, *Histories* 2.134), while Aristophanes later in the same century refers explicitly several times to animal tales by Aesop: *Birds* refers to the fable of the lark and its crest while *Peace* and *Wasps* both allude to the fable of the dung beetle who climbed to the eagle's nest. Plato narrates that in Socrates' final imprisonment in 399 BCE he tried his hand at writing poetic versions of Aesop's (prose) fables.[122] But the fables transmitted under his name are unlikely to be genuine works of any historical Aesop; even in antiquity the name in effect covers the whole genre of animal tales with a moral. The Greek prose Aesopic fables we actually have are likely to have been written under the Roman Empire from the second or third century CE onwards, and are not found collected together before the tenth century CE; they generally take the form of a brief story involving speaking animals of less than a modern page, often with an added moral at the end.[123] For example, here is Perry *Aesopica* 346, 'The Wolf, the Dog and the Collar':

> A comfortably plump dog happened to run into a wolf. The wolf asked the dog where he had been finding enough food to get so big and fat. 'It is a man', said the dog, 'who gives me all the food to eat'. The wolf then asked him, 'And what about that bare spot there on your neck?' The dog replied, 'My skin has been rubbed bare by the iron collar which my master forged and placed upon my neck'. The wolf then jeered at the dog and said, 'Keep your luxury to yourself then! I don't want anything to do with it, if my neck will have to chafe against a chain of iron!'[124]

Aesopic tales, which may ultimately have roots in animal fables in both Egypt and Mesopotamia,[125] enjoyed a strong transmission in the Greek-speaking parts of the ancient world for a millennium or more; several Aesop-derived animal fables are found in demotic Egyptian tale collections from the time of the Roman Empire (second to fourth centuries CE).[126] As Michael

Psellos had done for Homer in the eleventh century (see Chapter 4), the thirteenth-century scholar Maximus Planudes provided a prose paraphrase of Aesop's fables in Byzantine Greek for the benefit of his contemporaries. Greek appreciation of Aesop was helped by the 143 Greek animal tales of Babrius, written in iambic verse before the end of the second century CE and acknowledging Aesopic inspiration in a prologue (15–16), and by the wide circulation of the colourful Greek narrative of a fictional *Life of Aesop* (usually known as the *Aesop Romance*) in a number of versions.[127]

In the Latin-speaking West, Aesop descended principally through the iambic Latin versions of ninety-five tales written by Phaedrus in the first half of the first century CE; in his prologue (1–2) Phaedrus claims that Aesop found the material before him and he has now polished it in iambic verse.[128] Likewise, the late Roman poet Avianus' versions of forty-two tales in Latin elegiacs, written *c.*400 CE and probably addressed to the scholar Macrobius, acknowledge Aesop as well as Phaedrus and Babrius in their preface. Both these texts were known largely through prose and verse paraphrases and imitations in the late antique and medieval period; for example, *Romulus Ordinarius* or *Romulus Vulgaris*, eighty-three tales from the ninth century CE in simple Latin prose much used in education.[129] Aesopic-style beast fables of various kinds were a popular form in medieval literature; for example, in an illuminated Old French fourteenth-century verse version in the Bodleian Library (**figure 36**).[130]

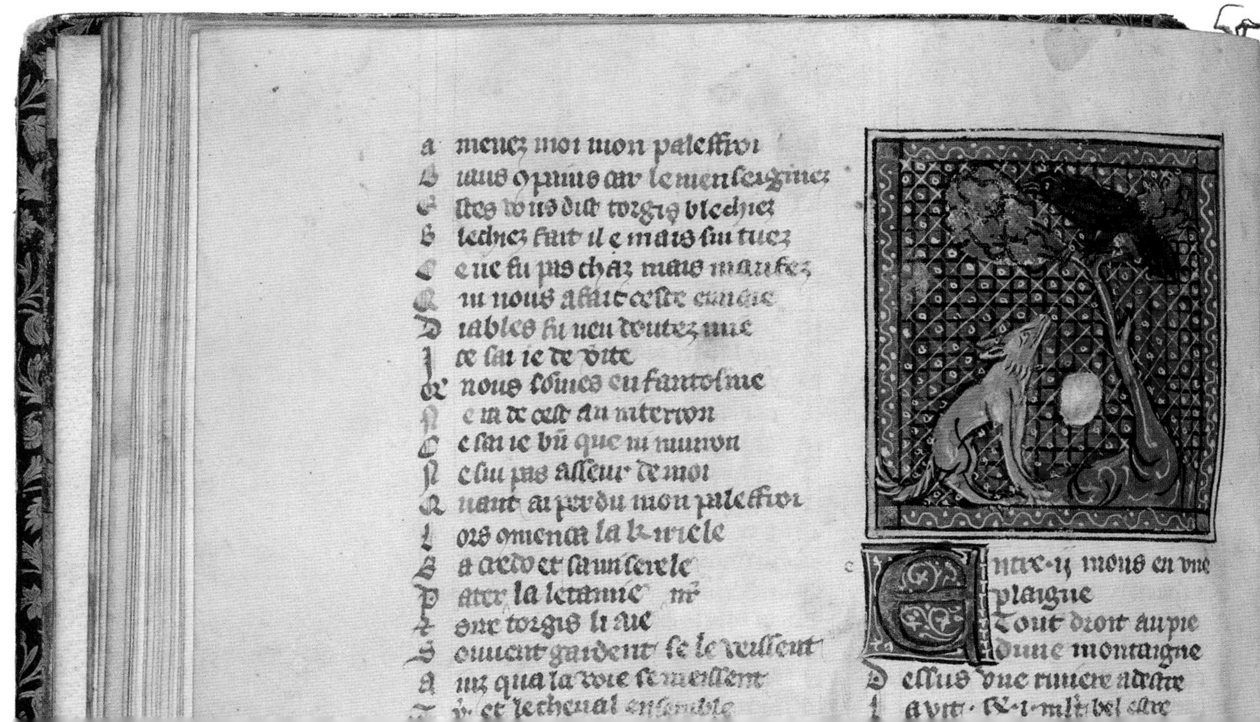

36 An Old French fourteenth-century verse version of various Aesopic fables, here with an illumination illustrating the fable of 'The Fox and the Crow' (Perry *Aesopica* 124). Bodleian Library, MS. Douce 360, fol. 29v.

He that is sure and wel garnysshed yet by fals counceyll may be bytrayed/ wherof Esope reherceth suche a fable/ ¶ An Egle was somtyme vpon a tree/ whiche held with his bylle a nutte/ whiche he coude not breke/ The rauen came to hym/ and sayd/ Thow shalt neuer breke it/ tylle thow fleest as hyghe as thow mayst/ And thenne late it falle vpon the stones/ And the Egle beganne to flyhe and lete falle his proye/ and thus he lost his notte/ ¶ And thus many one ben deceyued thorugh fals counceylle/ and by the fals tongue of other

¶ The xv fable is of the rauen and of the foxe

They that be glad and Joyefull of the praysynge of flaterers oftyme repente them therof/ wherof Esope reherceth to vs suche a fable/ A rauen whiche was vpon a tree/ and held with his bylle a chese/ the whiche chese the foxe desyred moche to haue/ wherfore the foxe wente and preysed hym by suche wordes as followen/ O gentyll rauen thow art the fayrest byrd of alle other byrdes/ For thy fethers ben so fayr so bryght and so resplendysshynge/ and can also so wel synge

Aesop in translation: from print to children's literature

It was only in the age of print that Aesop's tales became known in Greek in the West.[131] The *editio princeps* of the Greek text (Milan, 1480, with a Latin translation and the *Life of Aesop*) had been preceded by Heinrich Steinhöwel's important Latin and German edition (Ulm, 1476–77, with splendid woodcuts). This was one of a range of vernacular and classical sources employed by William Caxton in the first English translation of 1484, produced in the first decade of printing in England (**figure 37**).[132] About the same time, the Scottish poet Robert Henryson (*fl.*1460–1500) adapted a number of Aesopic fables from similarly mixed sources in his *Morall fabillis of Esope*, which were printed only in the sixteenth century (1570). He was not the first or last vernacular poet in the British Isles to use Aesopic-style material; in the 1390s Chaucer had used the story of Chanticleer and the Fox, recognizably related to 'The Fox and the Crow' (Perry *Aesopica* 124), in *The Nun's Priest's Tale*, while Shakespeare employs 'The Stomach and the Body' (Perry *Aesopica* 130) in Act 1 Scene 1 of *Coriolanus* (1608–09). Aesop's wide diffusion in the first century of print is evident from his appearance in the New World by 1700: a number of the fables were translated (from the 1538 Latin version of Joachim Camerarius) into the Mexican indigenous language of Nahuatl in the sixteenth or seventeenth century for educational purposes, a version preserved in manuscript in the Biblioteca Nacional de México.[133]

Perhaps the most famous vernacular versions of Greek Aesopic fables are those to be found in the French *Fables* of Jean de La Fontaine (published in twelve books overall, 1668–94), already mentioned above as an indirect inheritor of the Sanskrit tradition of the *Panchatantra*. The preface to the first collection of 1668, dedicated to the Dauphin, the then six-year-old son of Louis XIV, shows ostentatious classical learning but suggests that the stories are suitable for children (just as they had been used in education in the medieval period; see above). La Fontaine combines the material of Aesop with verse form, as in Phaedrus, Babrius and Avienus; 65 of the 124 fables of Books 1–6 are Aesopic in origin, with most of the rest deriving from the other classical poets. Editions of La Fontaine's work have been especially richly illustrated since the beginning (**figure 38**),[134] and in turn inspired other forms, for example a children's game from 1820 which uses figures and scenes from his tales.[135]

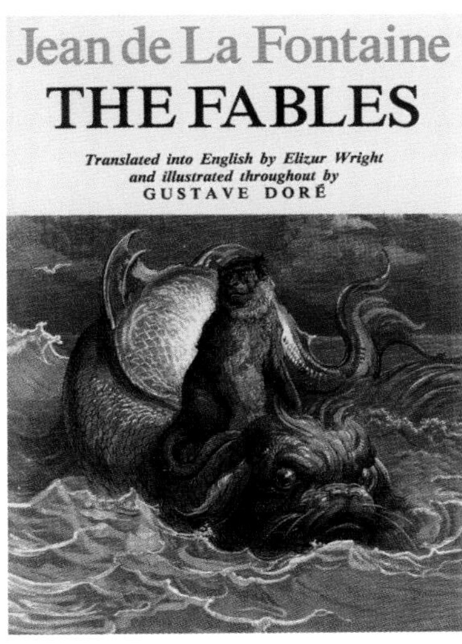

37 *left* Caxton's edition of Aesop's fables (1484), the first English translation produced in the first decade of printing in England, with a woodcut depicting the fable of 'The Fox and the Crow' (Perry *Aesopica* 124). Bodleian Library, Arch. G d.13, p. 256.

38 *above* Front cover of the American Elizur Wright's 1841 much-reprinted English version of La Fontaine's *Fables*, published in 1975 with Gustave Doré's 1867 illustrations. Author's collection.

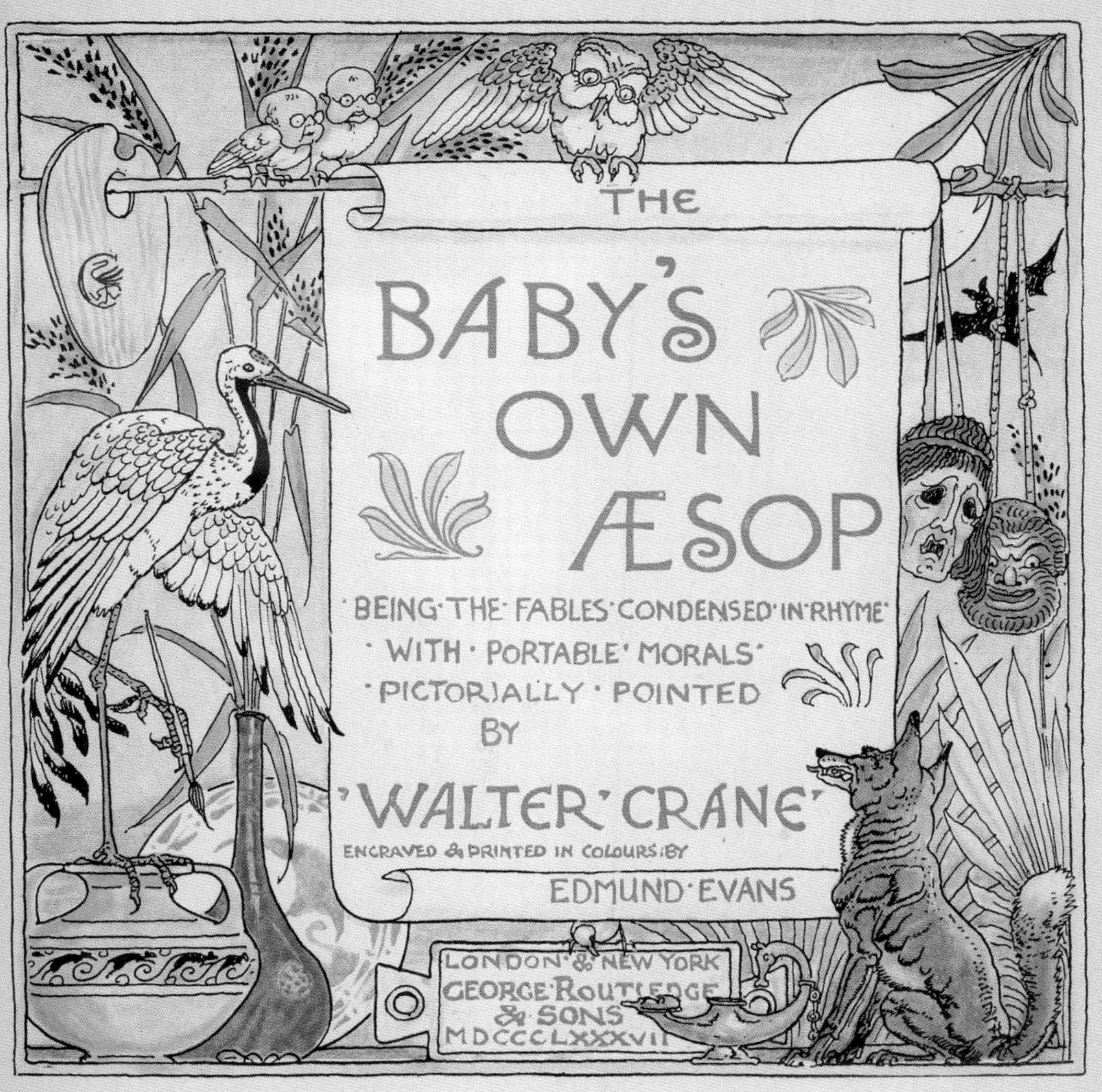
THE
BABY'S
OWN
ÆSOP
BEING THE FABLES CONDENSED IN RHYME
WITH PORTABLE MORALS
PICTORIALLY POINTED
BY
WALTER CRANE
ENGRAVED & PRINTED IN COLOURS BY
EDMUND EVANS
LONDON & NEW YORK
GEORGE ROUTLEDGE
& SONS
MDCCCLXXXVII

39 *previous spread* Title page and frontispiece from *The Baby's Own Aesop*, illustrated by Walter Crane, London, 1887. A beautiful children's version illustrated by one of the great book artists of the period. Bodleian Library, Dunston D85.

La Fontaine's versions in the *Fables* firmly established Aesop as a children's author in the modern world, and ensured the continuation of splendid illustrated editions, a kind of translation into images (**figure 39**).[136] Some of the most famous children's writers of the twentieth century have used the Aesopic tradition, such as Beatrix Potter in *The Tale of Johnny Town-Mouse,* one of her later animal tales (1918); this story reworks 'The City Mouse and the Country Mouse' (Perry *Aesopica* 352), a source recognized by its dedication 'To Aesop in the shadows' (**figure 40**).[137]

The natural appeal of anthropomorphic animal stories and their convenience as vehicles for advice or moralizing have ensured the wide diffusion of such tales across large areas of world literature since its earliest beginnings, and a rich tradition of illustration. This literary form shows an exceptional capacity to move rapidly via translation and adaptation across different cultures, languages and literatures, owing to its ease of assimilation and universal comprehensibility. Moreover, it covers a wide spectrum of readership from monarchs to children. It remains a fully living tradition.

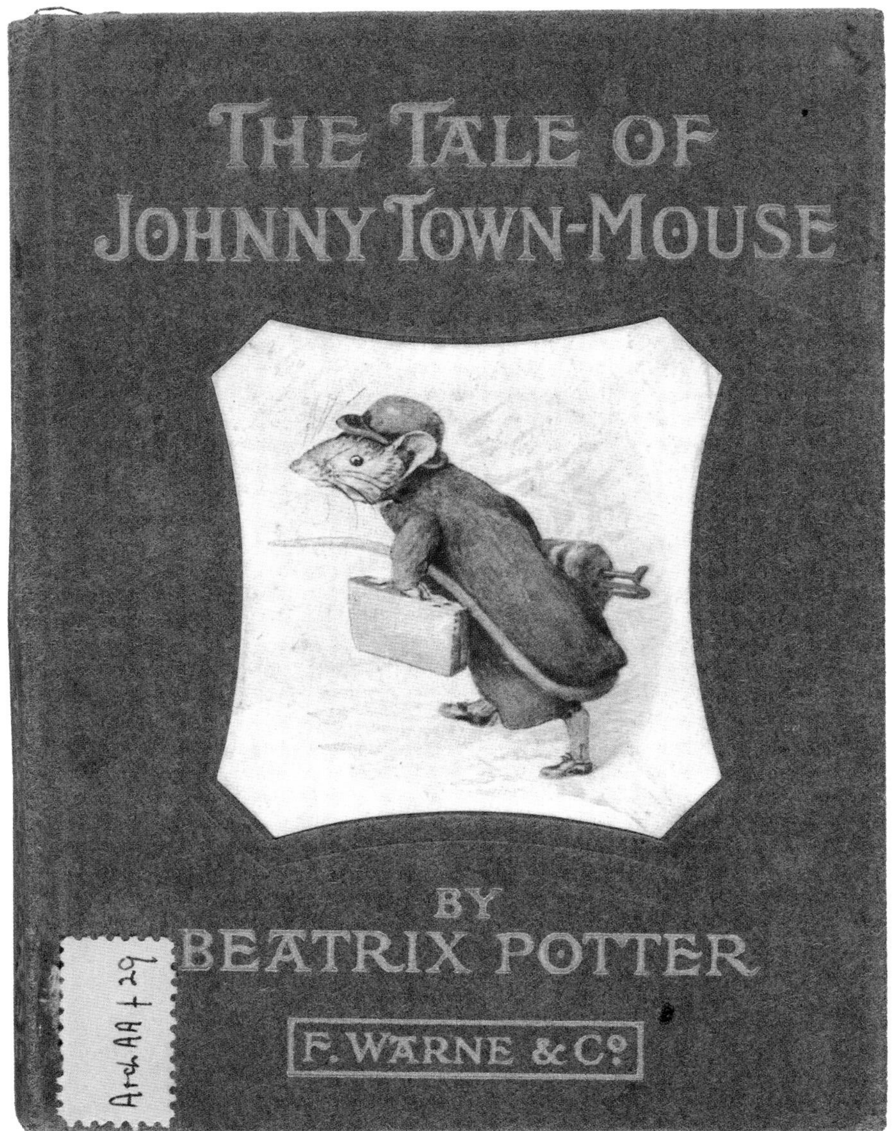

40 Perhaps the most widely read version of an Aesopic fable, by one of the best-known English children's authors. Front cover of Beatrix Potter, *The Tale of Johnny Town-Mouse*, Warne, London, 1918. Courtesy Frederick Warne & Co Ltd, Bodleian Library, Arch. AA f.29.

6 Traversing Realms of Fantasy

Katrin Kohl

nce upon a time ... stories that speak to age-old human concerns like hierarchy, love and jealousy have the power to appeal across eras, places and cultures. The stock beginning of English fairy tales mirrors the French 'Il était une fois …' or the German 'Es war einmal …', signalling the beginning of events that magically transcend the constraints of ordinary existence. The imagination knows no bounds – but for dissemination to happen the magic needs to be translated. Translation from one language to another offers scope for setting the story in a new time or place and giving it a new significance, a new moral, a new twist.

A magical plot stimulates the creativity of both writers and translators, and an entertaining story invites retelling and embellishment. Languages may play an important part. Fairy tales generally liberate their protagonists from communication problems as they fly to far-off places on magic carpets and still manage to make themselves understood at their destination, or talk effortlessly to animals who accost them in well-formed sentences. The translator can then simply transpose the speech into the language in which the tale is being (re-)told. But many writers have also made use of modified or invented languages to give life to strange lands and peoples, and linguistic difference may serve an important role in conveying a past or invented world. This presents translators with the complex challenge of creating an equivalent effect for the new readership – a challenge that is often mastered with inventiveness and linguistic humour drawn from the creative scope provided by the interplay between languages and movement from one into another.

41 *right top* Charles Perrault's 'Contes', or fairy tales, became immediately popular and were quickly disseminated, not least in pirated editions such as this one, printed in Amsterdam in 1708. The illustration by Antoine Clouzier, part of the first edition (1697), appears here in reverse. Bodleian Library, Douce P 646, pp. 90–91.

42 *right bottom* The third edition of Robert Samber's 1729 translation of Perrault's collection, entitled *Histories, or Tales of Passed Times. With Morals*, was printed in 1741 for a London bookseller and for 'J[oseph] Pote, at Eton'. The prefatory matter draws attention to an earlier bilingual edition designed to teach French. Bodleian Library, Vet. A4 f.1869, p. 120.

Translation from rags to riches

Some of our oldest stories have been passed down to us from origins and sources we can no longer reconstruct. When it comes to the Bible, or the works of Homer, it matters where and when they are thought to

MORALITE'.

LEs Diamans & les Pistoles,
Peuvent beaucoup sur les esprits;
Cependant les douces paroles
Ont encor plus de force, & sont
d'un plus grand prix.

AUTRE MORALITE'.

L'Honnêteté coûte des soins,
Et veut un peu de complai-
sance,
Mais tôt ou tard elle a sa recompense,
Et souvent dans le tems qu'on y pense
le moins.

CEN-

CENDRILLON, OU LA PETITE PANTOUFLE DE VERRE.

CONTE.

IL étoit une fois un Gentil-homme qui épousa en secondes nopces une femme, la plus hautaine &c

&c.

ains the
kes her
s dying
hes how
a good
liums to
y inspire
d tender

DE-

CINDERILLA; OR THE LITTLE GLASS SLIPPER.

TALE VI.

ONCE there was a gentleman who married, for his second wife, the proudest and most haughty woman ever was seen. She had, by a former husband, two daughters of her own humour, and were ... exactly like her in all th... thing have originated, and who is considered to have created them or who is credited with recording what happened. Even now, theologians and scholars argue about the provenance of these texts and the connections between their different versions in an effort to pin down their origins. Establishing the originator is important when the work serves as the founding text for a religion, cultural group or textual tradition. With popular oral tales, however, the origin may not be crucial, and indeed the legitimacy of the work may hinge precisely on the lack of artistic design. For the Romantic mindset it was desirable to find folk tales that could be assumed to have originated 'naturally' in the communal psyche rather than in the mind of a learned individual.

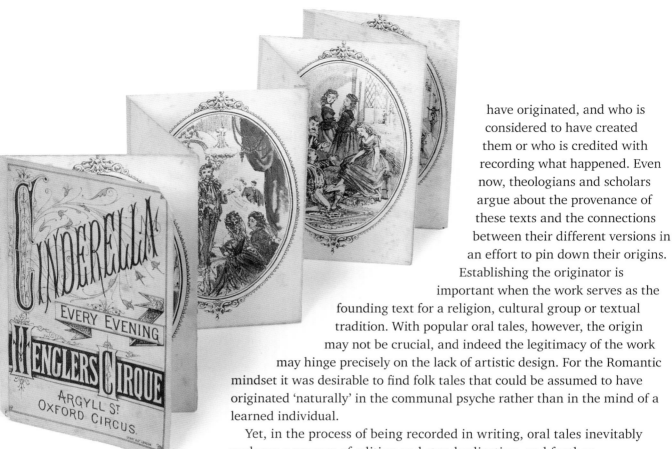

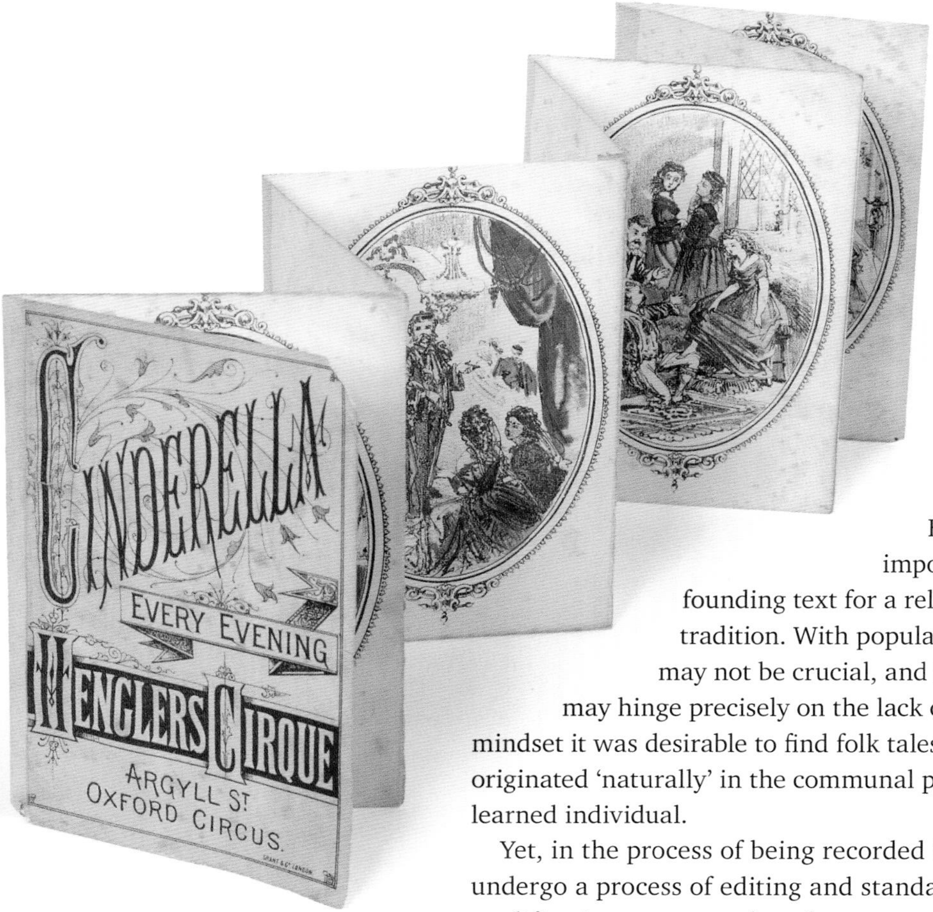

Yet, in the process of being recorded in writing, oral tales inevitably undergo a process of editing and standardization, and further modifications occur as the tales are transposed into other media such as music, visual art, theatre or film. Translation interacts with such transpositions in complex ways, as can be seen in the narrative pathways of *Cinderella*, one of the most enduringly popular stories in the European tradition and beyond.

In Britain, the tale of *Cinderella* became established after Robert Samber translated it in 1729 from Charles Perrault's French tale *Cendrillon, ou*

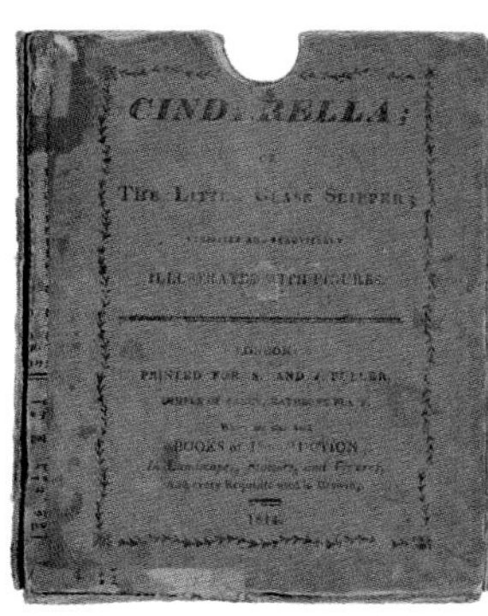

la Petite Pantoufle de Verre. Perrault's *Histoires ou Contes du Temps Passé. Avec des Moralitez* with their fictional storyteller 'Mother Goose' had first appeared in 1697 and had been reproduced within and beyond France (**figure 41**).[138] In the nineteenth century the story became a hot favourite in Britain and it was taken up in many forms, including poetry and pantomime, with film adaptations following in the twentieth century. The tale of the lovable heroine with her hidden beauty triumphing over an abusive stepmother and two odious sisters captured the popular imagination, as did the elements of disguise and revelation, the magical transformation of a pumpkin into a carriage and mice into men, the test of the slipper, and the marriage to Prince Charming.

Samber's book reproduces the title illustration from the French version for his rendering entitled *Cinderilla; or the Little Glass Slipper* (**figure 42**), and he keeps close to Perrault, though he occasionally diverges in order to clarify a point or take account of the reader's different cultural context.[139] While Perrault establishes the familial tensions that drive the plot simply by commenting that the father is marrying for the second time ('en secondes nopces'), leaving the reader to infer the differing parentage of the girls, Samber additionally explains that the wife's two daughters are 'by a former husband' and the husband's daughter 'by another wife'.[140] The translator here takes on the role of a mediator who is not only concerned to render the text accurately in the other language but who also interprets it for the reader and acts independently to ensure that his reader grasps the salient elements of the plot. Later, when Perrault has one of the sisters declare before the first ball that she will wear 'mon habit de velours rouge & ma garniture d'Angleterre', Samber adorns the 'red velvet suit' not with English trimming but with '*French* trimming'.[141] By transposing the cultural

43 The growing popularity of Cinderella's adventures is evident from early nineteenth-century theatre and pantomime programmes. The changing clothes in the story lent themselves – then as now – to toy adaptations. These cut-outs accompany a poetry version: *Cinderella, or the Little Glass Slipper* (1814). Bodleian Library, Opie EE 334a and Opie E 31.

44 *Aschenputtel* became one of the most popular of the Grimm Brothers' tales. In this 1825 edition of the *Kinder- und Haus-Märchen*, with fifty tales, it is among seven that are accompanied by an illustration. The heroine's domestic plight and animal helpers are highlighted here rather than her adventures at court. Bodleian Library (Taylorian), Fiedler.K.1341, pp. 104–5.

reference, he gives his reader an equivalent sense of the girl's apparel, her access to fashionable clothing, and her vanity.

In his prefatory dedication, Samber associates the tales with 'Apologue and Fable', which commend themselves as 'delightful and diverting, and, at the same time, instructive'.[142] Accordingly, he reproduces Perrault's versified 'morals' at the end of the tale. The publishing details and prefatory matter of this edition also suggest that it was closely associated with educational purposes, including language instruction, given that one of the booksellers specified is J. Pote 'at Eton',[143] and a bilingual version is advertised beneath the list of contents as 'Lately Published': 'Mother Goose's Tales, etc. in *French* and English. ... *N.B.* The above is very proper to be read by young Children at Boarding Schools, that are to learn the *French* Tongue, as well as in private Families.' In the subsequent decades and centuries the story was translated not only into many more languages but also into a wide variety of genres, media and toy re-creations (**figure 43**).[144] It is a long way from the eighteenth-century classrooms of Eton College to the continuing English Christmas pantomime tradition with its Commedia dell'arte heritage, and the world of Disney – not least within varieties of English.

45 The tale known in English as *Cinderella* forms part of a rich tradition of tales from Eastern and Western parts of the world, with new twists being added in modern retellings and versions. There are innumerable variations – in the setting, the provenance of the slipper, the magical helpers, the ending. *Angkat: The Cambodian Cinderella* (1998) is a retelling of an ancient Cambodian tale by Jewell Reinhart Coburn, illustrated by Eddie Flotte. The stepsisters' treatment of the heroine is more violent than in Charles Perrault's tale, and the ending has a more pronounced spiritual dimension. Courtesy of Shen's Books, an imprint of Lee & Low Books Inc. (2014 edition).

While Perrault's version of the story formed the lasting basis for the English tradition, the origins of the tale can be traced further back and indicate the complex routes by which popular tales take shape and evolve across language traditions. A Neapolitan version with the title *La gatta cenerentola* ('Ash Cat') had been published in 1634 as part of Giambattista Basile's *Il Pentamerone*, a collection of tales embedded in a narrative framework evidently inspired by Boccaccio's *Decameron*. Perrault's version reveals additional plot elements such as the magical transformation of the pumpkin and the mice, which do not appear in Basile. Parts of the plot are configured differently; for example, Perrault dwells on the two sisters' attention to their hair and attire, a feature of the tale that is regularly embellished to humorous effect in pantomime depictions of 'the Ugly Sisters'. Perrault's tale also ends with a considerably longer poetic 'moral'.

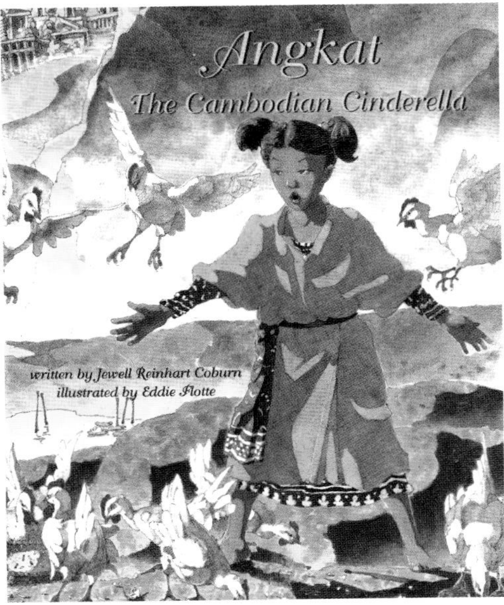

A century later, Basile's tale served as a source for Jacob and Wilhelm Grimm, who became important disseminators of his contribution to the European folk-tale tradition with their *Kinder- und Haus-Märchen* ('Tales for Children and the Home') (**figure 44**).[145] They published *Aschenputtel* (a name combining 'ash' with a dialect word from Hesse for 'slatternly girl') in 1812, expanding it in 1819. They also drew on Perrault in their work, both directly and indirectly, given the strong Huguenot legacy among the storytellers who contributed to their repertoire. Their tale differs from his in important respects and is made more moving by the heroine's visits to her mother's grave and – instead of Perrault's fairy godmother – the inclusion of a magically helpful bird that lives in the tree she plants there and that gives her the clothes she needs for the ball. For this motif, the Grimms evidently draw on a friendly dove found in Basile, and they also transform it into a tool for punishing the sisters. In their version, the stepmother advises her daughters to chop off their toe and heel respectively so they can make the slipper fit, a ploy that is revealed to the prince by doves calling attention to the blood in the slipper. Moreover, while Basile has the sisters learn from their mistakes and Perrault deploys his heroine's forgiveness to exemplify that the true gift of the fairies is graciousness, *Aschenputtel* ends with the sisters having their eyes pecked out. Rather than culminating in an explicit moral, the tale concludes with an act of natural justice.

Like Perrault, the Grimm Brothers were creating their tales on the basis of oral and written sources, and in both cases translation, adaptation and invention are inextricably intertwined. Both projects formed part of a concern to give the vernacular traditions higher status and independence from the classical canon. Differences are in part a matter of context and purpose, though patterns of reception tend to be fluid. Perrault – a 'modern' in the battle with the 'ancients' – aimed to entertain members of the court and children, and, notwithstanding the concluding 'morals', his tales have a genial lightness of touch which contributes to the humour that alleviates the trials of Cinders in the English tradition. The Grimm Brothers were compiling tales not for the court – unlike France, the German-speaking lands were a politically fragmented territory – but primarily for domestic enjoyment and edification.

For the Grimm Brothers, collecting such folk tales was part of an ambitious project to map the German linguistic heritage and establish a unifying German culture. They worked with protagonists of Romanticism such as Clemens Brentano, who put them in touch with *Märchenfrauen*, women known for their talent as storytellers; *Aschenputtel* was recounted

20 LOOKING-GLASS HOUSE.

manage this one a bit; it writes all manner of things that I don't intend——"

"What manner of things?" said the Queen, looking over the book (in which Alice had put '*The White Knight is sliding down the poker. He balances very badly*'). "That's not a memorandum of *your* feelings!"

There was a book lying near Alice on the table, and while she sat watching the White King (for she was still a little anxious about him, and had the ink all ready to throw over him, in case he fainted again), she turned over the leaves, to find some part that she could read, "—for it's all in some language I don't know," she said to herself.

LOOKING-GLASS HOUSE. 21

It was like this.

JABBERWOCKY.

'Twas brillig, and the slithy toves
Did gyre and gimble in the wabe;
All mimsy were the borogoves,
And the mome raths outgrabe.

She puzzled over this for some time, but at last a bright thought struck her. "Why, it's a Looking-glass book, of course! And if I hold it up to a glass, the words will all go the right way again."

This was the poem that Alice read.

JABBERWOCKY.

'Twas brillig, and the slithy toves
Did gyre and gimble in the wabe;
All mimsy were the borogoves,
And the mome raths outgrabe.

46 Alice's encounter with 'Jabberwocky' in Lewis Carroll's *Through the Looking Glass* (1872) happens through a textual soundscape that abounds in neologisms. They stimulate imaginative translation without yielding conclusive solutions, while enough of a story emerges to make the poem meaningful: '*somebody* killed *something*: that's clear, at any rate—' (p. 24). Bodleian Library, Opie AA 885, pp. 20–21.

to them by the impoverished spinster Elisabeth Schellenberg.[146] The tale transmitted by the Grimms is informed by an imagination altogether darker than those by Basile and Perrault. It seems likely that this quality derives at least in part from the version passed down by Schellenberg. By what complex pathways that tale might be connected with the Neapolitan and French sources before becoming part of the tale of the Brothers Grimm must remain a matter of conjecture.

Other threads that may have contributed to the tale include the Latin story of Cupid and Psyche from the second century CE[147] and, intriguingly, a story recorded in China during the Tang Dynasty: *Ye Xian*, part of a miscellany published by Duan Chengshi around 850 CE.[148] This probably absorbed Hindu and Buddhist influences, and it shares narrative elements especially with Basile's and the Grimm Brothers' versions. It is by no means implausible that the story originated in China and entered Europe via the great port of Naples. It centres on a slipper that will fit only the heroine, who has exceptionally tiny feet – an attribute of beauty highly prized in Chinese women. And it may have been transmitted by tradespeople or perhaps by Jesuit missionaries as they exchanged knowledge and no doubt stories with people in China. If so, the linguistic and cultural traces have become seamlessly assimilated into European tradition, and via Perrault and Samber into the American fantasy world created by Walt Disney.[149] But, as Jewell Reinhart Coburn's *Angkat: The Cambodian Cinderella* (1988; **figure 45**) and Robert D. San Souci's *Cendrillon: A Caribbean Cinderella* (1998) indicate,[150] the retellings and adaptations continue …

'It's all in some language I don't know' – populating new worlds

47 J.R.R. Tolkien invented languages for the peoples of his 'legendarium' that would make each culturally distinctive. Galadriel's Lament from *The Lord of the Rings* is written in the Elvish language Quenya. Tolkien has here used Latin script and provided an English translation underneath. Bodleian Library, MS. Tolkien 21, fol. 2. © The Tolkien Estate Limited, 2019.

While translation from one language to another enables stories to be disseminated across territories and cultures, and holds the potential of opening up worlds of magic to new audiences, it may also take on a role in the plot as the characters encounter people speaking an unfamiliar language. Invented languages engage the reader or audience in the activity of translation and interpretation as part of the reading or listening experience.

In Lewis Carroll's *Through the Looking Glass, and What Alice Found There* (1872) the heroine begins to grasp something about how the mirror world works when she seeks to understand a book she is unable to read, '– for it's all in some language I don't know' (**figure 46**).[151] The author does not just

The word-order and style is 'poetic': it makes concessions to metre. In a clearer and more normal order the words would run as below. Compounded words are shown by hyphens. A literal translation is written underneath.

Ai! lassi lantar laurië sūrinen, yēni ū-nōt-ime ve
Alas! leaves fall (pl) goldenly wind-in, long-years un-count-able as

rāmar aldaron! Yēni ve linte yuldar avānier
wings trees-of. Long-years as swift draughts have-passed-away (pl)

lisse-miruvōre-va mí oro-mardi Andūne pella Vardo nu
sweet-mead-of in-the high-halls West beyond under Varda's

luini tellumar, yassen tintilar i eleni ōma-ryo
blue (pl) domes which-in (pl) twinkle (pl) the stars voice-her-of

līrinen, aire-tário. Sī man i yulma nin en-quant-uva?
in-song-in, holy-queen-of Now who the cup me-for re-fill-will?

An sī Varda, Tintalle, Elen-tāri ortane mā-rya-t Oio-lossë-o
For now Varda, Spark-kindler, Star-queen raised hand-her-two Ever-snowy-from

ve fanyar, ar lumbule undu-lāve ilye tiër; ar sinda-nōrië-llo
like clouds, and heavy shadow down-licked (sc. swallowed) all (pl) roads; and grey-country-from

caita mornië i falma-li-nna-r imbe met, ar hīsië
lies darkness the foaming-many-upon (pl) waves between us-two [sc. Varda & Galadriel] and mistiness

un-tūpa Cala-ciryo mīri oiale. Sī vanwa ná, Rōmello
[down-roofs] covers over Kalakirya's jewels for-ever. Now lost is, [to those] from East

vanwa, Valimar! Namārië! Nai hiruvalye Valimar.
lost, Valimar! Farewell! May-it-be-that find-shalt-thou Valimar.

Nai elye hiruva. Na-mārië!
May-it-be-that even-thou find-shall (it). Farewell.

The text and punctuation as printed were defective in these points. 1) the first 2 lines go together: the leaves and years are the same (cf I p. 389). 2) únótime – tí is printer's error. 3) line 5: read mí (mi!) 'in the' for mi 'in'. 4) line 6 a comma required after luini. 5) line 11 (;) required after lumbule. At this point ends what Varda did in remote past (hence in Q. the past tense), then follows the still existing results (to which sí now properly applies). 6) line 15 read ná (is) 'is' give the reader a description of the mirror text but allows them to share the incomprehension Alice experiences. While the title, in capitals, provides a way into understanding the mirror effect, the use of italics makes the main text harder to follow, and it comes as a relief when her use of a looking glass turns the puzzling text into 'the poem that Alice read'.

Yet Carroll continues to make the process of comprehension gradual and ultimately elusive. The reader first has to convert the mirror text into ordinary script, and then try to translate a text that is semi-English into a comprehensible poem. Familiar grammar and standard function words indicate that the language is not foreign, yet the content words withhold an unequivocal meaning. Meanwhile powerful alliteration, rhyme and rhythm encourage 'translating' the visible words into spoken performance, supported by John Tenniel's full-page illustration centred on the prominent mouth of the Jabberwock (see above, p. 116). Unlike Alice, the reader appreciates the humour, which is enhanced by her understated response that '"It seems very pretty, … but it's *rather* hard to understand!" (You see she didn't like to confess, even to herself, that she couldn't make it out at all.).' In fact, as the poem 'fill[s] [her] head with ideas', she grasps the basic plot – '*somebody* killed *something*'. Using processes of translation and interpretation, she is opening up a story that is imbued with the heroic battles of ancient mythology.

J.R.R. Tolkien – initially Professor of Anglo-Saxon and then Professor of English Language and Literature at Oxford – took the invention of languages into a new dimension as he populated his world of Middle-earth. Having written *The Hobbit* (published in 1937), he set out to give a firm grounding to his mythology, an undertaking he saw as 'primarily linguistic in inspiration', 'begun in order to provide the necessary background of "history" for Elvish tongues'.[152] He created languages complete with grammatical and lexical systems and special scripts, allowing both the peoples and the languages scope within his capacious imagination to evolve in response to each other.

The Elvish languages are created out of the fabric of the ancient languages of the Germanic peoples and their interaction with the evocative world of the Elves in Norse, Anglo-Saxon and Celtic myths. Much as 'Middle-earth' may be seen as a translation and creative adaptation of 'Midgard' (the name for Earth, one of Nine Worlds in Norse mythology), the languages are constructed in a continual process of translation, adaptation and invention.

A moving experience in the early travels of Frodo and the Company in *The Lord of the Rings* is their 'Farewell to Lórien',[153] marked first by a song the royal elf Galadriel sings in English, and then by the poem 'Namárië', her lament in 'the ancient tongue of the Elves beyond the Sea' (**figure 47**). While Frodo appreciates the beautiful music, he only later makes sense of the words: 'as is the way of Elvish words, they remained graven in his memory, and long afterwards he interpreted them, as well as he could: the language was that of Elven-song and spoke of things little known on Middle-earth.' By incorporating a poem in the Elven language Quenya, and only then giving the reader Frodo's translation, Tolkien evokes a world that is both mysterious and meaningful. While the language is fictional, it draws so richly on the ancient languages Tolkien had studied that it seems like a living root reaching deep into our pre-textual past.

Tolkien's invented languages left a vibrant legacy. He used the same human capacity for linguistic creativity that has over the years brought us both languages such as Esperanto, constructed to facilitate practical communication (see chapter 2), and new vocabularies that enable us to talk about innovative technologies such as IT or AI. But the Elvish languages are not constructed to serve as tools of communication. They evoke living voices that articulate a particular cultural vision. Similarly, the languages spoken in *Dungeons and Dragons* or *Game of Thrones* engage players and audiences in imagining other ways of life and experimenting with different ways of seeing the world.

Translating local magic

Much fantasy is set in real-life contexts or derives its fascination from the way in which it grows out of realistic situations. The cartoon characters around the Gaulish warrior Astérix – developed by writer René Goscinny and illustrator Albert Uderzo from 1959[154] – inhabit an outpost of the historically documented Roman Empire in 50 BCE, but the magic potions of the resident Druid liberate them from normal human constraints. Comic moments in the French original arise from historical clichés and anachronisms combining with irreverent use of modern national stereotypes. A linguistic dimension adds to the humour with pseudo-Latin names, mistranslations, non-verbal expletives, puns and dialect variations, posing a challenge that was taken up with relish by translators into other languages (**figure 48**).

48 A Germanic attack on Astérix's Gaulish village is conveyed in the French original (first published in 1961) by Germanically pronounced French and a humorous hint of World War II in 'addentzion!'. The English translators add Germanic script while turning the aggressors anachronistically into 'Germans'. Meanwhile the German translator renders their linguistic provenance distinctive with Swabian dialect. (For the sources, see p. 170, note 154.)

The role of the translators here goes far beyond transposing the 'content' from one linguistic form into another since they need to create an equivalent effect for a reader with a different cultural perspective. Where the effect depends on at least rudimentary appreciation of the cultural and linguistic diversity that characterized the actual Roman Empire, the translation still needs to retain the lightness of touch that comes with quick comprehension. National stereotypes therefore have an important role in these mock-historical cartoon books. They may verge on being politically incorrect but they are safe so long as the setting is sufficiently far removed from a modern context and the humorous intent is clearly communicated.

By contrast with the historical expanse of the Roman Empire, the world depicted at the beginning of the *Harry Potter* series is stultifyingly ordinary, with small-minded characters exemplifying the dullness of contemporary English suburbia. Even Hogwarts School of Witchcraft and Wizardry in some respects resembles a peculiarly English boarding school. The crucial ingredient that gives J.K. Rowling's books global appeal is the imaginative force of magic that drives the epic battle between good and evil.

By contrast with the slow and meandering processes of dissemination that have over a period of many centuries given Cinderella's adventures global reach, *Harry Potter and the Philosopher's Stone* (1997)[155] gained a global audience almost immediately, aided by English having gained the status of a global lingua franca, and supported by a global publishing and media trade.

Translation has, however, played a crucial part in the process of dissemination. While Harry and his friends and foes are largely monoglots – though Harry discovers that he is mysteriously able to speak Parseltongue, and Dumbledore numbers multilingualism among his many accomplishments[156] – there has been no question of relying on global English to reach readers and audiences across the world. Some eighty published translations to date include a rich array of languages and scripts, and more ad hoc translations no doubt abound (**figure 49**). Translation into Braille, and sign-language captions and name equivalents have increased inclusiveness of access. Versions in Ancient Greek and Latin are the result of a passion for keeping ancient languages alive. Meanwhile versions in Scots, Breton and Catalan demonstrate the desire of culturally distinctive groups to sustain their identity through literature even though they could easily access the text in a more widely spoken lingua franca.

Realms of fantasy are brought alive by people – people who talk. These characters may use lingua francas that transcend barriers between countries or even species, or they may express their identities, needs and desires in a language that is culturally rich and special to them. Readers and audiences have no difficulty moving between lingua francas and more culturally specific languages as they respond to the stimulus of adventure.

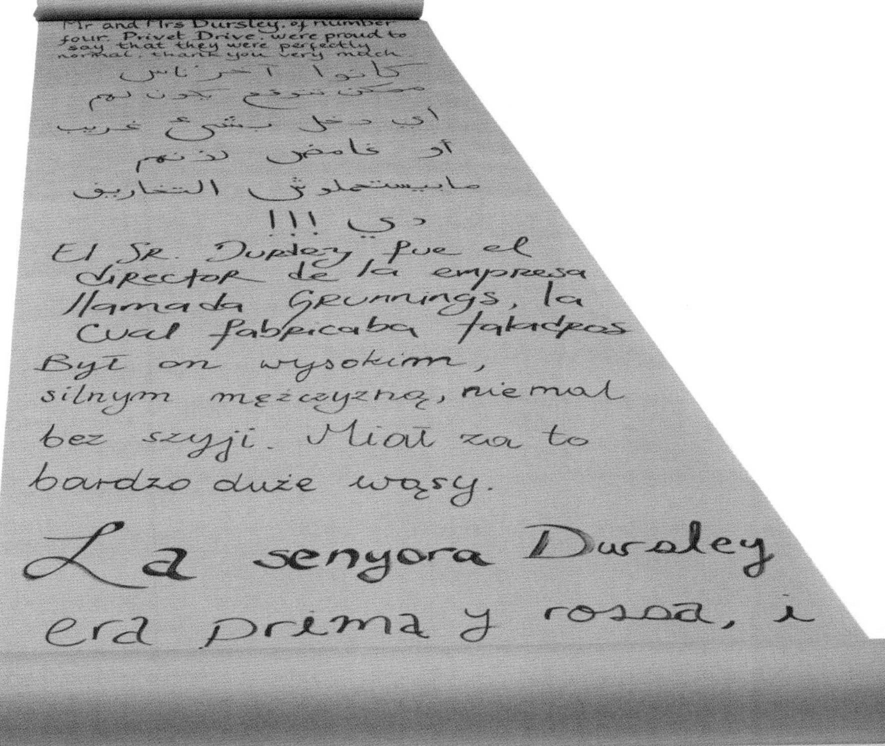

49 This giant scroll was rolled out in the Ashmolean Museum during a LinguaMania event in January 2017 to collect translated sentences from the beginning of J.K. Rowling's *Harry Potter and the Philosopher's Stone* (1997). The crowd-sourced translation incorporates fifty-one different languages. *Harry Potter and the Philosopher's Stone*: Copyright © J.K. Rowling 1997. Image courtesy of Creative Multilingualism, Henriette Arndt, Annina Hessel and Anna-Maria Ramezanzadeh.

degré.

Teat a little — un peu

To Ted To scatter. de
avec le ~~[illegible]~~ foin, pendant qui [illegible]
(peutetre de Teat un peu. pa[illegible]
on on le mette en [illegible]

Drik. wearisom tedious

Gab. Mouth. Bouche. Os.
— dit gape i.e ouvrir la [illegible]
disent aussi les Hollan[illegible]

7 Negotiating Multilingual Britain

Katrin Kohl

The British Isles were the cradle of English – now the lingua franca of the world. But what we know as 'English' was formed out of many immigrant languages, and English has never been the only language in England or Great Britain, let alone the British Isles. The processes of linguistic contact, transfer and mingling have been, and still are, as varied as the interactions between ethnic groups and cultures in England, Scotland, Wales and Ireland. Much of this process is lost in the mists of time. Languages meet and mix above all in ephemeral speech, informal exchanges and peaceful cooperation or violent clashes between groups that then form new social units and hierarchies, or go their separate ways.

We can try to reconstruct oral language transformations that have left no written traces, for example by analysing place names and word borrowings. By contrast, written records give us extended evidence of encounters between languages. The very fact that texts were produced which translate an administrative document, a historical account or a fictional narrative into another language provides an insight into the ways in which cultures learned from each other, shared their knowledge and practices, and shaped their identities in relation to each other. Manuscripts and books that show translation in action allow us to witness a meeting of minds, communication systems and cultural interests. Information leaflets that reach out to different language groups give us hard evidence of administrations responding to linguistic diversity. Reliance on electronic media is once more making such evidence more elusive while also creating new, more fluid forms of communication.

50 Translation from Latin was crucial in establishing 'English' as a written medium. This version of Boethius's influential *De consolatione philosophiae* (524–525 CE) was produced *c.*890–950 as part of the educational programme established by King Alfred. It survives in complete form only in this manuscript from *c.*1100–1150 CE. Bodleian Library, MS. Bodl. 180, fol. 1r.

The British Isles – translation in an evolving linguistic landscape

Historically, translation must have played a crucial part in shaping the ancient languages of the British Isles as they emerged and developed in interaction with the languages of continental Europe. In the Stone Age,

ÆLFRED KUNING WÆS WE-
ALHSTOD ÐISSE BEC 7 HIE OF
boclædene on englisc wende swa hio nu is gedon. Hwilum he sette word be worde. hwilum andgit of andgite. swa
swa he hit þa sweotolost 7 andgitfullicast gereccan mihte
for þam mistlicū 7 manigfealdum wordū. 7 bisgum þe hine
oft ægðer ge on mode ge on lichoman bisgodan. Ða bisgu
us sint swiþe earfoþrime þe on his dagum on þa ricu beco-
man þe he underfangen hæfde. 7 þeah ða þas boc hæfde ge-
leornode. 7 of lædene to engliscū spelle gewende. 7 geworh-
te hi eft to leoðe. swa swa heo nu gedon is. 7 nu bit 7 for godes
naman he halsað ælcne þara þe þas boc rædan lyste. þæt he
for hine gebidde. 7 him ne wite gif he hit rihtlicor ongite þo-
nne he mihte. forþam þe ælc mon sceal be his andgites mæ-
ðe. 7 be his æmettan sprecan þæt he sprecð. 7 don þæt þæt he deþ.

wæs hu gotan gewunnon romana rice. 7 hu boetius
hi wolde eft bereðan. 7 ðeodric þa þæt anfunde. 7 hine het
on carcerne gebringan.

Hu boetius on þam carcerne his sar seofiende wæs.

Hu se wisdom com to boetie æfter inne on þā carcerne 7 hine on-
gan frefrian.

Hu boetius hine singende gebæd. 7 his earfoðu to gode mænde.

Hu se wisdom hine eft rete 7 rihte mid his andswarum.

Hu he him rehte bispell bi þære sunnan. 7 be oðrum tunglum
7 be wolcnum.

immigrants from other parts of Europe will have travelled across the broad land bridge that connected the east coast of Great Britain to what was to become the Netherlands and western and northern Germany. But habitation was not continuous and there are no records of the languages spoken in pre-Celtic Britain. The earliest languages in the British Isles of which we have records are Celtic languages, which spread from central Europe and Gaul to the Iberian peninsula and the British Isles by the third century BCE.[157] Tacitus observes that the inhabitants of Britain 'nearest to the Gauls are also like them' and that their 'language differs but little'.[158] He probably came from an area in southern France or northern Italy where a Gaulish language was spoken, so his observation may well be reliable.

From 43 CE, the Roman conquest made Latin increasingly influential alongside Celtic languages, and we may assume that there was considerable traffic between the languages in daily life. It is likely that Latin was dominant especially in eastern Britain while the rest of lowland Britain was mixed with widespread bilingualism; and that varieties of the Celtic language Brittonic were dominant in highland Britain, though Latin was spoken, probably especially along Hadrian's Wall. Evidence for the interaction between the languages hinges on the borrowing of Latin words into Brittonic to name objects or express ideas for which there was often no indigenous equivalent, such as *papyrus* or *calendae* (first day of the month).[159]

Spoken Latin is thought to have died out by 700 CE, though especially its written form continued to be important in education, learning, the law and, with the rise of Christianity, the Church. Celtic languages survived primarily in Ireland, Scotland, Wales and Cornwall while migrants from northern Germany and Denmark established Old English in powerful Anglo-Saxon kingdoms between Sussex and Northumbria in the course of the fifth and sixth centuries. During this period, Anglo-Saxon (or Old English), with its Germanic grammar and vocabulary, became dominant in the central areas of Great Britain and formed the lasting basis of English, with Viking raids around 800 CE leaving traces of Old Norse in many areas of vocabulary such as warfare, as in 'slaughter' (from *slátr*, butcher's meat) and 'club' (from *clubba*).

Translation became a key medium of education that went hand in hand with the promotion of Christianity. Alfred (849–899 CE), King of Wessex, established a magnificent legacy, not only by driving back the Vikings

51 'The Oxford Roland' was probably produced in England around 1125–1150. It is the oldest surviving manuscript of France's national epic *La Chanson de Roland* and indicates how closely intertwined the two cultures and languages were in the period following the Norman conquest. Bodleian Library, MS. Digby 23, Part 2, fol. 43r.

Gryttaen oreu or ynyssed yr hon
aelwit gynt y wen ynys yg gorllew
inawl eigyawn. Y rwg ffreinc ac
iwerdon y mae gossodedic. wyth
cant milltir yssyd yn y hyt. a deu cant yny
llet. A pha beth bynnac a vo reit y dynyawl
arver o anniffygedic ffrwythlonder hi ae
gwassanaetha. Ygyt a hynny kyflawn yw
or maes tired llydan amyl. a brynneu ar
derchavel y dir dywyllodraeth. drwy y
rei y daw amrauaelon genedloed frwyth
eu. Yndi hefyt y maent koetyd a llwyneu
kyflawn o amgen genedloed anniueileit a bw
ystuileit. Ac y gyt a hynny amlaf kenue
moed or gwenyn o blith y blodeuoed yn
kynullaw mel. Ac y gyt a hynny gweirglo
dyeu amyl a dan aruchel vynyded. Yn
y rei y maent ffynhoneu gloew eglur.
or rei y kerdant ffrydyeu. ac a lithrant gan
glaer seinyaw murmur arwystyl kerd. a
hun yw y rei hynny yr neb a gyscco ar eu
glan. Ac y gyt a hynny llynneu ac avono
ed kyflawn o amrauaelon genedloed pyscawt
yssyd yndi. Ac eithyr y ffrwytheduor yd eu
drossant y ffreinc. Teir avon bonhedic yssyd
yndi. Nyt amgen. temys. a hvmyr. a
hafren. A rei hynny megys teir breich y
maent yn rannu yr ynys. Ac ar hyt y rei
hynny y deuant amravael gyfnewitye
... or gwladoed tramor. Ac y gyt a hynny
gynt yr oed yndi wyth prif dinas ar hugei
nt ynys theckau. A rei o nadunt bedw yssyd
diffeith. gwedy diffeithaw y muroed yn
vallus. a e rei ereill etwa yn sefyll yn iach. a the
mleu seint yndunt yn moli duw. a muroed
a chaeroed arderchawc yn eu teckau. Ac
yny temleu kenueinoed o wyr a gwraged
a chrefydwyr yn talu gwassanaeth dyledus
yn amseroed kyfreith y eu creawdyr yn he
rwyd cristonogawl fyd. Ac or diwed ynys
kenedyl yssyd ynys y chynnhalbedu. Nyt am

lat yr eidal y rhon gwlat rutuli. Ac yna yr amser hwn
nw yd oed latinus yn vrenhin yn yr eidal. Y gwr a
arvolles eneas yn anrydedus. Ac yna gwedy gwe
let o turn brenhin rutul. llityaw a oruc ac ymlad
a vnaeth ac ef. A gorvot a vnaeth eneas a llad
turn brenhin rutul. A chaffael yr eidal. A lauinia
merch latinus yn wreic idaw. Ac yna gwedy
ymlenwi dieuoed buched eneas, ascanius y
vab yntev a vnaeth yn vrenhin. A gwedy
drychavel ascanius ar brenhinawl gyuoeth.
ef a adeilwys dinas ar avon tiberis. a mab a anet
idaw. ac a rodet ar y enw silvius. Ar gwas hwn
nw gwedy yn rodi yledradawl odineb gordercha
a oruc nith y lauinia ae beichogi. A gwedy y gwy
bot o ascanius y dat ef hynny. erchi a vnaeth
oe dewinyon dywedut idaw pwy a bechogassei
y vorwyn. A gwedy dewinaw o nadunt a chaf
fel dihewrwyd or peth hwnnw wynt a dywedassant
bot y vorwyn yn veichyawc ar vab a ladei y vam
ae dat. A gwedy darffei idaw dreiglaw llawer o
wladoed y dayar or diwed y deuei ar blaenhed gwr
uchelder anrydet. Ac ny thwyllwys eu dewinia
aeth wynt kanys dyuot eu dewinyaeth. Ac
yna gwedy dyuot oet yr vorwyn y escor ar y thy
wyd velly y bu marw. Ac velly y lladawd ef y vam
ar mab a rodet arnaw. ac y dodet brutus ar nav.
A gwedy meithrin y mab ac bot yn bymthec
mlwyd. dwyn a wnaeth y dat y gwas yn y gyt yn
y dat yn hely. Ac val yd oedynt velly nachaf
karw yn kerdet heibyaw. Sef a oruc brutus a ne
lu bwa a gellwg saeth ac yn keissaw llad y karw
y brathawd y dat ar saeth y a dan y vron ac y
bu marw. Ac velly y lladawd ef y dat. A gwedy
marw y dat or eglwyt hwnnw y deholes gwyr yr
eidal brutus. kanyt oed deilwg gynnwyt yn
brenhin arnunt gwr a ladei gyflauan kyn
ent a llad y vam ac dat. A gwedy y dehol y daeth
yntev hyt yg groec ac y gwelas gwelygord o etif
ned elenus vap priaf yg keithiwet y dan ban
drassus brenhin groec. Pyrr vab achelarwy
a dugassei y genedyl honno gantaw gwedy dis

but also by establishing schools and fostering a culture of scholarship and wisdom. In the preface to an Anglo-Saxon version of *De consolatione philosophiae* ('The Consolation of Philosophy') by Boethius, he is credited with having produced the translation himself and is portrayed as a ruler who looks to philosophy for guidance (**figure 50**):[160]

> King Alfred was the interpreter of this book, and turned it from book Latin into English, as it is now done. Now he set forth word by word, now sense from sense, as clearly and intelligently as he was able, in the various and manifold worldly cares that oft troubled him in mind and body.[161]

The translation of this late Roman work shows how English was being refined through Latin by King Alfred's circle and connected to the most important currents of medieval Western thought. The ideal of translating partly 'word by word' and partly 'sense from sense' points to an approach that accommodated adaptation and allowed texts to become conduits for cultural transformation.

The Norman conquest in 1066 brought a further wave of immigration, with a decisive shift in power structures that was mirrored in the use of French by the nobility and the administration, and in an influx of French words into the (Middle) English that continued to be used by much of the population. Words were gradually assimilated from French – and ultimately Latin or indeed Greek – especially in such fields as 'government' (from Old French *governement*), the 'military' (from French *militaire* or Latin *militaris*) and areas associated with 'politics' (with 'policy' deriving from Old French *policie*, while the semantic field as a whole draws on Greek *polis* and *politeia*). The differing social status of the cultures is still reflected in the difference between the lower register of Germanic words such as 'home' (related to German *Heim*) and more formal, high-register equivalents like 'residence' (from Old French, or Latin *residentia*). Borrowing and translation will have united in day-to-day life to enrich the language and differentiate meanings, creating a more supple medium of expression in the process.

Our modern image of the Middle Ages is shaped by tales of heroic knights and their illustrious deeds – stories that were shared across Europe through manifold processes of translation, adaptation, appropriation and elaboration. Among the earliest are the legends surrounding Charlemagne, epitomized in the genre of the *chanson de geste*, 'song of deeds', of which the most famous

52 Welsh myths and legends, poetry and history make up one of the four Ancient Books of Wales: *The Red Book of Hergest* or *Llyfr Coch Hergest* (c.1375–1425). It contains early sources for the Arthurian legend that inspired Wales and captured the European imagination, including a translation of Geoffrey of Monmouth's Latin *History of the Kings of Britain* into Welsh. Jesus College, MS. 111, fol. 8v. By kind permission of Jesus College, Oxford.

is *La Chanson de Roland* ('The Song of Roland').[162] Composed around 1100, the poem recounts the military exploits and eventual death of its impetuous protagonist with his famous 'olifant' (hunting horn made from an elephant's tusk) in Charlemagne's campaign against the Saracens (**figure 51**).

It became the French foundational epic, celebrating the patriotism of a hero who fought with his emperor for sweet France, *dulce France*. It might seem ironic that the earliest surviving manuscript, written in the second quarter of the twelfth century, evidently originated in England and has resided in Oxford since the thirteenth century. Yet it is in Anglo-Norman, a variety of the Norman dialect of French that was used in England during this period when Norman culture, too, was becoming increasingly influential in English lands.

A mysterious feature of the 'Oxford Roland' is the periodic inclusion of the letters 'AOI' in the right-hand margin, which occurs in no other medieval manuscript. Early hypotheses assumed it to be a notation relating to the oral recitation and performance of the poem, perhaps giving an instruction to a minstrel, or signalling a potential omission to shorten the time of some five hours otherwise needed for a complete rendition. A more recent explanation is that the manuscript was not intended for use in performance and that the letters – perhaps an abbreviation of Latin *avoco* – mean 'I divert' and signal the scribe's departure from (now lost) earlier versions of the poem.[163]

While the Matter of France focuses on Charlemagne's conquests in continental Europe, the Matter of Britain centres on a leader with very slight, if any, historical roots. The legendary leader Arthur supposedly defended his people against the Saxons in the post-Roman era between 400 and 600 CE, with his claim to world fame resting above all on the chivalrous prowess and love life of his knights while the magical Merlin provides supernatural spice. Arthur inspired and enriched many Celtic and English tales, with his court being located variously in Cornwall, Wales and further north, but the influence of the Arthurian legends extended far beyond Britain, capturing the imagination of poets across Europe.

The seminal work that inspired some of the greatest poets of the Middle Ages in France, Germany and other parts of Western Europe was Geoffrey of Monmouth's *Historia Regum Britanniae* ('History of the Kings of Britain'), written around 1136. He was a cleric who is likely to have come from Wales or the Marches of Wales, and he claims to have used various sources for his work, including Welsh tales, while certainly drawing extensively on his

53 *The Annals of Inisfallen* are associated with the monastery on Innisfallen Island, Killarney (late eleventh to fifteenth century). They chronicle world and Irish history from a Munster perspective in Latin and Irish. Monks established a veritable industry of translation, mediating between global Latin and the local vernacular in disseminating Christian texts. Bodleian Library, MS. Rawl. B. 503, fol. 24v.

Domnall hua Uactarain
dofec. Hua Ccid ferleigind
do marbad do Airaib.
Mac Donnocain ri iar-
Ciaraige do marbad.
Dirgal choichisid i Thersid b
isin bliadain-sin co Domnall
na toirchi. Cairu ra-
caiti achaid bo dor.
Muirchertach hua Angil
ri Cheneoil Fergail mor.
Amalgaid mac Flaind
ri Callraige do mar.
do chnaran 7 do bruinaid.
Kl. En. f. [illegible]
Hua Flaind chuia co-
marba Ailbi [illegible]
Hua Cairpre ... Flaind
ri Eoganachta Locha
Lein do marbad. Hua
Cerbaill rigdamna
Irlan do marbad.
Dal Lac arid fer ta
dobrissed don taid ro
gelain. Art hua Ruai-
rc ri Connacht do m-
arbad. Hua Bilcoci
ferleigind Arda Macha
quieuit in Christo. ... hUachi
Kl. En. f. ... 7 hoss
fri. Snechta mor
isin bliadain-sin o feil Brig-
te co feil Patraicc

connaclos nec imbuasi
arslaiti. Niall hua
Ruairc ri Breifne do
marbad. Comarba Br-
igti dormiuit.
Kl. En. feria ... xii. [illegible]
Mac Conmara do mar-
bad u...ill. Clothna
muinech comarba Ailbi
quieuit in Christo. Inis Locha Eirne do thogail
7 a innriud do hu Cho-
buir do rig Connacht.
Hua Cuill primeces Her-
[illegible] dofec. Fedmat
[illegible] Maccnaric. Ai-
chir mac Domnaill do m-
arbad. Sadb ingen
Briain dofec. Fin.
Kl. En. f. dom. [illegible]
Amalgaid comarba
Patraicc dofec. Assid
mac Domnaill ri Cor-
cu Baiscind do marbad.
Conchobur hua Cind
.i. la hua ndaill gab
faelad do marbad.
Slogad la mac in Briain
co tuc gialla Laigen
7 Osraige ... [illegible]
Kl. En. f. ... 7 iiii. Hua
Cairn mor oc mac Bri...
Mac Cathail ri ... rua
dri do chenntruich dofec. b

hu Chonchobuir do rig
Connacht. Cell dara
do loscud fecht la ac 7
durthech. 7 Glend Uisen
do loscud isin bliadain
chetna. Cluain mac Nois
do chreachad fa thri do
nOsraighaib. Maelan
fer leigind Cluana Iraird quieuit.
Conall fer leigind Cille
mo Chelloc quieuit.
Mac ceticid fer leigind ri Ua
... Gall gab mor
Kl. En. f. ... 7 xii. [illegible]
Mac Bricc ri Uathfirte
do marbad. Mac Cath-
ail do dallad do Aed
hu Chonchobuir. Uile-
maige Adair do char-
cair do Aed hu Conco-
buir. Diarmait hua
Briain do marbad do
Murchad hu Briain.
Hua Bruic rigdamna
Osraige do marbad i tai-
bac ... mor do mac
Abraich 7 do fuc fri
dechitrai ... [illegible]
Slugad la mac in Briain
co loch Eirne ... Con-
chobuir 7 no cotuc
gialla na hAirthir.
Kl. En. f. ... [illegible]

inventive imagination. While the choice of Latin facilitated an enormously varied development of Arthurian mythology beyond Britain, translations into indigenous vernaculars embedded the adventures of King Arthur and his Knights of the Round Table in British literature and eventually other media including film. One of the most famous translations is in Welsh and included in the celebrated *Red Book of Hergest*, preserved in the holdings of Jesus College, Oxford (**figure 52**);[164] here Geoffrey's work connects with the *Mabinogion*, the earliest and most famous collection of Welsh prose tales.

For modern readers it can be frustrating to find that our understanding of the early history of the British Isles is to a considerable extent dependent on the transmission and translation of fragile texts and fictitious tales that move across shifting groups and territories, with individuals and groups adapting the material to new purposes and settings. Yet much of what informs our understanding of the post-Roman era and still prompts new excavations and discoveries would not have survived at all without the enthusiasm for a good story that sustained the rich and international literature of the Middle Ages. Moreover, adaptation and translation of texts contributed in multifarious ways to articulating the identities of nations and regions, interest groups and cultural communities.

Monks and nuns played a vital part in preserving legacies and recording important occurrences and intellectual developments. While illustrated manuscripts can give us vivid pictures of real and imagined people, and events and situations, the innumerable translations produced in monasteries and convents afford glimpses of cultural transformations that happen through linguistic exchange, and illuminate the pathways of ideas across communities and territories. For example, the *Annals of Inisfallen* give us a rare insight into the world-view of the community of monks on Innisfallen in Lough Leane, a lake in Killarney (**figure 53**). They moved continuously between Latin, the lingua franca of the Church, and the Irish language spoken by the Munster people around their monastery, founded in 640 to take forward the project of Christianization introduced to Ireland by Saint Patrick and other missionaries in the fifth century. In their chronicle the scribes envision the history of the world from the point of view of Munster and connect it with the world they know first-hand. It was their ability to read, write and translate that allowed them to give that global history imaginary shape and make it meaningful for their community.

Celtic languages – sustaining distinctive identities

Celtic languages have formed part of the linguistic fabric of the British Isles for longer than the Germanic languages, Latin and French from which English evolved. The Celtic languages continued to thrive – mainly in Scotland, Wales, Cornwall and Ireland – from Roman times onwards, interacting with the languages and varieties spoken in the central parts of Great Britain but retaining distinctive identities. With strengthening control of central government, Celtic languages increasingly came under pressure, though their role has varied enormously over time across the different countries of the British Isles. Their status continues to be an issue that engages hearts and minds today, often becoming the focus not only of differences with Westminster but also a driver of internal division, as in the contested role of Irish in Northern Ireland. In such contexts, the argument that bilingualism should be enshrined in public life is driven not by practical communication needs but by the conviction that language embodies and represents identity (**figures 54** and **55**).

In these debates we can trace two complementary tendencies: on the one hand the trajectory of abandoning the 'native' language or variety in favour of a language that is more widely spoken and/or dominant, and on the other the urge to preserve the minority language – by philological work, cultural activity, educational policies and political activism. Pressure from 'outside' may indeed strengthen the perceived value of the language as the medium through which a particular group can form and articulate its sense of self and its view of the world.

An urge to preserve distinctiveness is a powerful force in motivating scholarly work designed to record a language, and make its value tangible by giving it lasting written form and a shared standard. Etymological explanations, and translations into a more widely shared, politically dominant or culturally prestigious language, frequently play an important part in situating and enriching the language. The work of grammarians and lexicographers thereby becomes an important resource for writers, who contribute to enhancing the language's status and allow readers to appreciate its beauty and value.

54 and **55** These signs are a reminder that the British Isles have never been monolingual. Today, Wales has two official languages with equal status. In Ireland, the Irish language – or Gaelic – is the first official language, though the second official language, English, is far more widely spoken. In Northern Ireland, meanwhile, the status of the Irish language is a highly political issue at the heart of debates about cultural and national identity. Shutterstock / Wikimedia Commons.

To howk to dig. fodere.

To bend to drink. Bibere. sumere largos hau
to bend originairement signifie plier Or se plie on s
Hantil ou Hankil much. Beaucoup. multum.

Shairn Cow's dung. Bovium Excrementum.

Grise Pig. Cochon de lait.

Lave The rest. Reliquuum. (a leave linque

To birsle ou Birstle to toast. rotir a un certa
degré.

Teat a little – un peu.

To Ted To scatter. de comme on fa
avec le ~~[illegible]~~ foin, pendant qui se seche
(peutetre de Teat un peu. parceque qu
on ; on le mette en petites quan

Drih. wearisom tediosus

Gab. mouth Bouche. Os. En anglois
dit gape i.e. ouvrir la bouche comm
disent aussi les Hollandois.

Bairn Child. Enfant.

Swither doubt. dubitatio.

Powney A little horse parvus equus ut Poney
– sed etiam a Turkey. Dindon.

Yole ou Yoal. a Skuller. naviculum

Chield a lad. un Garçon. Child as un bon en

To Stou to cut. scindere.

[illegible] tete la [illegible]
[illegible] pas de ce phrase ils disent le Tou.

56 John Jamieson's 'Specimen of a dictionary of the Scottish language', produced during his work on the *Etymological Dictionary of the Scottish Language* (1808), indicates the importance of translation in making the vocabulary of a minority language accessible beyond the circle of its speakers. Bodleian Library, MS. Eng. lang. d. 68, fols 12v–13r.

The eighteenth and early nineteenth centuries were an important period for philology across Western Europe and laid foundations for the standardized languages we take for granted today as linguistic markers of nation-states. Users of English still build on the pioneering achievements of Samuel Johnson (1709–1784). His career benefited from his increasingly influential position in London, political centre of the British nation, from which Johnson drew the authority to establish a standard that would be accepted throughout the realm. By contrast, the Scotsman John Jamieson (1759–1838) produced a dictionary of 'the Scottish *Language*' in 1808 that is motivated by the need to defend it against the increasing cultural dominance of its linguistic neighbour to the south; for, unlike Scottish Gaelic, spoken primarily in the Highlands, Scots was considered by many as being 'on a level with the different provincial dialects of the English'.[165]

It is worth dwelling on Jamieson's groundbreaking project of recording and standardizing Scots (**figure 56**), for even the title of his dictionary elucidates the complex role language plays as a medium that both connects a people with others and distinguishes it from them. Language embodies and facilitates interplay between many aspects of identity – past and present, geographical and political, cultural and national, ritual and institutional:

> An Etymological Dictionary of the Scottish Language: illustrating the words in their different significations, by examples from ancient and modern writers; shewing their affinity to those other languages, and especially the northern; explaining many terms, which, though now obsolete in England, were formerly common to both countries; and elucidating national rites, customs, and institutions, in their analogy to other nations.[166]

Jamieson's preface highlights the role lexicography plays in translating a language across time from one generation to the next, in order to 'render … intelligible' texts ranging from legal documents to the great literary works of the people's ancestors.[167] His analysis highlights tensions that are characteristic of processes of interaction between lingua francas and more local languages, and he articulates pressures that shape the role of the Celtic languages in Britain to this day.

The political, cultural and, not least, linguistic diversity of Britain has continued to evolve, and the interplay between English and Celtic languages has been made even more complex by different waves of immigration over the centuries from the politically connected countries of colonial rule, the Commonwealth and continental Europe, and by the exchange – not least through film, television and the Internet – between Britain and the United States.

Living diversity

Every British passport testifies to a diversity that remains in flux and raises a multitude of questions. It gives the bearer the right to 'pass without let' – but what does that now obsolete phrase mean?[168] What is the UK's relationship with a 'Europe' of which it geographically forms a part but which a majority of British voters declared they wished to 'leave' in 2016? And what is the status today of all those European languages that entered the small print of British passports in the process of European integration – how do they compare in ongoing practical importance in England, Scotland, Wales and Northern Ireland with the languages that became part of modern Britain with migration from Commonwealth countries? Should children in Wales be taught Welsh as their first language even though English is a more useful passport to the world? Does Irish currently play a more prominent part in Northern Irish homes than Polish or Urdu?

Britain tends to see itself as monolingual. Yet many schools and places of work are multilingual spaces – not only in London, Birmingham and Glasgow but also in Oxford, Bangor and Leicester. And even within English, people move between a standard lingua franca and local languages or dialects, between varieties spoken in public and official contexts and varieties spoken with friends and family. The English spoken in Liverpool is diverse within the city and very different from the English spoken in Truro or Belfast. American films may be fully intelligible for British people but is it 'their' language? The Internet and social media have created networks in which 'global English' is complex and fluid as it interacts with a multitude of local and global Englishes.

This diversity means that translation is an intrinsic part of our daily lives. Indeed it becomes second nature to all of us from an early age. We learn to translate when we negotiate the gap between children's language and adult language, when we mediate between friends who come from different backgrounds or parts of the country, or when we translate an unfamiliar piece of jargon into the words we know. For many British families,

57 *following spread* Sign language builds on the gestural, performative and consequently visible aspect of language. While standardization has increased the communicative reach of, for example, British Sign Language (BSL) and American Sign Language (ASL), other varieties have developed – or been invented – especially among minority groups excluded from mainstream educational provision. © Rinkoo Barpaga (Artist), Nick Drew (Design), Rajinder Dudrah (Curator, Birmingham City University), Simon Redgrave (Co-curator, Punch Records).

www.punch-records.co.uk

BRITISH SIGN LANGUAGE

Eight Examples

LIE

A false statement made with deliberate intent to deceive.

Hand up against chin with forefinger outstretched. Mouths the word "lie" while moving hand away.

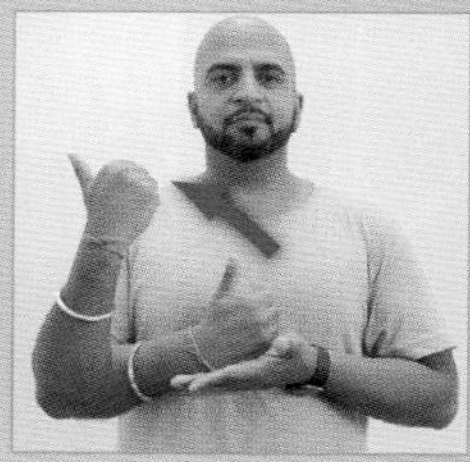

BRILLIANT

Satisfactory in quality, quantity, or degree.

Hand with raised thumb on open hand moves upwards.

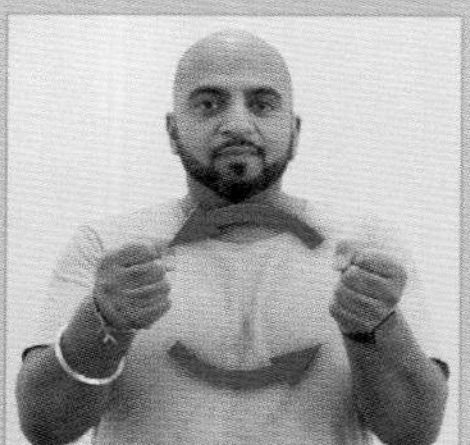

DRIVE

To convey in a vehicle.

Both hands grasp an imaginary driving wheel and move in a circular motion.

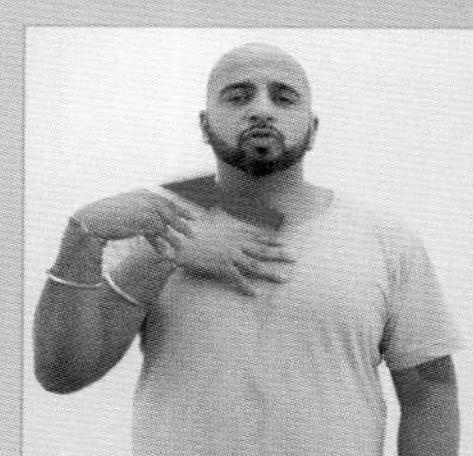

JEWELLERY

Articles of gold, silver, precious stones, etc., for personal adornment.

Hand moves across top of body to denote wearing of jewellery.

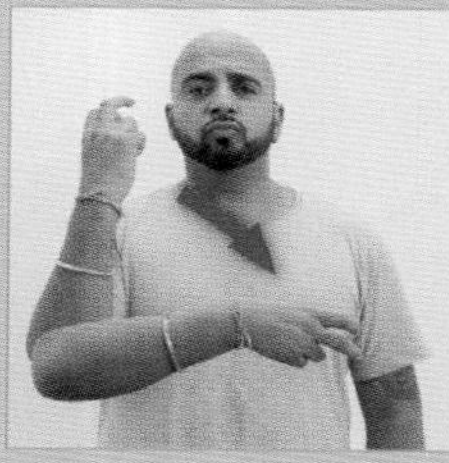

DRUNK

State in which one's physical and mental faculties are impaired by excess of alcohol.

Fingers extended to make 'V' shape. Make backward and forward movements.

GREAT

Wonderful, first-rate, very good.

Same as BRILLIANT, showing the limitation of conveying slightly different meanings in sign language.

RELAX

To release or bring relief from the effects of tension, anxiety.

Hands make repeated backward and forward movements with fingers outstretched.

COMPLETE

The act of achieving attainment or accomplishment.

Both hands raised with thumb outstretched move downwards.

www.punch-records.co.uk

URBAN SIGN LANGUAGE

Eight Equivalents

BULLSHIT

Not believing something someone says.

Thumb touching middle finger on one hand snaps down with fingers outstretched.

COOL, SICK

Cool, tight, wicked, sick, sweet, nice, etc.

Slight open hand gesture. This one is all in the facial expression!

DRIVE

To drive a car in a "cool" way like a "gangster".

Hand simulating holding a driving wheel with one arm stretched out on car door and turning it with small moves.

BLING

Jamaican slang denoting expensive, ostentatious clothing or jewellery, or materialistic attitudes.

Both hands outstretched and indicating neck or clothes.

PISSED

Out of your head on alcohol.

Hand touching side of the head with a small round twisting movement to indicate pain.

POW, GREAT!

Expressing the sound of a blow or gunshot, cool.

Hand raised with pointing finger symbolising a gun then pointing forward to symbolise shooting.

CHILL

Hang loose.

Hands outstretched with palms facing down and slightly outwards.

SMASHED IT!

Achievement, make progress or perform in a "cool" way.

First finger of both hands pointing towards signer then coming forward to point forward.

translation between very different languages is an everyday activity if one or more family members grew up in another country or perhaps use sign language (**figure 57**).[169]

How many languages are spoken in the British Isles today, and how many people speak them? The answer is that we have no idea. Even the 2011 UK census did not give us that information – because it arguably asked the wrong question: 'What is your main language?'[170] Some 4.2 million people (7.7 per cent) reported a main language other than English (or, in Wales, other than English or Welsh), with Polish being the most widespread 'other' main language, followed by Punjabi and Urdu. But the questionnaire took no account of bilingualism or multilingualism: individuals might have two or more 'main languages', different languages might be 'main' depending on the context, or a language might not be the 'main' one for practical purposes but nonetheless play an important role in their everyday lives.

In recent decades, policymakers in national, regional and local government, and in areas such as health, immigration and housing, have engaged in different ways with the need to reach a population that is linguistically as diverse as it is culturally. Languages other than English are spoken in many homes, and documentation in English officialese as well as advice on complex matters such as tenancy rights and preventive health screening can be hard to understand, especially for people whose first language is not English, or who have a disability that precludes access to written documentation.

If you are unable to read this letter or the enclosed leaflet because English is not your first language, please ask someone who speaks English to telephone the Freephone helpline on **0800 707 60 60** for further information and help.

Albanian	Në rast se nuk jeni në gjendje ta lexoni këtë letër apo broshurën bashkëngjitur për shkak se anglishtja nuk është gjuha juaj e parë, ju lutemi t'i kërkoni dikujt që flet anglisht që të telefonojë linjën e ndihmës falas në 0800 707 60 60 për informata të mëtejshme dhe ndihmë.
Arabic	إن كنت غير قادر على قراءة الرسالة المرفقة أو النشرة لأن اللغة الإنكليزية ليست لغتك الأم، فيرجى منك أن تطلب من أحد الأشخاص الذين يجيدون تحدث اللغة الإنكليزية الاتصال بنا على الهاتف المجاني رقم 0800 707 60 60 من أجل الحصول على معلومات إضافية ومساعدة.
Bengali	ইংরেজী আপনার প্রথম বা মাতৃভাষা না হওয়ার কারণে আপনি যদি এই চিঠি বা সঙ্গে দেওয়া প্রচারপত্র পড়তে না পারেন, তাহলে ইংরেজী বলতে পারে এমন কাউকে বলুন আরো বিস্তারিত তথ্য ও সাহায্যের জন্য 0800 707 60 60 নম্বরে ফ্রীফোন বা বিনা খরচের হেল্পলাইন-এ টেলিফোন করতে।
Chinese	如果你由於英文並非你的母語而不能瞭解此信件或隨附小冊的內容，請要求一位懂得英語的人士代你致電免費電話輔助熱線，號碼 0800 707 60 60，以獲得更多資料及協助。
Farsi	اگر انگلیسی زبان مادری شما نیست و قادر به خواندن این نامه و برگه همراه آن نمی‌باشید لطفاً از کسی که انگلیسی صحبت می‌کند تقاضا کنید که با شماره مجانی ۰۸۰۰۷۰۷۶۰۶۰ تماس گرفته و اطلاعات و راهنمایی لازم را دریافت دارند.
Gujarati	જો અંગ્રેજી તમારી પહેલી ભાષા ન હોવાને કારણે તમે આ પત્ર અથવા આ સાથે બીડેલી પત્રિકા વાંચી ન શકતાં હો, તો કૃપા કરીને અંગ્રેજી બોલતી કોઈ વ્યક્તિને કહો કે વધારે માહિતી અને મદદ મેળવવા માટે મફત ફોન હેલ્પલાઈન 0800 707 60 60 પર ફોન કરે.
Hindi	अगर आप इस पत्र या संलग्न पत्रक को नहीं पढ़ पाते हैं क्योंकि अंग्रेज़ी आपकी आम बोल-चाल की भाषा नहीं है, तो कृपया अंग्रेज़ी बोलने वाले किसी व्यक्ति से कहिये कि अधिक जानकारी और मदद के लिये फ्रीफ़ोन हैल्पलाइन (Freephone helpline) का यह नंबर मिलायें 0800 707 60 60.
Polish	Jeśli nie jesteś w stanie przeczytać ten list czy załączoną ulotkę ponieważ angielski nie jest Twoim ojczystym językiem, poproś kogoś kto mówi po angielsku żeby zadzwonił do bezpłatnej infolinii, pod numer 0800 707 60 60, po więcej informacji i pomoc.
Portuguese	Se o inglês não for a sua primeira língua e não conseguir, portanto, ler esta carta ou o folheto anexo, peça a uma pessoa que fale inglês que telefone para a linha verde de ajuda 0800 707 60 60 para obter mais informação e assistência.
Punjabi	ਜੇ ਤੁਸੀਂ ਇਹ ਖ਼ਤ ਜਾਂ ਨਾਲ ਭੇਜਿਆ ਗਿਆ ਪਰਚਾ ਇਸ ਕਰਕੇ ਨਹੀਂ ਪੜ੍ਹ ਸਕਦੇ, ਕਿਉਂਕਿ ਅੰਗਰੇਜ਼ੀ ਤੁਹਾਡੀ ਪਹਿਲੀ ਭਾਸ਼ਾ ਨਹੀਂ ਹੈ; ਤਾਂ ਕਿਰਪਾ ਕਰਕੇ ਕਿਸੇ ਅੰਗਰੇਜ਼ੀ ਬੋਲਣ ਵਾਲੇ ਨੂੰ ਕਹੋ ਕਿ ਉਹ ਹੋਰ ਜਾਣਕਾਰੀ ਅਤੇ ਮਦਦ ਲੈਣ ਲਈ ਫ੍ਰੀਫ਼ੋਨ ਹੈਲਪਲਾਈਨ ਨਾਲ ਨੰਬਰ 0800 707 60 60 'ਤੇ ਕਾੱਲ ਕਰੋ।
Somali	Haddii aadan akhrisan karayn warqaddaan ama buugyaraha kan la socda maxaa yeelay Ingiriisiga ayaanan luqaddaada hooyo ahayn, fadlan qof Ingiriisi ku hadla haddaba weydiiso in uu soo waco khadka caawinta ee Lambarkan bilaashka ah 0800 707 60 60 si aad uga hesho warbixin iyo caawimo dheeraad ah.
Turkish	İngilizce'nin anadiliniz olmaması nedeniyle bu mektubu veya ilişikteki broşürü okuyamayacak olursanız, daha fazla bilgi ve yardım için, lütfen, İngilizce bilen birisinden, ücretsiz olarak telefon edilebilen 0800 707 60 60 numaralı yardım hattını aramasını rica edin.
Urdu	اگر آپ اس خط کو یا ساتھ بھیجے جانے والے لیف لیٹ کو نہیں پڑھ سکتے کیونکہ انگریزی آپ کے استعمال کی پہلی زبان نہیں ہے، تو براہ کرم کسی انگریزی بولنے والے شخص سے کہیے کہ مزید معلومات اور مدد کے لئے فری فون ہیلپ لائن کو 0800 707 60 60 پر فون کرے۔

58 Over the last few decades UK society has become increasingly multilingual in ways that are not always visible when the 'other' language is spoken mainly in the home. Organizations in fields such as immigration, health, housing and education vary in the extent to which they provide for linguistic diversity. While some rely increasingly on the availability of digital translation tools, this health screening letter actively seeks to reach members of the population beyond those who are confident with English. Royal Surrey County Hospital NHS Foundation Trust.

The 1990s and 2000s saw documentation increasingly being made available in a wide range of languages, and at best this practice continues (**figure 58**).[171] Yet cuts in public spending have contributed to authorities often relying instead on individuals fending for themselves. The availability of Google Translate – sometimes supported proactively by publicly available translation and interpretation services – on the one hand provides a practical alternative to resource-intensive provision of multilingual information, and on the other acts as a fig-leaf for relying solely on the communicative efficacy of English. However, recognition that communication with all parts of the population is vital has also prompted a more systematic approach to communicating practical information in 'plain English' and using pictograms where appropriate.

While linguistic diversity has been increasing across the British Isles, especially but by no means exclusively in cities and towns, local varieties of English continue to evolve. Moreover, 'global' English is continually changing the languages spoken within the United Kingdom and Ireland. Just as trade fuelled language change from the Dark Ages onwards, business and commerce are important drivers of change as companies seek to establish themselves on the global stage (**figure 59**).[172] Meanwhile artists, too, respond in highly inventive ways to the rich opportunities offered by evolving linguistic diversity. Indeed, innovative use of language(s) is a mark of our times as social media become a shared arena for articulating individual feelings and conducting human relationships. The dynamics of Babel are keeping people in touch with each other, and increasingly connect the British Isles to all corners of the world.

59 The Cheltenham-based Superdry brand fuses English with Japanese to establish its global credentials, incorporating two scripts used in Japanese. The Chinese characters mean 極 'extreme'; 度 'degree'; 乾 'dry on the outside'; 燥 'dry on the inside'. The Japanese characters inside the brackets しなさい mean 'do' (an imperative form). © Superdry.

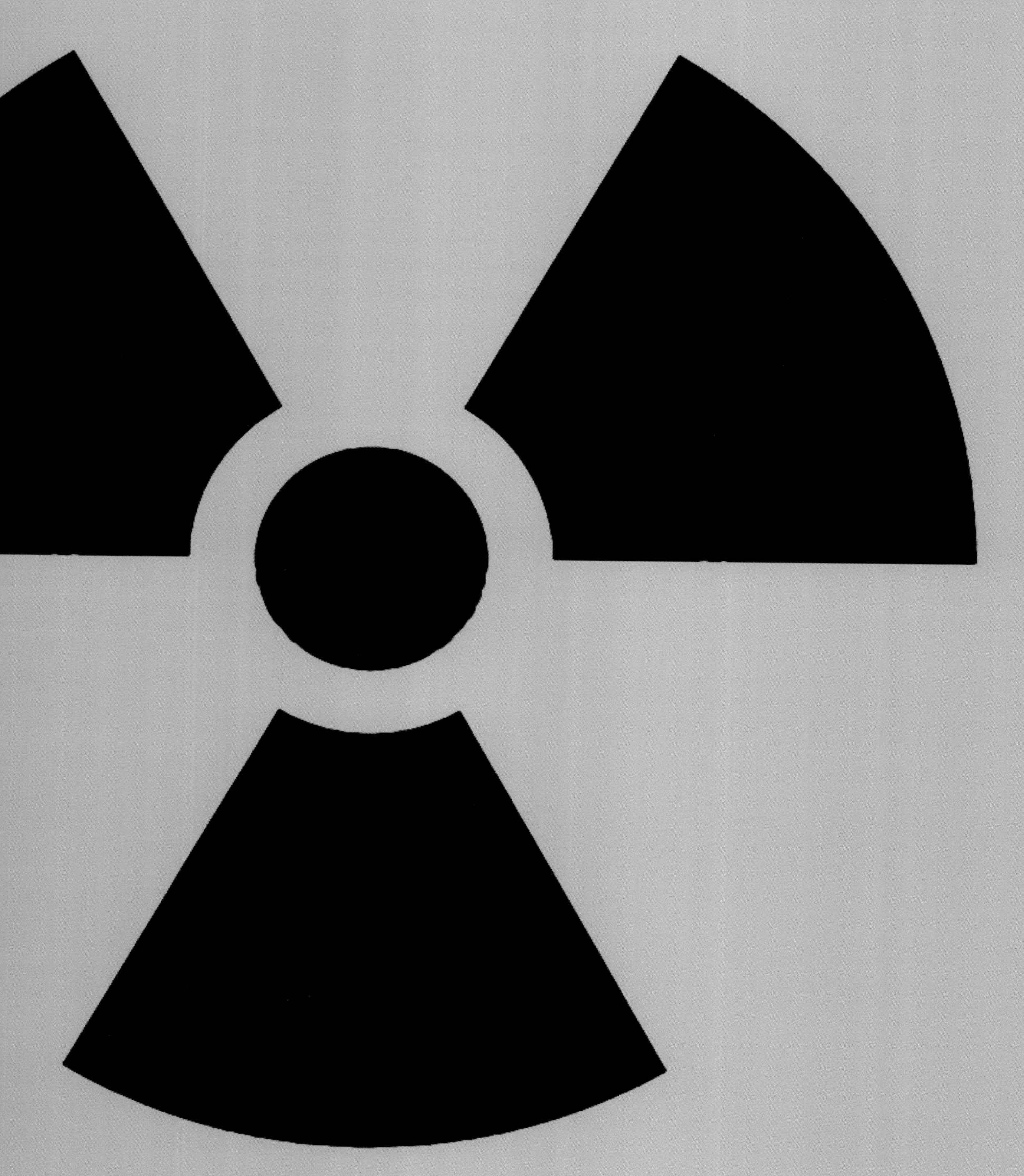

8 Languages Lost in Time

Dennis Duncan

In 1768 the antiquary Daines Barrington paid a visit to a small hut in the fishing village of Mousehole in Cornwall. Barrington hoped that he might find there a woman named Dolly Pentreath, who had been described to him as the last fluent speaker of the Cornish language. Introducing himself as having laid a wager that no such Cornish-speaker could be found, Barrington found himself the target of a sustained volley of abuse from the small woman in her late seventies:

> Dolly Pentraeth spoke in an angry tone of voice for two or three minutes, and in a language which sounded very much like Welsh.
>
> The hut in which she lived was in a very narrow lane, opposite two rather better cottages, at the doors of which two other women stood, who were advanced in years, and who I observed were laughing at what Dolly Pentraeth said to me.
>
> Upon this I asked them whether she had not been abusing me; to which they answered, very heartily, and because I had supposed she could not speak Cornish.[173]

The other women explained to Barrington that, having grown up ten years or so later than Pentreath, they were able to understand her, but could not readily speak Cornish themselves. Dolly, concluded Barrington, was the end of the line.

And yet, as any modern visitor to the county will know, Cornish is patently *not* a lost language. It is there in street signs (*Kernow a'gas dynergh* – Welcome to Cornwall), guidebooks, radio bulletins and magazines. You can even buy *Tintin* books translated into Cornish. To use Barrington's term, Cornish may have *expired* with Dolly Pentreath; but it was never *lost* in the sense that, given the will, new life could not be breathed into it.

Not all languages, however, are so resilient, or so lucky. For one thing, Cornish has a large body of writing surviving from the period when it was originally spoken, including grammars, bilingual dictionaries and books, like the Bible, which could be compared with their equivalents in other languages. A substantial written corpus like this means that a language can be reconstructed even after it ceases to be spoken. Nevertheless, not all writing can be so easily resurrected, and not every ancient text comes down to us in a writing system that is still familiar.

Before we can translate a piece of writing we need to know how to read it. That is, we need to understand what its symbols represent: whether they are sounds that can be strung together to form words (as with the essay you are reading now), or whether each symbol stands for a word on its own. If an unfamiliar writing system can be *deciphered*, and if it maps onto a language we know, then a text in that script can be translated: what might have been lost can be recovered.

Cracking Cretan Linear B

Two artefacts discovered on the island of Crete in the Mediterranean (**figures 60** and **61**) are among objects that bear writing in writing systems quite unlike our own alphabet.[174] Both date from the second millennium BCE – the period of the Minoan civilization. A hundred years ago both inscriptions were equally obscure; but the writing on the tablet has now been deciphered, while the script on the bowl – although similar – is in a writing system that is still impregnable to us, its meaning lost.

Both writing systems were discovered, in modern times, by the archaeologist Arthur Evans, keeper of the Ashmolean Museum in Oxford, who in the 1890s began a series of extensive excavations at Knossos on Crete. These excavations turned up a large number of artefacts that bore writing – carved, stamped or inscribed – on their surfaces. Evans was able to divide the writing that he found on Crete into three categories, used during different periods on the island. The earliest, dating roughly from 2000 to 1650 BCE, Evans would call 'hieroglyphic'. This is not to suggest that the writing is related to Egyptian script, but only that it consists of pictorial signs, often recognizable forms – a head, a hand, and so on. Overlapping slightly in period with the Cretan hieroglyphs, the second type of writing that Evans identified he termed 'linear script of Class A' – it is now known as Linear A. This dates from around 1800–1450 BCE. While not obviously pictorial like the hieroglyphs, some of its forms appear to have their origin

in the earlier shapes. Evans's final category, which we now call Linear B, was used from 1450 to 1200 BCE and inherits many forms from its predecessor. After Evans published these findings in *Scripta Minoa* (Clarendon, Oxford, 1909), a community of academic classicists went to work on deciphering the Cretan scripts. Four decades later, however, although some important progress had been made, all three scripts remained unreadable.

In 1936 an elderly Evans gave a talk on Cretan archaeology at Burlington House in London. In the audience was a schoolboy named Michael Ventris. As Ventris's future friend the classicist John Chadwick would have it, 'In that hour a seed was planted.'[175] On learning that Linear B was undeciphered, the fourteen-year-old Ventris resolved that he should be the one to crack it. Over the next decade and half, while Ventris served in the war, trained as an architect, married and raised two children, his passion as an amateur scholar of Linear B was undimmed. He kept up with the latest theories and

60 *left* Bowl excavated at Knossos on Crete. The inscription is in Linear A, used between *c.*1800 and 1450 BCE. © Ashmolean Museum, University of Oxford, AN 1938.872.

61 *above* A tablet excavated from Knossos on Crete. The inscription is in Linear B, used between *c.*1450 and 1200 BCE. © Ashmolean Museum, University of Oxford, AN 1910.211.

corresponded with the leading academic authorities, meanwhile testing out his own hypotheses. In the early 1950s he had a breakthrough.

Ventris noticed that while tablets bearing Linear B script had been unearthed both on Crete and at Pylos on the southern mainland of Greece, certain combinations of symbols only occurred on the Cretan tablets. This led him to wonder whether those site-specific combinations might be place names – a hypothesis that allowed him to decode these symbols as syllables that could then be fed back into other parts of the inscriptions. What Ventris discovered was that the Linear B tablets contained not an unknown language but an early form of Greek, written in signs that represented its syllables. The lost language on tablets like **figure 61** had been recovered.

What does this mean for Linear A? After all, the earlier writing is fairly similar in its symbols to Linear B. Unfortunately, such similarities would not necessarily indicate that the underlying languages are the same. (English and French, for example, use largely the same alphabet, but are not mutually intelligible.) It is thought that when conquerors from mainland Greece took control of Crete in around 1450 BCE the writing system already in use on the island was pressed into action to represent the language of the new settlers. As John Chadwick puts it, 'Linear B is the result of adapting the Minoan script for the writing of Greek'.[176] Cracking Linear B, then, does not allow us to read its predecessor. The earlier Minoan language – the language of Linear A and the Cretan hieroglyphs before it – remains obscure.

Communication across deep time

When we look at an artefact like **figure 60**, then, we can see that it has writing on it but it has lost its value as a meaningful communication. The message has endured across three and a half millennia, but we have lost the ability to understand it. Many of the inscriptions from the excavations at Knossos and elsewhere on Crete have survived through happenstance. Ordinarily, the clay tablets on which they were written would only have been baked in the sun – a process that would make them hard enough to store for a short time, but soft enough to be reused by being pounded in water. When the palace at Knossos was destroyed by fire, however, the intense heat from its burning timbers fired the tablets like pottery, making them hard enough to survive the elements ever since. These texts were not originally intended to last – or, rather, that they should come down to us across so many centuries was not one of their intended functions. But what if we *did* want to pass a message down the generations, not just across a distance of three millennia, but of thirty, or three hundred? How might we ensure that it remains readable in the far-off future: decipherable and translatable like Linear B, and not obscure like Linear A?

This is not merely idle speculation, but rather a question of critical importance in today's nuclear energy industry. The reason is that the production of nuclear power produces waste material which is highly radioactive and which needs to be disposed of in such a way that it will not present an immediate hazard to people or to the environment. The current method of disposal is to isolate the waste in deep geological repositories – that is, to bury it in specially created bunkers at depths of 300 metres or more underground. Since high-level waste can remain dangerously radioactive for hundreds of thousands of years, it is essential that these repositories are able to withstand the types of shock that might arise over such vast periods of time: earthquakes, the effects of glaciation in a future ice age, or accidental human interference. But how can one warn generations in the almost unimaginable future of the cataclysmic radiation risks that these sites present if tampered with? How, essentially, do you write 'DON'T DIG HERE' in a format which will still be meaningful in a hundred thousand years – far, far longer than the lifespan of any language we know? Is the fate of every language to become a lost language one day? If so, how can we send a message that will translate itself whenever it is in danger of losing its meaningfulness? The curse of Babel – the ancient problem of the multiplicity of languages – is being felt with a new urgency, and within the world's nuclear agencies a surprising range of consultants – philosophers, linguists, historians and psychologists – have been marshalled for their advice.

In many of their reports, the type of translation under consideration is *intermedial* – that is, translation broadly conceived, not into other words but into other forms entirely. The warning message can be 'translated' iconographically, as in the familiar black trefoil on a yellow background which has been used since the 1940s to represent radiation hazards (**figure 62**).[177] But icons cannot guarantee their meaningfulness; as in the case of the Cretan hieroglyphs, it is easy to imagine future readers unable to decipher

62 The radiation warning symbol, designed in 1946 at the University of California Radiation Laboratory in Berkeley, represents activity radiating from an atom. Wikimedia Commons.

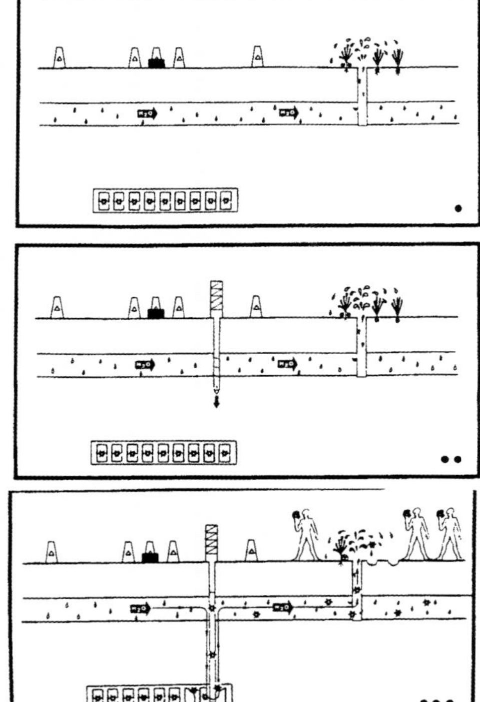

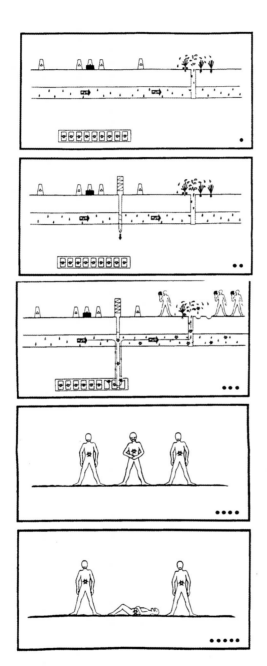

the icon's intent. Even a pictographic warning, like the one in **figure 63**, will not necessarily be universally intelligible.[178] The message could perhaps be encoded geologically: 'Brilliantly colored layers of materials laid beneath the surface may provide a warning when brought to the surface by conventional drilling.' Nevertheless, the report goes on to note that this type of sign 'might go unnoticed when drilling is performed by lasers').[179] Another surprising suggestion, put forward by a French sociologist and an Italian semiotician, is to breed a species of cat – 'radiation cats' or 'ray cats' – that would change colour when exposed to high radiation.[180] Here, then, the message is encoded biologically. There have been proposals for an architectural solution, as in Michael Brill's 'Landscape of Thorns' or 'Spikes Bursting Through Grid', both prepared for the 1993 report *Expert Judgment on Markers to Deter Inadvertent Human Intrusion into the Waste Isolation Pilot Plant* (**figures 64** and **65**).[181] There is an obvious objection here, however, as the behavioural psychologist Percy Tannenbaum has pointed out, that 'certain individuals are attracted to danger, particularly danger associated with challenge'.[182] We need only think of Howard Carter and Lord Carnarvon entering the tomb of Tutankhamun to be reminded that there is a certain adventuring mentality that regards the monumental 'Keep Out' structure merely as a challenge to be overcome.

Perhaps the best known and most influential report, however, Thomas Sebeok's *Communication Measures to Bridge Ten Millennia*, has translation 'proper' at its core. In the early 1980s, Sebeok, one of the pre-eminent academics in the field of semiotics, was commissioned by the US Human Interference Task Force to give his professional opinion on the problem of marking waste sites. The report he produced is a rather extraordinary and highly readable document.[183] It comes down to us in strikingly official covers, with a reassuring stamp informing us that, as of 2006, this information is 'publicly releasable'. The content, however, is anything but the dry officialese we might therefore expect. Among other things, Sebeok presents a brief and very good introduction to semiotics, a discussion of German Expressionist painting, and some grumbling about mistranslations of the early Greek poet Hesiod, before finally arriving in the last few pages at his main hypothesis for how a message might be passed on intact over 10,000 years. Sebeok's solution essentially involves two parts, which he terms the 'folkloric relay' and the 'atomic priesthood'. Let's look at these in turn.

The translation relay – the translation of a translation, to whatever number of iterations – is not a new idea. This was in essence the process when classical authors such as Euclid were lost, during the Dark Ages, to Western European readers, and rediscovered/retranslated via Arabic. But Sebeok does not have in mind simply that clear information about the nature and whereabouts of the waste sites be retranslated every few centuries. (This is part of his recommendation, but not the whole of it.) What the phrase 'folkloric relay' suggests is that where the detail is not important – and for most people a mere 'Don't dig here!' will suffice – narrative is a more robust vector than any specific language. Sebeok proposes that 'information be launched and artificially passed on into the short-term and long-term future with the supplementary aid of folkloristic devices, in particular a combination of an artificially created and nurtured ritual-and-legend'.[184] That is, rather than simply stating what the sites are and why they're dangerous, if a high-level warning about the location could be encoded into a myth or myth system, this message would be more likely to be passed on, not only between generations, but from one language to another. The 'Keep Out' message, then, should be inserted into folklore, an act which would be

> tantamount to laying a 'false trail', meaning that the uninitiated will be steered away from the hazardous site for reasons other than the scientific knowledge of the possibility of radiation and its implications; essentially, the reason would be accumulated superstition to shun a certain area permanently.[185]

It doesn't matter that people will avoid the site on the basis of (false) superstitious beliefs rather than (true) scientific ones. The effect is the same,

63 'Pictographic presentation of biohazardous caution message'. This sequence of images illustrates the effects through time of drilling at the isolation site. From William Hewitt, et al., *Reducing the Likelihood of Future Human Activities that Could Affect Geological High-Level Waste Repositories* (1984), p. 117. © US Department of Energy, Office of Scientific & Techincal Information: www.osti.gov/scitech/biblio/6799619.

64 and **65** *Landscape of Thorns* and *Spikes Bursting Through Grid*, view 2 (concepts by Michael Brill, art by Safdar Abidi), in Kathleen Trauth et al., *Expert Judgment on Markers to Deter Human Intrusion into the Waste Isolation Pilot Plant* (1993), pp. F-61 and F-66. These images, designed by Michael Brill for a 1993 report by Sandia National Laboratories, demonstrate how a message might be encoded architecturally. © Michael Brill, Safdar Abidi, Sandia National Laboratories. Images courtesy of Sue Weidemann.

and the durability of the principal message is the most important thing. Some genres stand a better chance of remaining in circulation. We pass on stories; we do not always pass on facts.

Not everybody, however, would be fed the folkloric version. Sebeok recommends that the actual truth about the nature of the radioactive site should be entrusted to 'a commission of knowledgeable physicists, experts in radiation sickness, anthropologists, linguists, psychologists, semioticians, and whatever additional expertise may be called for now and in the future'.[186] These experts should also be responsible for ensuring that the translation relay occurs so that the folkloric message is not forgotten by the wider population:

> The 'atomic priesthood' would be charged with the added responsibility of seeing to it that our behest [concerning the folkloric relay system] is to be heeded – if not for legal reasons, then for moral reasons, with perhaps the veiled threat that to ignore the mandate would be tantamount to inviting some sort of supernatural retribution.[187]

The terminology is almost mischievous: a 'priesthood' must inculcate a system of 'ritual-and-legend' in the wider public, using the 'veiled threat' of 'supernatural retribution' where necessary. *Communication Measures* is fascinating both for the insight it provides into the contemporary technological problem of nuclear waste management, and for its reading of the history of Christianity. A shrewd analysis of organized religion hovers discreetly behind most of what Sebeok proposes, from the successive retranslations of the central text and the use of awe-inspiring architecture to the establishment of an elite – a priesthood who are guardians of the true message – and the encoding of a lower-definition message in folklore.

To a certain extent Sebeok underplays all this – he doesn't mention the Bible explicitly, and suggests that he chose the phrase 'atomic priesthood' merely for 'dramatic emphasis'.[188] Yet in the similar reports which came after *Communication Measures* no one was fooled: the textual history of Christianity became one of the central paradigms of the emerging field of nuclear semiotics. Thus we find, for example, that a report with the rather academic title *The Vatican Archives: A Study of Its History and Administration* is the product of research commissioned by the Swedish Radiation Safety Authority.[189]

But perhaps the most astonishing and explicit reference to the power of the religious text to achieve the goals of the nuclear semioticians comes from the Norwegian professor of law Knut Selmer, in his remarks at a 1991 conference in Oslo on 'Transmittal of Information Over Extremely Long Periods of Time':

> It is my suggestion that the only possible way to influence human activity in a very distant future goes through religion. One must approach the leading circles of the great world religions, and persuade them that we are under an obligation to warn our distant descendants of the deadly dangers which we are creating in the environment. The danger symbols must be included in the set of holy symbols of each religion. The obligation to seek information and act upon it must be embodied in the central axioms. If the message could be given a form which was common to the world religions and which formed part of their rites and practices, one might hope that the message would survive and motivate people in a distant future.[190]

In Selmer's vision, the trick to maximizing the chances of a message's translation is to piggyback off those texts that have already shown themselves to be the most widely translated. But none of the religions Selmer has in mind is as old even as Linear A; all come up short by several orders of magnitude when compared to the timescale of radioactive decay in high-level waste. Beyond a few thousand years we are in uncharted territory, both linguistically and culturally. The Babel conundrum remains as pressing as it ever was.

Chapter 1

1 Philip Michael Sherman, *Babel's Tower Translated: Genesis 11 and Ancient Jewish Interpretation*, Brill, Leiden and Boston MA, 2013, p. 78.

2 The diagram is reproduced, with the kind permission of the authors, from Shahar Ronen, Bruno Gonçalves, Kevin Z. Hu, Alessandro Vespignani, Steven Pinker and César A. Hidalgo, 'Links that Speak: The Global Language Network and its Association with Global Fame', www.pnas.org/content/111/52/E5616, doi:10.1073/pnas.1410931111.

3 Mary Phil Korsak (trans.), *At the Start: Genesis Made New*, Doubleday, New York and London, 1993, pp. 41–2.

4 *Vetus testamentū multiplici lingua nūc primo impressum. Et imprimis Pentateuchus Hebraico Greco at[que] Chaldaico idiomate. Adiūcta vnicui[que] sua latina interpretatione. [Followed by] Nouum testamentum grece & latine [and] Vocabularium hebraicum at[que] chaldaicū totius veteris testamenti cū alijs tractatibus*, [Alcalá de Henares,] 1514–17.

5 Ibid., fols 1v–2r; James Kearney, *The Incarnate Text: Imagining the Book in Reformation England,* University of Pennsylvania Press, Philadelphia PA, 2009, p. 64.

6 Athanasius Kircher, *Turris Babel, sive Archontologia*, Amsterdam, 1679.

7 *The dictionary of syr Thomas Eliot*, London, 1538.

8 Jonathon Green, *Chasing the Sun: Dictionary-Makers and the Dictionaries they Made*, Pimlico, London, 1997, pp. 78–89; David Crystal, *The Stories of English*, Penguin Books, London, 2005, pp. 88–9; Stanford Lehmberg, 'Elyot, Sir Thomas (*c*.1490–1546)', *Oxford Dictionary of National Biography*, Oxford University Press, Oxford, 2004, online edition, January 2008, http://ezproxy-prd.bodleian.ox.ac.uk:2167/view/article/8782 (accessed 7 September 2017), doi:10.1093/ref:odnb/8782.

9 Green, *Chasing the Sun*, p. 81.

10 Robert Cawdry, *A Table Alphabeticall: conteyning and teaching the true writing, and vnderstanding of hard vsuall English wordes*..., London, 1604.

11 Janet Bately, 'Cawdrey, Robert (*b*.1537/8?, *d*. in or after 1604)', *Oxford Dictionary of National Biography*, Oxford University Press, Oxford, 2004, doi:10.1093/ref:odnb/69578; Crystal, *The Stories of English*, pp. 280–84; Green, *Chasing the Sun*, pp. 57, 149.

12 Codex Mendoza, Mexico, *c*.1541, Oxford, Bodleian Library, MS. Arch. Selden. A. 1.

13 Frances F. Berdan and Patricia Rieff Anawalt, *The Essential Codex Mendoza*, University of California Press, Berkeley, Los Angeles and London, 1997, pp. xi–xii.

14 D. Bleichmar, 'History in Pictures: Translating the *Codex Mendoza*', *Art History*, vol. 38, 2015, pp. 682–701, doi: 10.1111/1467-8365.12175.

15 Luis van Rooten, *Mots d'Heures: Gousse, Rames: The d'Antin Manuscript*, Viking Adult, New York, 1967.

16 For the first in the series, see Miles Kington, *Let's Parler Franglais*, Robson, London, 1979.

17 Francesco Colonna, *Hypnerotomachia Poliphili, ubi humana omnia non nisi somnium esse docet*, Venice, 1499.

18 Francesco Colonna, *Hypnerotomachia Poliphili*, ed. Marco Ariani and Mino Gabriele, 2 vols, Adelphi Edizioni, Milano, 1998, vol. 2, pp. lxv–vi.

19 Ibid., vol. 2, p. 602.

20 Ibid., vol. 1, pp. 41–2.

21 Anne Carson, *Nox*, New Directions, New York, 2009.

22 http://programmatology.shadoof.net/?translation (accessed 8 November 2017).

Chapter 2

23 Robert Recorde, *The Whetstone of Witte*..., London, 1557, sig. Ff1v.

24 John Wilkins, *An Essay Towards a Real Character, and a Philosophical Language*, London, 1668, p. 13.

25 Richard Wallace, 'Euclid', in Nigel Wilson (ed.), *Encyclopedia of Ancient Greece*, Routledge, London, 2005, pp. 278–9 (p. 278).

26 Euclid, *Elementa*, Books I–XV, Oxford, Bodleian Library, MS D'Orville 301.

27 Euclides, *Preclarissimus liber elementorum*, trans. Adelard of Bath, E. Ratdolt, Venice, 1482.

28 Euclid, *The Elements of Geometrie of the most Auncient Philosopher Euclide of Megara*, trans. Henry Billingsley, London, 1570, sig. ☞3r.

29 Francis Lodwick, *A Common Writing: Whereby two, although not understanding one the others Language, yet by the helpe*

thereof, may communicate their minds one to another, London, 1647, sig. A2v.

30 Ibid., sig. A2r.

31 Ibid., sig. A3r.

32 Wilkins, *An Essay Towards a Real Character*, p. 13.

33 Ibid.

34 Ibid., sig. b2v.

35 Ibid., p. 13.

36 Ibid., p. 414.

37 Ibid., p. 415.

38 Quoted in Dorothy Stimson, '"Ballad of Gresham Colledge"', *Isis*, vol. 18, no. 1, 1932, pp. 103–17 (p. 115).

39 L.L. Zamenhof, *An Attempt Towards an International Language*, trans. Henry Phillips Jr, Henry Holt, New York, 1889, p. 5.

40 Ibid., p. 6.

41 Ibid., p. 11.

42 Ibid., p. 12.

43 *Kondukanto al Belega Skotlando*. Higgie & Co., Rothesay, 1907.

44 Louis Couturat and Leopold Leau, *Complete Manual of the International Language* [i.e. Ido], Pitman, London, 1909, p. 3.

45 Otto Neurath, *International Picture Language: The First Rules of ISOTYPE*, Kegan Paul, London, 1936, p. 17.

46 Ibid., p. 13.

47 Ibid., p. 17.

48 Ibid.

49 Ibid., pp. 26–7.

50 Herman Melville, *Emoji Dick*, edited and compiled by Fred Benenson, trans. Amazon Mechanical Turk, New York, 2010.

Chapter 3

51 Tania Demetriou pointed this out to me. On divine speech in Greek tragedy, see Simon Goldhill, *How to Stage Greek Tragedy Today*, Chicago University Press, Chicago, 2007, pp. 189–224.

52 Theo Hermans, *The Conference of the Tongues*, St Jerome Publishing, Manchester and Kinderhook NY, 2007, pp. 1–3.

53 Dante Alighieri, *The Vision of Hell (Purgatory and Paradise)*, trans. H.F. Cary, illus. G. Doré, Cassell, London, 1893, p. 439.

54 Alfred, Lord Tennyson, *In Memoriam*, Edward Moxon, London, 1850, XCV.45–8.

55 Travis Zadeh, *The Vernacular Qur'an: Translation and the Rise of Persian Exegesis*, Oxford University Press in association with the Institute of Ismaeli Studies, London, 2012, pp. 1, 11.

56 Quoted and translated in Alasdair Watson, 'Untranslatability and the Qur'ān', M.Sc. thesis in Translation Studies, University of Edinburgh, 2007, p. 26; https://oxford.academia.edu/AlasdairWatson (accessed 13 November 2017).

57 Qur'ān, sixteenth century, Oxford, Bodleian Library, MS. Bodl. Or. 793.

58 Mañjuśrīnāmasaṅgīti, seventeenth or eighteenth century, Oxford, Bodleian Library, MS. Asiat. Misc. d. 8.

59 I am indebted to Camillo Formigatti for all the information in this paragraph.

60 *Ko Te Kawenata Hou: o to Tatou Ariki o te Kai Whakaora o Ihu Karaiti*, Ranana (NZ) [London], 1852.

61 https://biblesociety.org.nz/discover-the-bible/the-bible-in-maori; https://nzhistory.govt.nz/culture/missionaries/henry-williams-era (both accessed 13 November 2017).

62 Matthew Reynolds, *Translation: A Very Short Introduction*, Oxford University Press, Oxford, 2016, p. 69.

63 Fragment of a Greek translation of the Book of Ezra, fourth century CE, found in Oxyrhynchus. Oxford, Bodleian Library, MS. Gr. bib. g. 3(P)r.

64 Martha P.Y. Cheung (ed.), *An Anthology of Chinese Discourse on Translation*, Volume 1: *From the Earliest Times to the Buddhist Project*, St Jerome Publishing, Manchester, 2006, pp. 7–12; see also Reynolds, *Translation*, pp. 7–8.

65 Helen Moore and Julian Reid (eds), *Manifold Greatness: The Making of the King James Bible*, Bodleian Library, Oxford, 2011, pp. 91–2.

66 Ibid., pp. 14–22.

67 Ibid., p. 28.

68 Ibid., pp. 32–3.

69 Ibid., p. 91.

70 *The Holy Bible: Containing the Old Testament and the New. Authorised and appointed to be read in churches*. The Bishops' version, translation overseen by Matthew Parker [1568], London, 1602, with annotations in pencil for the King James Bible (1611). Oxford, Bodleian Library, Bib. Eng. 1602 B.1.

71 John 1.1–5, in William Tyndale, *The New Testament as it was Written, and Caused to be Written, by them which Herde yt*, [By me wyddowe of Christoffel [Ruremond] of Endhoue[n]], [Antwerpe,] 1534, n.p.

72 John 1.1–5, in *The Holy Bible, Conteyning the Old Testament and the New: Newly Translated out of the Originall tongues: & with the former Translations diligently compared and revised by her Maiesties speciall Comandment*, Robert Barker, London, 1611, n.p.

Chapter 4

73 For the influence of translation in English literature, see especially: Peter France et al. (eds), *The Oxford History of Literary Translation in English*, 4 vols to date (the beginnings to 1900), Oxford University Press, Oxford, 2005–10; Stuart Gillespie, *English Translation and Classical Reception: Towards a New Literary History*, Wiley-Blackwell, Chichester, 2011. For the role of Homer, see George Steiner and Aminadav Dykman (eds), *Homer in English*, Penguin, Harmondsworth, 1996; and

Edith Hall, *The Return of Ulysses: A Cultural History of Homer's Odyssey*, I.B. Tauris, London and New York, 2008.

74 Hawara Homer, second century CE, found in the Fayum area of Egypt in 1888, Oxford, Bodleian Library, MS. Gr. class. a. 1 (P).

75 See e.g. Martin Davies, *Aldus Manutius, Printer and Publisher of Renaissance Venice*, Arizona Center for Medieval and Renaissance Studies, Tempe AZ, 1999.

76 George Chapman, *The Odysseys of Homer* [vol. I], Nathaniell Butter, London, 1614.

77 See David Foxon, *Pope and the Eighteenth-Century Book Trade*, rev. and ed. J. McLaverty, Oxford University Press, Oxford, 1991.

78 In his 'Life of Pope', in *Samuel Johnson: The Lives of the Most Eminent English Poets: With Critical Observations on Their Works*, vol. IV, ed. Roger Lonsdale, Oxford University Press, 2006, p. 74.

79 *The Iliad of Homer*, trans. Alexander Pope, Whiston et al., London, 1771.

80 For Pope as Homeric translator, see Robin Sowerby, *The Augustan Art of Poetry: Augustan Translation of the Classics*, Oxford University Press, Oxford, 2006, pp. 228–336.

81 *The Iliad of Homer*, vol. I, trans. Alexander Pope, Bernard Lintot, London, 1715.

82 William Cowper, *The Iliad and Odyssey of Homer*, J. Johnson, London, 1791.

83 See Arnold A. Markley, *Stateliest Measures: Tennyson and the Literature of Greece and Rome*, University of Toronto Press, Toronto, 2004, pp. 101–3. For further Victorian debate about the use of hexameters to render Homer in English, see Y. Prins, 'Metrical Translation: Nineteenth-Century Homers and the Hexameter Mania', in Sandra Bermann and Michael Wood (eds), *Nation, Language, and the Ethics of Translation*, Princeton University Press, Princeton NJ, 2005, pp. 229–56.

84 See Stephen Harrison, 'Some Victorian Versions of Greco-Roman Epic', in Christopher Stray (ed.), *Remaking the Classics*, Duckworth, London, 2007, pp. 26–8.

85 James Joyce, *Ulysses*, intro. Stuart Gilbert, illus. Henri Matisse, Limited Editions Club, New York, 1935, p. 140.

86 See e.g. Thomas H. Carpenter, *Art and Myth in Ancient Greece: A Handbook*, Thames & Hudson, London, 1991.

87 Athenian black-figure lekythos (oil jar), 550–500 BCE, © Ashmolean Museum, University of Oxford, AN1943.249.

88 See Martin M. Winkler (ed.), *Troy: From Homer's Iliad to Hollywood Epic*, Blackwell-Wiley, Malden MA and Oxford, 2007.

89 See Joanna Paul, *Film and the Classical Epic Tradition*, Oxford University Press, Oxford, 2013, pp. 86–92.

90 For the effect on Classics in particular, see Edith Hall, 'Navigating the Realms of Gold: Translation as Access Route to the Classics', in Alexandra Lianeri and Vanda Zajko (eds), *Translation and the Classic: Identity as Change in the History of Culture*, Oxford University Press, Oxford, 2008, pp. 315–40.

91 See Jeremy Lewis, *Penguin Special: The Life and Times of Allen Lane*, Penguin, London, 2006.

92 See Hall, 'Navigating the Realms of Gold', p. 330.

93 E.V. Rieu, *Homer: The Odyssey*, Penguin, Harmondsworth, 1946, p. vii.

94 Ibid., p. 21.

95 See Amanda Wrigley and Stephen Harrison, *Louis MacNeice: The Classical Radio Plays*, Oxford University Press, Oxford, 2013.

96 For Logue's own version of how this came about, see Christopher Logue, *Prince Charming*, Faber & Faber, London, 1999, pp. 221–4.

97 Posthumously published in Christopher Logue, *War Music*, Faber & Faber, London, 2015; the individual sections had appeared in the period 1963 to 2005. We are grateful to Rosemary Hill for permission to publish a reproduction of draft material.

98 Derek Walcott, *Omeros*, Farrar, Straus & Giroux, New York, 1990. The work was also published in the same year by Faber, London.

99 Alice Oswald, *Memorial: An Excavation of the Iliad*, Faber & Faber, London, 2011.

100 For a sample reading by the author, see www.youtube.com/watch?v=pvJBxie9Dlw (accessed 22 August 2017).

101 Homer, *The Odyssey*, trans. Emily Wilson, Norton, New York, 2017. The first major published verse version of the *Iliad* by a woman is also very recent: Caroline Alexander's *The Iliad: A New Translation*, Vintage Classics, London, 2015.

102 Homer, *The Odyssey*, trans. Wilson, p. 105.

103 See the review by Helen Morales, *Times Literary Supplement*, 5980, 10 November 2017, p. 12.

Chapter 5

104 Aesopic fables are referred to using the standard numeration of Perry's edition (Ben Edwin Perry, *Aesopica: A Series of Texts Relating to Aesop or Ascribed to Him*, Volume I: *Greek and Latin Texts*, University of Illinois Press, Urbana IL, 1952) (e.g. 'Perry *Aesopica* 1').

105 Here I use the translation and introduction of Patrick Olivelle, *The Pañcatantra*, Oxford University Press, Oxford, 1997.

106 The reconstruction followed here (the original needs to be pieced together from later versions) is that of Franklin Edgerton, *Panchatantra Reconstructed*, 2 vols, American Oriental Society, New Haven CT, 1924, often recognized as the most plausible (cf. e.g. Olivelle, *The Pañcatantra*, p. xii).

107 Here I use the translation and introduction of Olivelle, *The Pañcatantra*, p. 8.

108 For these earlier traces, see ibid., p. xi.

109 See Francisco R. Adrados and Gert-Jan van Dijk, *History of the Graeco-Latin Fable*, 3 vols, Brill, Leiden, 1999–2003, vol. I, pp. 229–30.

110 See especially Johannes Hertel, *Tantrākhyāyika: Die älteste Fassung des Pañcatantra*, Weidmann, Berlin, 1910.

111 Tantrākhyāyikā, seventeenth century, Oxford, Bodleian Library, MS. Stein Or., f. 2. See the annotation on the Bodleian copy by the explorer and archaeologist Sir Aurel Stein.

112 For the information in this section, see Edgerton, *Panchatantra Reconstructed*; Hertel, *Tantrākhyāyika*; and D. Beecher, J. Butler and C. Di Biasi, *Sir Thomas North, The Moral Philosophy of Doni, Popularly Known as The Fables of Bidpai*, Dovehouse Editions, Ottawa, 2003, pp. 14–27.

113 See e.g. Munther A. Younes, *Tales from Kalila wa Dimna: An Arabic Reader*, Yale University Press, New Haven CT, 1989.

114 *Kalila wa-Dimna*, 1354 CE, Oxford, Bodleian Library, MS. Pococke 400, fols 45v–46r.

115 Cf. C. van Ruymbeke, *Kashefi's Anvar-e Sohayli: Rewriting Kalila wa-Dimna in Timurid Herat*, Brill, Leiden and Boston MA, 2016.

116 See G.M. Wickens, '*Anwar-e Sohayli*', in Ehsan Yarshater (ed.), *Encyclopaedia Iranica*, vol. II, Routledge & Kegan Paul, London, 1986, pp. 140–41.

117 The Bodleian Library holds the following edition: *The morall philosophie of Doni, englished by T[homas] North*, H. Denham, London, 1570.

118 North's version of Plutarch was the primary source for Shakespeare's Roman history plays.

119 Jean de La Fontaine, *Fables Choisies*, vol. 3, Thierry and Barbin, Paris, 1678, p. 2.

120 Arthur Tilley, 'La Fontaine and Bidpai', *Modern Language Review*, vol. 34, 1939, pp. 21–39.

121 For a sceptical view, see Martin L. West, 'The Ascription of Fables to Aesop in Archaic and Classical Greece', in Francisco R. Adrados (ed.), *La Fable*, Fondation Hardt, Geneva, 1984, pp. 105–36.

122 See *Birds* 471–2 (referring to the fable of the lark and its crest, Perry *Aesopica* 447), *Peace* 129 and *Wasps* 1446–8 (both alluding to the fable of the dung beetle who climbed to the eagle's nest, Perry *Aesopica* 3). For Plato's reference to Aesop, see *Phaedo* 60d.

123 The most convenient modern translation is Laura Gibbs, *Aesop's Fables*, Oxford University Press, Oxford, 2002. For the history of the fable more generally in Greek and Roman literature and for scholarship on the topic, see Niklas Holzberg, *The Ancient Fable: An Introduction*, Indiana University Press, Bloomington and Indianapolis IN, 1992, and especially Adrados and van Dijk, *History of the Graeco-Latin Fable*.

124 I cite the translation of Gibbs, *Aesop's Fables*, p. 5.

125 See Adrados and van Dijk, *History of the Graeco-Latin Fable*, vol. I, pp. 287–33.

126 See Miriam Lichtheim and Joseph G. Manning, *Ancient Egyptian Literature*, Volume III: *The Late Period*, University of California Press, Berkeley CA, 2006, p. 141.

127 On the *Aesop Romance*, see Niklas Holzberg (ed.), *Der Aesop-Roman: Motivgeschichte und Erzählstruktur*, Narr, Tübingen, 1992; Lesley Kurke, *Aesopic Conversations: Popular Tradition, Cultural Dialogue, and the Invention of Greek Prose*, Princeton University Press, Princeton NJ and Oxford, 2011.

128 For the many texts of the Latin tradition between Phaedrus and printing, see Perry *Aesopica* 553–74.

129 See Edward Wheatley, *Mastering Aesop: Medieval Education, Chaucer, and His Followers*, University Press of Florida, Gainesville FL, 2000.

130 Oxford, Bodleian Library, MS. Douce 360, fols 29v–31v. See e.g. Jill Mann, *From Aesop to Reynard: Beast Literature in Medieval Britain*, Oxford University Press, Oxford, 2009.

131 See David G. Hale, 'Aesop in Renaissance England', *The Library*, vol. 5, 1972, pp. 116–25.

132 *The book of the subtyl historyes and fables of Esope whiche were translated out of Frensshe by wylliam Caxton*, London, 1484. For its complex range of sources, see Hale, 'Aesop in Renaissance England', p. 122.

133 BN MS.1628 bis. See Andrew Laird, 'A Mirror for Mexican Princes: Reconsidering the Context and Latin Source for the Nahuatl Translation of Aesop's Fables', in Barry Taylor and Alejandro Coroleu (eds), *Brief Forms in Medieval and Renaissance Hispanic Literature*, Cambridge Scholars Publishing, Newcastle Upon Tyne, 2017, pp. 132–67.

134 François Chauveau was the first illustrator; major names since include J.J. Grandville (1855), Gustave Doré (1867), Arthur Rackham (1912) and Marc Chagall (1927–30). These have accompanied contemporary and later editions with versions in many languages. See, for example, the following volume in the Bodleian Library's holdings in a translation first published in Boston in 1841: Jean de La Fontaine, *The Fables: A selection rendered into the English language by Elizur Wright and adorned throughout with illustrations and decorations after Gustave Doré*, Jupiter Books, London, 1975.

135 *Le jeu des fables, ou Fables de Lafontaine: mises en action, avec figures coloriées et découpées*, Alphonse Giroux, Paris, 1820.

136 E.g. by John Tenniel (1848), which led to his illustrations for Lewis Carroll's Alice books; Randolph Caldecott (1883); E.J. Detmold (1909); and Arthur Rackham (1916). See also [W.J. Linton,] *The Baby's Own Aesop*, illus. Walter Crane, Routledge, London, 1887. For more recent illustrators for children, see Pat Pflieger, 'Fables into Picture Books', *Children's Literature Association Quarterly*, vol. 9, 1984, pp. 73–5; and for a rich online gallery of Aesop illustrations from the earliest printed editions onwards, compiled by Laura Gibbs, see www.flickr.com/photos/38299630@N05/collections/72157625472117156 (accessed 24 August 2017).

137 Beatrix Potter, *The Tale of Johnny Town-Mouse*, Warne, London, 1918.

Chapter 6

138 A copy of the first edition of Perrault's tales containing 'Cendrillon, ou La petite pantoufle de verre' is held in the Bibliothèque nationale de France: Charles Perrault, *Histoires, ou Contes du temps passé, avec des Moralitez*, Barbin, Paris, 1697. The earliest copy held by the Bodleian Library is a pirated edition, which appeared eleven years later. A first title page establishes that it is based on a 1698 Paris edition while the second title page gives the following details: *Histoires ou Contes du tems passé. Avec des Moralitez. Par le Fils de Monsieur Perreault de l'Academie François. Suivant la Copie de Paris*, Chez Jaques Desbordes, Amsterdam, 1708. Perrault had published under the name of his son, probably to preserve his reputation from being associated with folk tales.

139 The Bodleian Library holds a copy of the third edition of Robert Samber's 1729 translation, published in 1741: *Histories, or Tales of Passed Times. With Morals. Written In French by M. Perrault, And Englished by R.S. Gent. The Third Edition, Corrected. With Cuts to every Tale*. London. Printed for R. Montagu, …, and J. Pote, at Eton, 1741. The description of editorial intervention suggests that changes were accepted and indeed expected in a translation for a new readership. This is likely to have been the case particularly with a work intended for educational purposes; it was evidently sold at Eton College.

140 Perrault, *Histoires*, p. 91; and Samber, *Histories*, pp. 69f.

141 Perrault, *Histoires*, p. 95; and Samber, *Histories*, p. 72.

142 Dedication 'to the Right Honourable the Countess of Granville', in Samber, *Histories*, pp. i–vi (p. iii).

143 Joseph Pote is named in the first edition as a London bookseller involved in the publication of the work, but he established himself at Eton College soon afterwards, also as the proprietor of a small boarding house; see R.S. Austen-Leigh, 'Joseph Pote of Eton and Bartlet's *Farriery*', *The Library* 4th ser., vol. XVII, no. 2, 1936, pp. 131–54 (p. 133).

144 See for example the programme for a 'panorama' performed by Hengler's Grand Cirque, Argyll Street, Oxford Circus: *Cinderella*, 1800, Oxford, Bodleian Library, Opie EE 334a. As in modern times, the different dresses worn by Cinderella offered opportunities for toys inspiring re-enactment, as in the following booklet with accompanying figures: Daniel Nathan Shury and S. and J. Fuller, *Cinderella; or, The little glass slipper, beautifully versified and illustrated with figures*, S. and J. Fuller, London, 1814, Oxford, Bodleian Library, Opie E 31.

145 The Grimm Brothers collected folk tales over many years and published them in successive editions. The earliest edition in the Bodleian Library is the following: *Kinder- und Haus-Märchen, gesammelt durch die Brüder Grimm, Kleine Ausgabe, mit sieben Kupfern*, Reimer, Berlin, 1825.

146 She is unlikely to have had access to written sources or transmission directly from the French. See Holger Ehrhardt, *Die Marburger Märchenfrau oder Aufhellungen eines 'nicht einmal Vermutungen erlaubenden Dunkels'*, Boxan, Kassel, 2016, and the press release in www.uni-kassel.de/uni/aktuelles/meldung/post/detail/News/kasseler-grimm-forscher-lueftet-das-geheimnis-der-aschenputtel-erzaehlerin (accessed 10 October 2018). For a wide-ranging discussion of aspects of the Grimm Brothers' use of sources in their *Märchen* and their collaboration with Brentano, see Heinz Rölleke, *Die Märchen der Brüder Grimm. Quellen und Studien…*, Wissenschaftlicher Verlag, Trier, 2000, pp. 9–37, 54–66 and *passim*.

147 See Detlev Fehling, *Amor und Psyche: Die Schöpfung des Apuleius und ihre Einwirkung auf das Märchen, eine Kritik der romantischen Märchentheorie*, Steiner, Wiesbaden, 1977. I am grateful to Stephen Harrison for highlighting the importance of this thread of the tradition.

148 Fay Beauchamp, 'Asian Origins of Cinderella: The Zhuang Storyteller of Guangxi', *Oral Tradition*, vol. 25, no. 2, 2010, pp. 447–96. See ibid., Appendix A, pp. 490f. for Arthur Waley's 1963 translation of the story. See also *Yeh-Shen: A Cinderella Story from China*, retold by Ai-Ling Louie, illus. Ed Young, Puffin, London, 1996.

149 *Cinderella* was produced as an animated musical feature film in 1950 by Walt Disney Productions. It was followed later by two sequels, and a remake with the same title was released in 2015.

150 Jewell Reinhart Coburn, *Angkat: The Cambodian Cinderella*, Shen's Books, Fremont CA, 1998; and Robert D. San Souci, *Cendrillon: A Caribbean Cinderella*, Simon & Schuster, New York, 1998.

151 Lewis Carroll, *Through the Looking Glass, and What Alice Found There*, Macmillan, London, 1872. For Alice's encounter with the poem, see pp. 20–24.

152 'Foreword to the second edition', in J.R.R. Tolkien, *The Lord of the Rings* HarperCollins, London, 1994, pp. xv–xviii (p. xv).

153 Tolkien, *The Lord of the Rings*, Book 2, ch. 8, pp. 358–70. For Galadriel's Lament, see p. 368.

154 See René Goscinny and Albert Uderzo, *Astérix le Gaulois*, rev. edn, Hachette Livre, [1961] 1999. See also the following translations: *Asterix the Gaul*, trans. into English by Anthea Bell and Derek Hockridge, rev. edn, Hodder & Stoughton, London, 2013; *Asterix der Gallier*, trans. into German by Gudrun Penndorf M.A., Egmont Ehapa Verlag, Berlin, [1968] 2013.

155 J.K. Rowling, *Harry Potter and the Philosopher's Stone*, Bloomsbury, London, 1997.

156 Among other languages, Dumbledore – whose name is derived from a dialect word for 'bumblebee' – understands Mermish, Parseltongue and the Goblins' language Gobbledegook. Harry Potter's ability to speak Parseltongue is both remarkable and suspicious because it is normally restricted to serpents and their ilk; see www.pottermore.com/features/everything-you-didnt-know-about-parseltongue.

Chapter 7

157 For a comprehensive overview, see John T. Koch, *Celtic Culture: A Historical Encyclopedia*, 5 vols, ABC–CLIO, Santa Barbara CA and Oxford, 2006.

158 Tacitus, *Agricola*, 11.

159 P.H. Sawyer, *From Roman Britain to Norman England*, 2nd edn, Routledge, London, 1998, pp. 69f.

160 Oxford, Bodleian Library, MS. Bodl. 180, fol. 1r.

161 Translation by Kevin S. Kiernan, 'Alfred the Great's Burnt Boethius', www.uky.edu/~kiernan/iconic/iconic.htm (accessed 5 November 2017).

162 For a digital copy of the manuscript see http://image.ox.ac.uk, Oxford, Bodleian Library, MS. Digby 23, Part 2.

163 See the discussion of the evidence in Nathan Love, 'AOI in the *Chanson de Roland*: A Divergent Hypothesis', *Olifant*, vol. 10, no. 4, 1984/85, pp. 182–7 (pp. 182f. and *passim*).

164 For a digital copy of the manuscript, see http://image.ox.ac.uk, Oxford, Jesus College, MS. 111.

165 John Jamieson, 'Preface', in *An Etymological Dictionary of the Scottish Language…*, 2 vols, Edinburgh University Press, Edinburgh, 1808, vol. 1, pp. i–viii (p. iv). For a study of Jamieson's contribution to Scottish lexicography, see Susan Rennie, *Jamieson's Dictionary of Scots: The Story of the First Historical Dictionary of the Scots Language*, Oxford University Press, Oxford, 2012.

166 Jamieson, *An Etymological Dictionary of the Scottish Language…*, vol. 1, title page.

167 Ibid., 'Preface', p. iii.

168 The noun 'let' (hindrance, stoppage, obstruction) originates in Middle English and is now archaic; see 'let, n.1', in the *Oxford English Dictionary*, www.oed.com/view/Entry/107493?redirectedFrom=without+let#eid39339517 (accessed 5 December 2017).

169 The poster exhibition *Slanguages* (first shown at Wolfson College, Oxford, in October–December 2017 under the auspices of the AHRC-funded research programme Creative Multilingualism) featured the urban sign language and deaf comedian Rinkoo Barpaga on posters that contrast standard British Sign Language (BSL) and non-standard Birmingham-based 'Urban Sign Language (USL)'.

170 See 'Household Questionnaire, England, Office for National Statistics, 2011 Census', Question 18, in 2011-census-questions-england_tcm77-186474.pdf, www.ons.gov.uk (accessed 2 December 2017). See also the form for Wales, which includes a further question about the respondent's command of Welsh (2011-census-questions-wales_tcm77-186475.pdf, Question 17).

171 By way of example, the Southern Bowel Cancer Screening Programme Hub goes some way towards ensuring that its invitation to cancer screening will be understood even if the addressee is not familiar with English. While the information itself is provided only in English, the reverse of the letter includes an instruction in a wide range of other languages.

172 Cheltenham-based SuperGroup plc is an example of a company responding linguistically to globalization. In the Superdry logo, Chinese and Japanese characters appeal to a global market while also signalling an ethos of embracing diversity of corporate culture; see https://careers.superdry.com/about-ys/equality-and-diversity (accessed 10 December 2017).

Chapter 8

173 Daines Barrington, 'On the Expiration of the Cornish Language', *Archaeologia*, vol. 3, 1775, pp. 279–84 (pp. 281–2). Barrington spells the woman's surname 'Pentraeth'. However, 'Pentreath' is now the accepted spelling, appearing, for example, on the memorial to her in Cornwall.

174 Bowl with inscription in Linear A, Knossos, Ashmolean Museum, University of Oxford, AN 1938.872. Tablet with inscription in Linear B, Knossos, Ashmolean Museum, University of Oxford, AN 1910.211.

175 John Chadwick, *The Decipherment of Linear B*, 2nd edn, Cambridge University Press, Cambridge, 1967, p. 1.

176 Ibid., p. 14.

177 See https://upload.wikimedia.org/wikipedia/commons/b/b5/Radioactive.svg (accessed 10 December 2017).

178 William M. Hewitt et al. (Human Interference Task Force), *Reducing the Likelihood of Future Human Activities that Could Affect Geological High-Level Waste Repositories*, Office of Nuclear Waste Isolation, Columbus OH, 1984, p. 117.

179 Kathleen M. Trauth et al., *Expert Judgment on Markers to Deter Human Intrusion into the Waste Isolation Pilot Plant*, Sandia National Laboratories, Albuquerque NM and Livermore CA, 1993, p. D-5.

180 Françoise Bastide and Paolo Fabbri, 'Lebende Detektoren und komplementäre Zeichen: Katzen, Augen und Sirenen', *Zeitschrift für Semiotik*, vol. 6, no. 3, 1985, pp. 257–64.

181 Trauth et al., *Expert Judgment*, pp. F-61, F-66.

182 Hewitt et al., *Reducing the Likelihood*, p. 39.

183 Thomas A. Sebeok, *Communication Measures to Bridge Ten Millennia*, Office for Nuclear Waste Isolation, Columbus OH, 1984.

184 Ibid., p. 24.

185 Ibid.

186 Ibid.

187 Ibid., p. 27.

188 Ibid., p. 24.

189 Suzanne Pasztor and Stephen C. Hora, *The Vatican Archives: A Study of Its History and Administration*, NKS/KAN 1.3(91)6, NKS, Roskilde, 1991.

190 Quoted in Ola Wikander, 'Don't Push This Button: Phoenician Sarcophagi, "Atomic Priesthoods" and Nuclear Waste', in H. Rahm (ed.), *Vetenskapssocieteten i Lund: Årsbok 2015*, Vetenskapssocietete, Lund, 2015, pp. 109–24 (p. 116).

Further Reading

Matthew Reynolds, *Translation: A Very Short Introduction* (Oxford University Press, Oxford, 2016) and David Bellos, *Is That a Fish in Your Ear? Translation and the Meaning of Everything* (Particular Books, London, 2011) provide overviews of the broad field of translation; George Steiner's *After Babel: Aspects of Language and Translation* (Oxford University Press, London, 1976) is a classic account of the Babelic nature of European literature.

Explorations of different translation practices can be found in Martha P.Y. Cheung (ed.), *An Anthology of Chinese Discourse on Translation*, 2 vols (St Jerome Publishing, Manchester, 2006) and Ronit Ricci and Jan van der Putten (eds), *Translation in Asia: Theories, Practices, Histories* (St Jerome Publishing, Manchester, 2011). The *Oxford History of Literary Translation in English*, 5 vols planned (Oxford University Press, Oxford, 2010–) gives an insight into the richly varied ways in which translation has interacted with literature in English.

Efforts to overcome the curse of Babel are described in Umberto Eco, *The Search for the Perfect Language*, trans. James Fentress (Blackwell, Oxford, 1995), and Otto Neurath, *From Hieroglyphics to Isotype: A Visual Autobiography*, ed. Matthew Eve and Christopher Burke (Hyphen Press, London, 2010).

On translations of the Bible, see Helen Moore and Julian Reid (eds), *Manifold Greatness: The Making of the King James Bible* (Bodleian Library Publishing, Oxford, 2011) and David Norton, *A History of the English Bible as Literature* (Cambridge University Press, Cambridge, 2000).

Reworkings of classical epics are gathered in George Steiner and Aminadav Dykman (eds), *Homer in English* (Penguin, Harmondsworth, 1996), and explored in Edith Hall, *The Return of Ulysses: A Cultural History of Homer's Odyssey* (I.B. Tauris, London and New York, 2008) and Alexandra Lianeri and Vanda Zajko (eds), *Translation and the Classic: Identity as Change in the History of Culture* (Oxford University Press, Oxford, 2008).

On fables, see Niklas Holzberg, *The Ancient Fable: An Introduction* (Indiana University Press, Bloomington and Indianapolis IN, 1992), and Jill Mann, *From Aesop to Reynard: Beast Literature in Medieval Britain* (Oxford University Press, Oxford, 2009).

David Crystal, *The Stories of English* (Penguin Books, London, 2005) recounts the history of the English language in all its variety; fascinating detail about dictionaries is in Jonathon Green, *Chasing the Sun: Dictionary-Makers and the Dictionaries they Made* (Pimlico, London, 1997).

For discussions of identity and political power in a Babelic world, see Eric Cheyfitz, *The Poetics of Imperialism: Translation and Colonization from 'The Tempest' to 'Tarzan'* (Oxford University Press, New York, 1991), Sherry Simon, *Gender in Translation: Cultural Identity and the Politics of Transmission* (Routledge, London, 1996), and Ziad Elmarsafy, *The Enlightenment Qur'an: The Politics of Translation and the Construction of Islam* (Oneworld, Oxford, 2009).

John Chadwick's *The Decipherment of Linear B* (Cambridge University Press, Cambridge, 1957 and much reprinted) is a classic and still fascinating account of the translation of a very ancient language; on translation's contemporary importance, see Michael Cronin, *Translation in the Digital Age* (Routledge, Abingdon, 2013), and Mona Baker's urgent book *Translating Dissent: Voices from and with the Egyptian Revolution* (Routledge, Abingdon, 2016).

Acknowledgements

Work on this book has been intimately connected with curating the associated exhibition, and it is the result of a collaboration with many people who contributed vital expertise.

The exhibition was developed in close cooperation with Madeline Slaven, whose creative ideas were vital to its design. We are also most grateful for the input from her exhibition team, notably Sallyanne Gilchrist and Jennifer Varallo. In the course of our work we were advised by a large number of Bodleian curators, from whom we gained fascinating insights into textual worlds with which we had not hitherto been familiar: Bruce Barker-Benfield, Gillian Evison, Camillo Formigatti, Martin Kauffmann, Julie Anne Lambert, César Merchán-Hamann, Judith Priestman, Alasdair Watson, Sarah Wheale.

The Ashmolean Museum, University of Oxford, contributed valuable items and we are grateful to Marianne Bergeron and Anja Ulbrich for their advice.

Copyright holders are acknowledged in the captions to the illustrations, on the copyright page and in the endnotes to the chapters. We should, however, particularly like to thank Rosemary Hill for her permission to publish handwritten drafts from *War Music* by Christopher Logue.

Contributions to publication and public engagement costs were provided by the following organizations, to whom we should like to extend our thanks: the Charles Oldham Trustees, Corpus Christi College, Oxford; Jesus College, Oxford; and the Arts and Humanities Research Council, which contributed through the research programme Creative Multilingualism (Open World Research Initiative).

This book forms part of a wide array of means by which the exhibition seeks to engage with diverse audiences. It is in the nature of the topic, and the books and other materials at the heart of the project, that we should like to involve language learners, language enthusiasts and the communities that are familiar with the many different languages represented. We are grateful to the colleagues who contributed to this endeavour, in particular Suzanne de la Rosa and Rosie Sharkey in the Bodleian, colleagues from the Faculty of Medieval and Modern Languages, and Bhee Bellew and Katy Terry from the Creative Multilingualism team. In designing suitable activities we were able to benefit particularly from the expertise of the schoolteachers in our Modern Foreign Languages Advisory Group.

Many colleagues and students have contributed in multifarious ways to the ideas that are explored in this book. In particular, we should like to thank Tania Demetriou for her advice, and especially Stuart Gillespie, who contributed his expertise and was instrumental in making the exhibition happen.

We are grateful to Samuel Fanous, Janet Phillips, Leanda Shrimpton, Susie Foster, Dot Little and the other members of the publication team for their advice, help and patience in seeing the book through the production process and for their consistent attention to the detail of the text and the quality of the images.

Working on this book and the associated exhibition has been a pleasure throughout. This is due above all to the marvellous holdings of the Bodleian Library and to the Bodleian's wonderful staff.

About the Authors

Dennis Duncan is Munby Fellow in Bibliography, University of Cambridge.

Stephen Harrison is Professor of Latin Literature, University of Oxford, and Fellow and Tutor in Classics, Corpus Christi College, Oxford.

Katrin Kohl is Professor of German Literature, University of Oxford, and Fellow and Tutor in German, Jesus College, Oxford.

Matthew Reynolds is Professor of English and Comparative Criticism, University of Oxford, and Fellow and Tutor in English Language and Literature, St Anne's College, Oxford.

References to both illustrations and captions are in *italics*.